MW00604722

THRU AND BACK AGAIN

A Hiker's Journey on the North Country Trail

THRU AND BACK AGAIN

A Hiker's Journey on the North Country Trail

North Dakota

Minnesota

Wisconsin

Michigan

New York

Ohio

Pennsylvania

Luke Jordan

Thru and Back: A Hiker's Journey on the North Country Trail
© 2017 by Luke Jordan
All Rights Reserved. No part of this publication may be reproduced,
stored in a retrieval system, or transmitted, in any form or in any means
– by electronic, mechanical, photocopying, recording or otherwise –
without prior written permission.

Published in collaboration with
Fortitude Graphic Design and Printing & Season Press LLC
Cover and book design by Sean Hollins
Pencil drawing of Luke Jordan by Haley Frost Creative
All images courtesy of Luke Jordan Archives

The use herein of selected brief quotations and character names is be-
lieved to be compliant with the four Fair use factors listed in 17 U.S.C.
107, or otherwise within public domain. For bulk orders, speaking en-
gagements, to view pictures and videos taken during the 2013 journey, or
to order copies of other books written by Luke Jordan,
visit <www.stridernct.com>,
or on Facebook at StriderNCT@facebook.com.

Thru and Back Again/ Jordan, Luke- Non-fiction
p.cm

1. Hiking-Personal account 2. National Trail System-North Country Trail
3. Travel-United States 4. Backpacking-transcontinental

Library of Congress Control Number:
2017940056
ISBN-10: 0-692-88090-9
ISBN-13: 978-0-692-88090-6

Printed in the United States of America

FIRST EDITION
10 9 8 7 6 5 4 3 2 1

Table of Contents

Special thanks to
Susan Carol Hauser and Amelia Rhodes

FOREWORD

Ron Strickland-Founder
Pacific Northwest National Scenic Trail

On October 17, 2013, Luke "Strider" Jordan, 23, arrived on foot at Maine Junction (near Killington, Vermont) after a 6½ month North Country Trail (NCT) trek from North Dakota. He was not the first of the handful of thru-hikers in the trail's 33-year history. But his hike's significance was not only that he walked 4,600 miles but also that he made a point throughout his trip to educate the public about both the NCT and long distance hiking. In this fine book, he makes his trek come alive for even the most couch-bound reader.

I urge you to read Luke's daily journal entries with an active sense of how you yourself would react to the places and people that he saw. What would you do? What would you feel? Though thru-hikers such as Luke point the way, the vast majority of NCT visitors experience the trail a day or a weekend at a time. Part of the charm of Luke's narrative is that it piques our imaginations with the possibility of our setting out on our own adventures.

By the way, I also admire Luke for having used his trek to help promote the development of a transcontinental Sea-To-Sea Route (C2C), an ocean-to-ocean enhancement of the National Trails System. Do you know that the NCT is double the length of its celebrated cousin, the north-south Appalachian Trail? Have you heard that America has eleven "national scenic trails?" And that the NCT is the key to linking them together to create the world's finest hiking network?

That is the ultimate significance of Luke's spectacular hike and of his subsequent Pied Piper-like trails advocacy. When I met Luke at Maine Junction, he spoke of the need to fill in an 800-mile Sea-To-Sea gap in North Dakota and Montana. "America needs a new Big Sky Trail," he said, "to connect west from the NCT to the Continental Divide National Scenic Trail." Luke thinks big! He dreams that the NCT and his new Big Sky Trail will be the linchpin in a recreational pathway from the Pacific Ocean to the Atlantic Ocean.

I have feared that eventually, there will not be enough new blood to ensure the future of the National Trails System. However, at Maine Junction on that October day in 2013 I felt overjoyed and grateful to meet a visionary hiker from our next generation of trail activists.

America's National Scenic Trails

Our nation's National Scenic Trails have been established to provide access to some of the most spectacular scenic areas of the nation while providing healthy outdoor recreation opportunities. An important aspect is also to expose hikers to some of the historical, natural, and cultural elements within the areas these trails pass.

The National Trails System Act of 1968 established two NST's, the Appalachian and Pacific Crest Trails, and additionally called for the study of 14 other potential routes. As of 2015, eleven such trails exist that wind through some of the most spectacular scenery this continent has to offer. The North Country NST is one of these trails, the fourth to be designated and the longest at nearly 4,600 miles.

The 11 National Scenic Trails include:

Appalachian Trail
Arizona Trail
Continental Divide Trail
Florida Trail
Ice Age Trail
Natchez Trace Trail
New England Trail
North Country Trail
Pacific Crest Trail
Pacific Northwest Trail
Potomac Heritage Trail

The North Country NST was established to provide a world-class hiking and backpacking experience though the northern heartland and Great Lakes region of America. Originally envisioned to stretch about 3200 miles, that original vision has drastically expanded to an estimated 4600 miles since the trail's designation in 1980. What the final distance may be is anyone's guess, as the trail continues to grow mile-by-mile every year as new trail gets built and some gets rerouted (including a 400-mile reroute in Minnesota known as the Arrowhead Reroute).

To date, about 2,700 miles of hike-able off-road trail have been built to national hiking standards, with the remaining miles temporarily routed on shared use trails or roads. In the trail's relatively short history, there are already more miles of off-road trail than the length of the entire Pacific Crest Trail.

After beginning at Lake Sakakawea State Park the trail travels across the open plains of North Dakota and roughly follows the Sheyenne River, including the state's only registered waterfall outside Fort Ransom. Continuing east the trail leaves the river valley and crosses the much flatter Lake Agassiz basin where it enters Minnesota. Much diversity can be found hiking through the "Land of 10,000 Lakes", leaving the prairie behind and entering the North Woods.

After passing through Tamarac National Wildlife Refuge, Itasca State Park and the Chippewa National Forest a change in the trail via the "Arrowhead Reroute" brings the trail through the Iron Range and into Minnesota's Arrowhead Region. The Reroute takes in 400 miles of world class scenery along the Canadian Border and down the Superior Hiking Trail, providing great views of Lake Superior and countless waterfalls in the many state parks along the route.

Crossing into Wisconsin, the trail continues through classic north woods scenery past historic sites and more waterfalls as it winds its way back to the Lake Superior shore, crossing into Michigan. Here the trail passes through some of its most remote areas crossing the Porcupine Mountains in the Upper Peninsula, and then follows Lake Superior's Shoreline for many miles through Pictured Rocks National Lakeshore and beyond.

Heading south, the trail meets Tahquamenon Falls before reaching the straits of Mackinac at St. Ignace. A hiker must take a shuttle across the Mackinac Bridge to the Lower Peninsula. In lower Michigan the trail skirts Little Traverse Bay and heads south through the Manistee National Forest where the trail leaves the north woods behind and enters more developed and agricultural areas, including the town of Lowell, the approximate halfway point of the trail.

In Ohio, the trail first takes in the Oak Openings Region before heading south along historic canals to Dayton, the largest city on the trail. The NCT follows the Buckeye Trail for much of its route through the state, passing near several historical sites and through the Hocking Hills region. Leaving the Buckeye Trail behind, the NCT enters Pennsylvania where it crosses more rocky terrain into New England.

At the New York state line the NCT joins with the Finger Lakes Trail which it follows for over 400 miles through the heart of upstate New York. The FLT offers many spectacular gorges and waterfalls as it threads its way east until the NCT leaves it behind and heads for the finale in the Adirondack Mountains. Home of many lakes and 5,000 feet high peaks, Adirondack Park is a vast wilderness area and the trail threads its way over peak and valley to the Eastern Terminus at Crown Point State Historic Site on Lake Champlain at the Vermont state line. Plans are currently underway to extend the trail into Vermont to connect with the Appalachian Trail, as the original plan intended.

Follow along with Strider as he hikes this trail of great diversity from the vast plains of North Dakota to the high peaks of the Adirondacks. If you're wondering whether or not his trail name comes from the tales of J.R.R. Tolkien, it does not, though he is a big fan of the books and even read the entire Lord of the Rings Trilogy while out on the trail. Any fans of Tolkien will notice a few hints here and there within this book of references to Tolkien's vast mythology. Some of the sights and locations Strider encountered on his journey reminded him of specific places Tolkien mentioned in his work.

PROLOGUE

Luke "Strider" Jordan
North Country Trail - 2013

For many people hiking 4,600 miles in one go may seem like a crazy, even foolish idea. But for some others it is an opportunity to see isolated places, to discover oneself, and of course to have fun doing it! Such is the case with me.

A few years ago I had never even heard of the North Country Trail. I had no idea that such a daunting task of building a continuous footpath across seven northern states was underway, and had been for more than thirty years. I first heard about it one weekend in my college years volunteering on a Superior Hiking Trail project from another volunteer. I was immediately excited and fascinated with the idea. After doing a little research and finding out what the trail was all about I began to feel a sense of longing, a desire to hike beyond Minnesota and see what else the North Country had to offer.

When I was a young kid my family used to take trips up to the North Shore of Lake Superior every summer and I always enjoyed hiking around exploring the many excellent state parks in the area. I was awe struck by the beauty of the region and developed an appreciation and love for it. Then as I grew older the crowds started to get larger. On our family trips we found it was harder to find a campsite without a reservation many weeks or even months in advance.

Since we loved it up there so much we decided to avoid planning our trips in advance and buy a piece of land instead. A year later we had a chunk of land with a nice little cabin on it that we built ourselves. We would visit the North Shore more frequently now that we had a place of our own. It was during this first year that I discovered, only a few hundred feet away from our cabin, a hidden gem of the North Shore… The Superior Hiking Trail (SHT).

It was 2003, I was 13 years old. I had lots of energy and was eager to explore new places. Little did I know that just down the road was a fantastic section of the SHT known as Section 13, with many scenic vistas from atop nameless peaks. After that initial discovery, every family trip we took up to "The Shack" I would spend time by myself hiking the nearby sections. When I was old enough to drive I would make solo trips with the main objective of hiking new sections of the SHT. This was my life for a few years until I had a life-changing experience on the Continental Divide Trail (CDT) in Colorado.

This was in 2008, after I had graduated from high school. I signed up as a volunteer for the Forest Service's Passport In Time program in Twin Lakes, Colorado for a week in July doing historic preservation work at a remote location. The project was located right on the CDT, the old Dexter Cabin at the Interlaken Resort. I met many interesting hikers, all with cool stories of traveling around the country. One person in particular caught my attention. This individual had been backpacking all over the United States and Europe.

He recounted one of his journeys across Ireland and the Isle of Man, as well as telling me about his Appalachian and Colorado Trail thruhikes. His stories stirred something up inside me that made me want to move on to bigger things in the world of hiking: Backpacking.

In 2010 I read an article in the Ridgeline newsletter that the SHT was nearing completion and they were asking for volunteers to help construct the last remaining miles between Duluth and Two Harbors to complete the trail. I decided to sign up for a work weekend to learn the art of trail building, to contribute to society and give back to the trail. I enjoyed the experience so much I signed up again the following year and have a been a regular on the trail crew ever since. It was at that first trail building weekend in 2010 that I first learned of the NCT.

After that first experience on the trail crew I headed to Alaska for a month on yet another Forest Service Project, this time as an actual paid intern for an organization called Historicorps, and traveled by plane, car, boat, and foot way into the interior near the Yukon border. It was my first real experience working in the world of natural resources and was my first real adventure outside of Minnesota. I experienced a lot of firsts on that trip, and while it's not necessarily related to backpacking, it sparked my wanderlust and the desire to experience America.

Back in school once again I immediately began research to find out more about this North Country Trail I had heard about, and during my research I stumbled upon the videos of Nimblewill Nomad's epic thru-hike of the NCT in 2009. Watching his journey gave me a surge of inspiration and the desire to complete an "odyssey" of my own. I was hooked, and there was no turning back.

In 2011 I bought my first backpack, the same one I would later take on my NCT journey, and made the first concrete step toward my new dream on a camping trip in the Northwest Angle of Minnesota. I had just finished an eight day trip in the Boundary Waters Canoe Area and my mother Roxanne had planned a camping trip of her own, so we decided to meet up once I had exited the BWCAW and see a few of the state parks in far northern Minnesota.

On the third night, sitting by the fire in Scenic State Park, I told her about this incredibly long trail that had been on my mind for a year and how the desire to hike it had been unquenchable ever since. I asked her opinion on my thoughts of ignoring the pressure of society to get a job right out of college, and instead pursue this dream that had recently come into being to hike over 4000 miles and know that at the end would be an uncertain future.

She didn't hesitate at all, "Go for it," she told me. "Do it now or you'll regret it later."

It was decided, no matter what I was going to attempt a thru-hike of the NCT once I graduated college. The next day was another milestone, as I stumbled upon my trail name by luck. We were hiking along and I was told to slow down, it was impossible to keep up with my long strides. Strides… "Strider!" It was no secret that I had an abnormally fast walking pace. The name fit well, and it stuck.

Only a month later I headed out to the Rocky Mountains for the rest of the summer for another internship on many projects in Colorado, Idaho, and Wyoming. I took a day to myself in between projects for a visit to that site on the CDT that had inspired me many years prior. I was in the Rockies for over two months, but even then the NCT was on my mind, all the time until I returned home. And that's when the planning began, way back in 2011.

In 2012 several important milestones took place. By the beginning of the summer I finally had all the gear I would need for my thru-hike attempt of the NCT, now less than a year away. Right before my final semester of college I spent a week backpacking around Isle Royale National Park in the middle of Lake Superior. My mission was two-fold, first to give all my gear a final field test before I made the decision to rely on it for more than six months.

The second was to force myself to do 20-mile days while I was there to give my body a taste of what I would need to do on the trail. For the Midwest, Isle Royale is pretty strenuous, basically just mountains sticking up out of the surface of the world's largest lake. The trip was a success, all my gear worked perfectly, the high-mile days didn't bother me and I even had my first dose of trail magic on the island.

Earlier in August I had a weekend free so I decided to spend it logging a few miles with my gear. I headed across the river to Wisconsin for a weekend on the Ice Age National Scenic Trail. Nimblewill Nomad was thru-hiking it at the time and was within a few days of finishing. I left my car at a trailhead nearly 40 miles from the trail's Western Terminus at Interstate Park where I got dropped off and began my hike. I camped that night on the St. Croix River and began early in the morning, intending to do a high-mile day with a heavier-than-normal pack to get used to the weight.

About mid-day I encountered a group of hikers coming towards me, and the guy in the middle was non-other than Nimblewill Nomad himself. I couldn't believe this, I thought he was still a few days away, but here he was, the guy that had inspired me to do my first ever thru-hike, on the North Country Trail no less. I introduced myself and explained what an inspiration he was to me, and of my plans to thru-hike the behemoth North Country Trail. We talked for maybe fifteen minutes, he gave me some good advice, some rules to live by on the trail. He was on the final day of his Ice Age Trail thru-hike so I didn't want to hold him up. Our meeting was brief, but it was an amazing experience.

I graduated on time in December of 2012 with my Natural Resources degree and a few adventures under my belt, and then spent the next three months preparing for the journey ahead. I was consumed by cooking dehydrated meals, organizing food drops, pouring over maps, purchasing any last minute gear, making a list of contacts and ultimately mentally preparing myself for the 4,600-mile journey. After roughly a year and half of various stages of planning I was as ready as I was ever going to be. The longest backpacking trip I had been on up to this point was my six day trip to Isle Royale the previous summer to test out a lot of my gear.

This trek is the most ambitious thing I have done, and I knew it would undoubtedly be the hardest thing I had ever attempted. But all that planning paid off, as you know by reading this that I did in fact reach my goal and became the fourth person to successfully thru-hike the North Country National Scenic Trail. It was the journey of a lifetime, and I am grateful to have had the opportunity to grow because of it.

This book is intended for you, as a resource for any potential future hikers of the NCT, or simply as a campfire story to read while you're out on your own adventures or in your backyard.

Luke "Strider" Jordan

Nimblewill Nomad and Strider along the Ice Age
National Scenic Trail, WI August 2012.

REFLECTIONS

What Sue and I remember about the NCT is that every day was different. It began with canals and rail trails, these enabled us to walk along great rivers and through the dark hemlocks of Pennsylvania. New York brought rugged mountains, pristine lakes and summer snow!

Now headed west, we headed north into the forests of Michigan, across the spectacular Mackinaw Bridge and along the wild shores of Lake Superior. Wisconsin featured floating bridges, installed when the ground was frozen. Minnesota meant a return to Lake Superior along the Canadian Shield of the Superior Hiking Trail. We raced winter in North Dakota finishing in temperatures that hovered just above zero. The "Big Sky" here was unforgettable.

I have hiked most every major trail in the US and the North Country Trail is by far my favorite!

Ed Talone & Sue Lockwood – NCT 1994

The NCT is a very different experience than the better known long-distance trails like the Appalachian and Pacific Crest Trails. Most notably, it traverses a region of the country, not a mountain range, so there is much greater diversity in the path itself -- forested trails of course, but also canal towpaths, section line roads, rails-to-trails, farm lanes, irrigation ditches, and more.

Also, within "the north country," there is tremendous diversity longitudinally, coinciding the variables of precipitation, continental glaciation, and human development. In short, I thought the NCT gave me a broader understanding of the land, its history, and people than other trails had. The other distinct difference is the lack of hiking culture.

As a NCT thru-hiker, you're an anomaly and an instant hero, not just another mustached vagabond whose presence is as predictable as spring buds and fall colors. Locals are much more likely to interact and engage, which is an additional element with tremendous value.

Andrew Skurka – "C2C" 2004-2005

The question asked by so many today, as always, was: "Why?" The why meaning, why are you doing this; what drives a person to hoist a pack and walk over 4,000 miles? I used to tell folks that if you gotta ask the question, you aren't going to understand the answer...

It's the people, the places, the pain, and the trials.
It's the joy and the blessings that come with the miles.
It's a calling gone out to a fortunate few,
To wander the fringes of God's hazy blue.

MJ Eberhart (Nimblewill Nomad) – NCT 2009

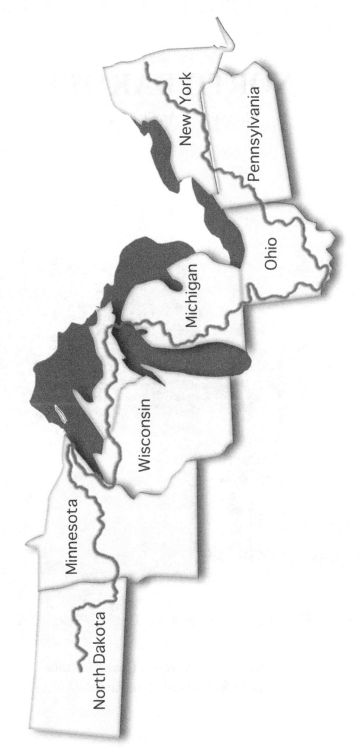

NORTH DAKOTA

March 27 - April 15, 2013

Western Terminus North Country Trail –
Lake Sakakawea State Park, ND

Wednesday, March 27, 2013
Trail Day 001
Miles hiked: 09
Sakakawea Motel - Pick City, ND

I enjoy being an early riser, and this morning was no exception. I was up at 4:30 a.m. to load the car with supplies for ten days. For the first leg of my hike, I will have a support crew to help me get through the areas of North Dakota that have no camping available along the trail. My mother Roxanne, has some vacation days saved up and has agreed to help. I will be staying in motels during this time and will get dropped off and picked up at the end of each day; which will allow me to slack pack for this first leg of the journey and cover more ground.

It's about a seven-hour drive from my home in central Minnesota, to the trail's western terminus at Lake Sakakawea State Park. We are there by 2 p.m. For the past few weeks I have been in contact with John, park manager, getting information about snow conditions and letting him know that I am arriving today. We arrive and find that the visitor center is locked and no one seems to be around.

John had mentioned that we should try the maintenance building if this happened. Sure enough we find John supervising a small construction crew. Before we know it he had let us in to the visitor center and we are looking over maps of the portion of the trail that I will be hiking today. He offers to drive us along the route before I start hiking and we accept.

As we are preparing to leave, John pulls a book out from his desk and hands it to me. I have heard about this book and I quickly realize how significant it is. This book is a special trail register that only the folks who have come to hike the North Country Trail have signed. Many of the names I recognize: Ed Talone (first NCT thru-hike), Peter Wolfe (first end-to-ender—not a thru-hike), Andrew Skurka (second thru-hike), Bart Smith (end-to-ender), Joan Young (end-to-ender—first woman), and Nimblewill Nomad, whom I know personally (third thru-hike). I add my name to this register, and as I hand it back to John it is time to start my hike.

The trail begins just a stone's throw away from the visitor center where a big wooden sign marked the spot. I take a picture in front of the sign before I finally turn and take my first steps on this 4,600-mile journey...it's 3:01p.m. Thank you John, for making this an extraordinary beginning to a grand adventure.

I hike the nearly two miles of trail in the park in no time and soon find myself at the Garrison Dam, where I will begin a road walk that will take me across the dam, through the town of Riverdale, and along some back roads. Along the route, I pass by a few signs marking the auto-tour route of the Lewis and Clark National Historic Trail.

There is plenty of breathtaking scenery along the route, some nice views of the Missouri River looking south from the dam, and a grand view over Lake Sakakawea from the high bluff where the road runs. I certainly hope they can eventually build some off-road trail along the rim of the bluff between the lake and the road (it would make a fantastic segment of trail). A few hours after beginning my trek, I end the day about a mile south of Wolf Creek Campground. In total, I had hiked about nine miles on the first day of this journey.

Thursday, March 28
Trail Day 002
Miles hiked: 25
R&H Motel, Trailer Park & Bait Shop - McClusky, ND

I got a late start today, didn't get going until 8:45 a.m. I get dropped off where I ended my hike last night near Wolf Creek Wildlife Management Area, and begin a long stretch of road walk through Audubon National Wildlife Refuge. It's a foggy morning and visibility is poor as I make my way down the quite gravel road, a layer of frost coating the fences and the branches of the few trees along the route.

I make a slight detour to stop in at the visitor center and tell the people there about my hike. They inform me that the auto-tour route would take me along the lake for the entire trip through the refuge, vs. the straight road that bypasses the refuge and misses the lake. So I take the auto-tour route. But unfortunately, the dense fog blocks my view of the lake. What I do see are dozens of pheasants, even after I exit the refuge.

A few miles east of the refuge I come to the second segment of certified trail in North Dakota. This segment follows along the McClusky Canal using the towpath, which is more of a service road through this area. I hike six miles of this before calling it a day. Roxanne intercepts me along the canal towpath and we head to the small town of McClusky a ways down the road. I hiked 25 miles today, the first of many such long days I will need to achieve if I hope to reach the end of the trail in New York before the snow falls once again.

Fri. March 29
Trail Day 003
Miles hiked: 29
R&H Motel, Trailer Park & Bait Shop - McClusky, ND

Today was a pretty uneventful. I started hiking at 8:40 a.m., my entire trek following along the McClusky Canal. Early in the day, I pass a few clumps of frost-covered trees, a few old abandoned farmsteads, and get a view of about 50 deer as I follow the colorful carsonite posts along the way marking the trail. At one point, I am presented with some surprising terrain where the towpath stops. I make my way up and through the prairie grass along the portion of the canal known as the "deep cut", on some significant slopes above the canal, which now looked more like a small canyon.

Back to the towpath again I pass through a series of campsites along the McClusky Chain of Lakes, one of the few designated camping areas on this side of the state. I pass by the first cluster of sites and end my hike at Hecker's Lake where Roxanne is waiting with the vehicle.

The hard surface of the canal towpath did a number on my feet today. The first blister is forming and my body is sore. The first thing I do back at the motel is get a nice soak in the tub, then a good night's sleep.

Saturday March 30
Trail Day 004
Miles hiked: 24
R&H Motel, Trailer Park & Bait Shop - McClusky, ND

Today is my last full day of hiking along the McClusky Canal. I'm looking forward to hiking through Lonetree Wildlife Management Area to give my swollen feet a break from the continuous pounding of the gravel towpath. The views along the canal have been better than I expected and have made for many good photos. Early on, I snap a good one looking across New Johns Lake.

I get the first five miles of my hike done in pretty good time until I hit the eastern edge of the chain of lakes and the re-emergence of the canal where I encounter some snow. It's the kind of snow that is deep enough to make your progress slow and treacherous but not deep enough to warrant using snowshoes. This unfortunate obstacle makes the going today painfully slow. Despite starting at 8 a.m., I don't have enough time to make it to my pre-determined end point at the pace I'm going, so I call ahead and let my ride know I need to bail out three miles sooner than I intended, not far from the town of McClusky.

After being intercepted at the canal towpath, I'm informed that an editor from the *McClusky Gazette* wants to interview me about my hike. Back at the motel the editor arrives and we have a fun-filled interview about the trail and my inspiration for hiking it. She brought me some homemade goodies, including some meatball soup and wheat bread. What a joy to be treated to some trail magic so early in the hike.

I spend the rest of the night soaking my feet and making plans for tomorrow, we will be moving to a new spot up the trail after spending the last three nights here in McClusky.

Sunday March 31 - Easter
Trail Day 005
Miles hiked: 22
R&R Hotel - Harvey, ND

Today is the first day I need to use my snowshoes. As a result, my progress is slow. It takes me most of the day to reach the end of the canal and the entrance to Lonetree Wildlife Management Area. I take a picture of the big brown sign and head on in. In the summer, the trail through Lonetree is a mowed path through the prairie. But now I am able to see a white ribbon through the snow where there is no vegetation to indicate the mowed path. The trail is also marked with yellow carsonite posts along the entire route, so I easily find my way.

During the day the sun is blazing overhead and I can feel it burning in my face. I quickly come to the painful realization that while packing for these first few weeks in winter I completely overlooked packing sunscreen. My face felt a bit warm last night already, and I'm sure by the time I get back to the motel my face is going to be in pretty bad shape. I end my hike at the Jensen Campground after watching 50 deer dash away as I arrive. Roxanne snaps a few photos of me arriving at the campground wearing big snowshoes. Then we load up and head to the motel in Harvey, a step up from our place in McClusky.

Monday, April 1
Trail Day 006
Miles hiked: 22
R&R Hotel - Harvey, ND

The snow has been steadily getting deeper little by little since I began hiking the off-road segments. We had a fresh snowfall last night and there is a foot of snow all along the trail today, making for another painfully slow day.

Today's hike takes me all the way through Lonetree WMA. There isn't a whole lot to see because of the deeper snow, but the trail here does pass through a few campgrounds, some sunflower fields, and scenic some lakes. I manage to take a good video from the hill which over looked Sheyenne Lake with a bit of artificial "prairie art" in the foreground. Unfortunately, there is some illegal snowmobile and ATV use on the trail near the campgrounds; a disappointing sight for sure. Just as I pass the sign declaring the eastern edge of Lonetree WMA, a large Jackrabbit scampers away toward the New Rockford Canal where I hike a few more miles before calling it a day.

Back at the motel, I discover that my lower lip actually got the worst of the sunburn from the past few days. Additionally, my legs, feet, and toes took a beating today from the continuous use of the heavy snow shoes. So, I am very sore at the end of the day. A nice hot soak in the tub and a cold beer go a long way to ease the discomfort.

Tuesday, April 2
Trail Day 007
Miles hiked: 26
Bison Lodge - New Rockford, ND

Today I got a late start in an attempt to get well rested after the hard day yesterday. Despite starting at 10 a.m., I still manage to make good time and get 26 miles in by 7 p.m. The New Rockford Canal is much straighter and more snow-free than the McClusky Canal, so it is an easy hike (though there isn't much interesting to see). I see a fox scamper away into the nearby field early in the day as I hike along the incredibly flat towpath, marking my only sighting for the day. With more hard-surface pounding, a few more blisters have appeared and I spend a good deal of time back at the motel tending to my feet.

Wednesday, April 3
Trail Day 008
Miles hiked: 28
Bison Lodge - New Rockford, ND

Today is my last day hiking along the New Rockford Canal. It also happens to be my last day hiking a long continuous segment of trail stretching from the western end of the McClusky Canal to the eastern end of the New Rockford Canal, with Lonetree WMA between. These canal towpaths—no more than a narrow gravel road—are not typical routing for National Scenic Trails. But in this case, they happen to be the only continuous stretch of public land in central North Dakota, operated by the Bureau of Reclamation.

These canals were originally constructed to divert water from the interior of North Dakota west towards Fargo and other population centers. The project was shut down when it was discovered that it would affect watersheds that overlap with Canada. The project was never finished, and now the canals provide a public corridor for the NCT to utilize. I'll take this over the pavement any day.

I start out going at a pretty good pace; making it the 15 miles to the end of the canal by 2 p.m. From here it is a long roadwalk all the way to Lake Ashtabula where the next segment of certified trail awaits. I'll be completely on the road for at least the next two days.

After leaving the canal behind, the route brings me through the town of New Rockford and right by our motel where I stop in for some tune ups and to have a quick snack. My ankle is bothering me and I have another blister forming, so it's time for some Moleskin and Biofreeze to ease the pain and discomfort.

Continuing on the roadwalk south of town, I pass an abandoned farm. Right along the road, right where I need to hike, is a skunk! This is bad news as I don't want to get sprayed. (I've heard, if you're close enough you can actually go blind.) I'm not taking any chances, so I get a little closer, shouting as I do so, but unable to get his attention. I resort to picking up a piece of gravel from the road and throwing it at him, landing it about six inches in front of him. Now I've got his attention. He slowly scampers off. A few more well-placed rocks gets him out of "firing range", and I am safe to pass.

A half mile further down the road I spot another skunk. I have to go through this all over again. This guy doesn't seem to notice me as I throw rocks, and instead, decides to chase after them rather than retreat. It takes a near-direct hit to finally get him to notice me before he finally scampers away, tired of being bombarded by projectiles.

Now safe from any unpleasant smells, I continue on the road walk until my feet have had enough. I get picked up at the 28-mile mark.

On the way back to the motel we spot three raccoons at the same spot I encountered the skunks not an hour before. Looks like the old farm nearby isn't abandoned after all. After some dinner and another hot soak in the tub I'm ready for bed.

Thursday, April 4
Trail Day 009
Miles hiked: 28.5
Westside Motel - Cooperstown, ND

Today's hike is all a roadwalk from where I left off yesterday to where I end the day a few miles west of the small town of Binford.

It starts out on gravel roads taking me past a few old farms and eventually turns to pavement. Along my route three locals stop as they drive past and ask if I am in trouble or "just getting some exercise." I let them know that everything is fine, that I'm just out for a walk. Everyone I've encountered so far on this trek has been really nice, ready and willing to help those in need.

The sunburn I received last week has finally taken its toll as my face. It has become blistered and the peeling causes great discomfort and pain most of the day. I'm still mostly in good spirits despite some discomfort in several places. I'm intercepted along the roadwalk at the end of another long day and I celebrate at the pizza ranch in Cooperstown. We have moved our base camp again and got a room at the motel here in town for the next two nights. After downing an entire pizza and getting hot shower, I'm ready to relax and drift off to sleep.

Friday, April 5
Trail Day 010
Miles hiked: 31
Westside Motel - Cooperstown, ND

Today's hike is another full day of roadwalking, mostly on paved roads. I start near Binford where I ended yesterday, and make pretty good time until the weather turns sour. First, a strong wind out of the south shows up and tries to blow me off the road. Then, the snow comes and I put on some blaze clothing because the visibility has become so poor. I pull off the road for a break and take shelter under a church awning out of the wind. Luckily, it only lasts for an hour or two and I'm in Cooperstown before long.

Cooperstown, ND—a nice little trail town if there ever was one— has got everything a hiker needs. There's a grocery store, some restaurants, post office, and some cheap motels. I stop in to our motel for lunch, since the strong wind and a busy shoulderless State Highway, discouraged me from stopping to eat earlier. It's about 4 p.m. and I realize I only need to hike two more miles to make it a 25 mile day. I decide to try and get a little ahead on the mileage. After nearly three hours of fighting against the wind, I finally call it quits in front of a small church and claim victory; 31 miles hiked today!

Saturday, April 6
Trail Day 011
Miles hiked: 19
Super 8 Motel - Valley City, ND

Getting up this morning was not easy. My feet are sore from the hard pounding of the pavement the past few days, and I'm exhausted from the long hours yesterday. I still manage to get going a little after 8 a.m., and make good time on the last seven miles of roadwalk I have today.

The remainder of the day is spent hiking along the next certified segment of trail in North Dakota along the shore of Lake Ashtabula. The lake and surrounding land is controlled by the Army Corps of Engineers, but much of the land also is used for cattle pasture...and there are land mines everywhere!

There are many fences to cross (hence today I come to my first stile of this trek). By the end of the day I will have encountered 13 of them, and it certainly is a pain in the butt to cross these things with snowshoes in your arsenal.

Before long, the snow gets too deep and I need to wear the snowshoes again. The stuff around here is over a foot deep in some places, making for very slow hiking. A point of interest I encounter today is a highline railroad bridge that crosses the lake.

I happen to walk under just as a train is passing over and I get some good video footage. From this point it is five miles to Sibley Crossing, one of two possible pick up points today. To my dismay, I find that the deep snow coupled with the rugged terrain only allowed me to hike eleven miles in the last seven hours of the day. I am forced to bail off here, four miles away from my planned pickup point as the daylight fades away and we head to our new motel in Valley City.

Sunday, April 7
Trail Day 012
Miles hiked: 17
Lake Ashtabula, about a mile south of Kate Olson's Landing

Waking up in a warm comfy motel and knowing you have to trudge on out into the cold is not a pleasant feeling. Even worse is knowing that you have to do it alone, no support crew to pick you up at the end of the day. Alas, today is my first day as an unassisted hike.

Roxanne was kind enough to use some vacation days to shuttle me out here to North Dakota to get me started on this trek over the North Country Trail. Between Lake Sakakawea and Lake Ashtabula there are no places to camp besides the one section along the McClusky chain of lakes, so thru-hiking this portion of the trail is impossible without a support crew. She had ten days available to spend with me, and today is the last one. So here, about a mile south of Sibley Crossing, it is time to say goodbye. Some photos are taken, some words spoken, some tears shed, and then I turn and start hiking.

The first quarter mile is uphill so I pause at the top and take a last glance back. I look toward the car and lift my trekking poles high, remembering a quote from a documentary we watched together a few months earlier about thru-hiking the Pacific Crest Trail. The finishing quote of that film was the final rule for a thru-hike: Rule #12 "Be Unstoppable".

Now as I look down toward the car, I am filled with determination. This is my first thru-hike and I do have doubts that I will even make it to the end. But I know I am going to give it my best, everything I have. *Thank You Mom, for driving me out here, taking care of me, and making the first leg of this trip more enjoyable.*

It isn't very long until I need the snowshoes, but then I don't need them for long. The trail is very "patchy". Short stretches of deep snow were followed by longer stretches of no snow, so progress is again very slow. Early in the hike I face my first obstacle, a frozen creek with no crossing visible.

I search for a safe place to cross and finally find one that looks suitable, about four feet wide. As I take my first step into the snow on the opposite side of the creek, I lose my balance as my leg plunges down into water up to my waist. I had not made it to the other side after all, it had only appeared that way because of the snow. I've been on my own only a few hours and already my feet are soaking wet and cold. I have no choice but to hike on, and since my feet are already wet, I decide to do without the snowshoes most of the day.

After hiking through miles of cow pasture I can see a row of houses appearing in the distance. I expected the trail to travel around them since these houses are right on the lakeshore, but no, as I arrive I discover that the trail goes right along the lake through people's backyards! I have to weave my way around boat trailers, picnic tables, and fishing docks behind people's houses to hike this trail. In the many years I've been hiking, I've never hiked on a trail like this before; it's a very goofy situation. I hike about a mile beyond this weird place and pitch my tent near a fence line for the night.

Monday, April 8
Trail Day 013
Miles hiked: 19
Super 8 Motel - Valley City, ND

It is very cold getting up this morning...even my shoes have frozen! It's a struggle to get them to fit, and afterwards comes about ten minutes of torture as I force my feet into icy cold shoes. Once my feet get pounding on the trail they warm up to a reasonable level. I have a five mile hike to the Baldhill Dam where this segment of trail ends. I need the snowshoes the whole way so it takes a few hours to get there.

The Army Corps of Engineers have an office here at the dam and I stop in to introduce myself. Here I meet Scott, the head guy, and we have a nice chat. He's hiked most of the trail between Lake Ashtabula and The Sheyenne Grasslands so he gives me the rundown on what I can expect the next few days. Then I fill up my water bottle and move on.

It's a ten-mile roadwalk from the dam to Valley City and it takes a few hours to get there. On the edge of town another certified segment of trail begins and wanders through the city for about four miles. The highlight of the day is crossing the many bridges across the Sheyenne River, including the Alumni Bridge at Valley City State University. This same bridge was sandbagged about four feet high when Nimblewill Nomad passed through in 2009 due to flooding. Luckily, the river won't reach flood stage for awhile and it remains open for me to cross. After passing through VCSU, the trail climbs the rim of the valley through the woods and enters Medicine Wheel Park providing a great view of the city. It's only a few blocks from here to the Super 8 Motel where I will be spending the night so I head on in.

Once settled into my room, I make a phone call and am soon

talking with Deb, one of the leaders of the Sheyenne River Valley Chapter of the NCTA. I had called her a few days earlier inquiring about a possible shuttle from Baldhill Dam into town, but never made it there because of snow. After our initial conversation she wanted to meet me, so we arranged a meeting at a diner across the street. I head on over and meet Deb, and another volunteer, Drew, and we have a nice chat about the trail. We go over details of new segments constructed in the area and conditions I will encounter further south. After downing a burger and two sodas (thanks Deb) it's time to head back to the motel and get a good night's sleep, safely indoors from the blizzard beginning outside.

Tuesday, April 9
Trail Day 014
Miles hiked: 20
Clausen Springs Park

I slept in this morning and didn't get out of bed until 7:30 a.m. It's probably my last night in a motel for a long while so I wanted to make the most of it. For breakfast I grab a cup of orange juice and downed three donuts while packing my gear. About an hour after eating, applying Biofreeze to my ankle, and sending a few emails, I am out the door and hiking south out of Valley City on a short segment of paved bike trail beginning right at the motel entrance, marked by an official NCT marker.

The route is mostly a roadwalk that parallels the Sheyenne River until it leaves the pavement and follows some gravel back roads and grassy field roads. Near the place where the gravel and field roads meet there is an interesting abandoned structure that if acquired and a little work done, could make a fine shelter for the NCT. A newly-constructed segment of trail begins at this point and heads south to Clausen Springs Park using field roads and a "chute" between two fence rows.

The park at Clausen Springs has several developed campgrounds and a day use area for fishing. The scenery is different from what I've encountered so far. There's a lake, some wetlands, and planted ponderosa pine trees all around. When I arrive, the freezing wind has picked up to about 40 mph, and with the ground completely frozen there is nowhere to drive a tent stake; making it impossible to pitch a tent without it blowing away. The temperature feels like it is dropping by the minute and I am getting desperate for warmth.

There is only one structure nearby with walls and it happens to be a restroom facility. I check the door and it is unlocked (luckily it appears to have been recently cleaned). I decide that taking shelter in this structure is a better choice than being out in the howling wind, so reluctantly I make a place for myself on the floor, using my sleeping pad as a mattress. The thought of spending the night in a bathroom had never occurred to me before today and I would feel grossed out by it had this place not recently been cleaned.

In times of desperation we all have to make tough choices, and I'm almost positive I'm not the only hiker who has resorted to this uncomfortable situation. Though I am out of the wind it is still frigidly cold and getting to sleep proves to be difficult.

Wednesday, April 10
Trail Day 015
Miles hiked: 24
Mineral Springs Campsite - Sheyenne State Forest

I awoke in my little "shelter" to find that everything had frozen during the night. My food, my water, and my wet shoes. It takes all the strength I have to get my frozen shoes to fit and then I'm out of there and back on the trail, fighting through about twenty minutes of frostbite until the shoes thaw.

From Clausen Springs, there is a four-mile segment of trail leading to the town of Kathryn along an abandoned railroad grade. I've hiked on several rail grades back in Minnesota and am used to them having a crushed limestone surface. The Luce Line Trail runs just over a mile from my house and I've had many pleasant walks along it, so my hopes are high for a quick start to the hike.

I arrive at the beginning of the trail to find that the surface is ballast, which makes for slow hiking. Ballast is basically the original railroad bed with only the rails and ties removed, leaving behind large chunks of loose rock. The going is slow, I have to calculate each step to avoid rolling an ankle.

I make it to Kathryn, there to begin a roadwalk along the Sheyenne Scenic Byway to Fort Ransom State Park. Two locals stop along the way to wish me well on my hike and warn me about the weather coming up tomorrow. It's a pleasant walk along the byway. The terrain here is pretty rugged compared to what I've encountered so far, lots of rolling hills with heavy tree cover and some steep canyon walls.

The river banks out here in North Dakota are some of the few places in the northern plains where the eastern hardwood forest is still around, and I have enjoyed these areas.
The scenic byway leads me directly into Fort Ransom State Park. Here I meet John, park manager. He takes my picture under the NCT Arch, and we stop into the office to chat. Unfortunately, I will miss most of the trail in the park because it is a dead-end segment. Hopefully, if I finish my hike before the snow flies, I will be able to come back and hike this section in the fall.

From the park it is about a mile and a half to the small town of Fort Ransom where I stop in at the Old Mill Grill for a burger and a few beers with the locals. They had just stopped serving food, but the cook fires it up again for one last burger. Nice folks here in Fort Ransom. I linger awhile and head out again before darkness descends.

From the bar it is about a three-mile hike to the Sheyenne State Forest where I hike in one mile on surprisingly snow-free trail to the first campsite and pitch for the night.

Thursday, April 11
Trail Day 016
Miles hiked: 14
Super 8 Motel - Lisbon, ND

I woke up this morning with snow all around me. It feels warm enough out, nothing in my pack is frozen. The snow is just a light dusting so I pack up and head out with no trouble. The Sheyenne State Forest has a three-mile section of NCT (the first to be certified in the state). Unfortunately, it is also a dead-end segment, so working it into a thru-hike is not practical. I also plan to come back in the fall and hike this section. There is a waterfall at the end of it that I do not want to miss, supposedly the only one in the whole state!

From the forest, it's about fourteen miles to Lisbon where I have my first food drop awaits. After only a few miles the snow starts to pick up intensity and visibility becomes poor. The wind picks up and the snow keeps getting deeper, making the trek even slower. Despite leaving before 8 a.m., I don't reach Lisbon until almost 1 p.m.

En route to the post office, a woman in a van pulls over and shouts over to me. "Are you the hiker? Would you mind stopping in to the *Ransom County Gazette* for an interview?"

I agree to her request, but also let her know that I need to retrieve my package first. She informs me that the newspaper office is right around the corner from the post office where she'll be waiting. Once I arrive to retrieve my package, I find that they don't open until 1:30 p.m., and I am a few minutes early. I remain inside (free of the snowstorm) and soon the same woman walks through the door. Hence I meet Jeanne. She offers to take me out to lunch at a cafe down the street where she will conduct the interview. Now this I just can't refuse.

It only takes a few minutes to retrieve my box then I'm off to the cafe. I order a Philly sub with a lemonade and work on demolishing them both during the interview. While I'm still eating the main course, she leaves for a few minutes and comes back with a large piece of chocolate cake—by far the best cake I've ever tasted! She asks me a few more questions, then it was time to continue on my way.

I find that my meal had already been taken care of, and the hostess wishes me "happy travels." *Thank you Jeanne, and the fine folks at Hotdenattes. The generosity and kindness you've shown me will be hard to match.*

I have another fifteen miles to reach the Sheyenne National Grassland, where I planned to spend the night. But with the pace I've been going so far today, and with the storm not letting up, there is no way I can make it there by dark. I decide to spend the night in Lisbon and hope the storm blows over by morning. I check in to the Super 8 in town, sort through my supply package, and catch up on journal entries. With any luck I can get an early start in the morning and make up some lost mileage caused by the blizzard.

Friday, April 12
Trail Day 017
Miles hiked: 26
Sheyenne National Grassland

I got up at 6 a.m. so I would have time to pack my gear after letting it dry, take a shower, and eat breakfast. A few incoming phone calls delay the process, but I am still out the door before 8 a.m. The roadwalk to the trailhead at the Sheyenne National Grasslands is slow going through the town of Lisbon because of the icy roads. Once on the gravel back roads though, I'm able to make decent time, despite getting confused a few times on where to go.

One thing I discovered on day one of this trek is, that many of these back roads in North Dakota are not marked. To make matters more confusing many of the roads that appear on most maps aren't really roads, but narrow two-tracks between farmer's fields. I encountered one of these spots today, completely drifted over with snow. Without a GPS unit it is often hard to determine if you are turning on the right street. Despite the confusion, I manage to cover the fifteen miles to the west trailhead of the grassland a few minutes after 1 p.m.

I'm surprised to find that the snow in here is not deep enough to require snowshoes, so my feet are wet most of the day as I trudge in. The trail is fairly easy to follow with large wooden posts marking the trail, although many of them have been knocked over by cattle and I do get off track a few times. Along most of the trail I can see evidence of a gravel tread way, I assume to keep the trail from being destroyed by cattle. There are plenty more landmines to watch out for. The highlight of the day is passing through a fairly large and thick pine plantation, reminding me of the great north woods back home.

After a few more hours, the sky starts to darken and I pitch for the night on snow-free ground just outside a large stand of oak trees.

Saturday, April 13
Trail Day 018
Miles hiked: 28
NDSU Ekre Grassland Preserve

My shoes are once again frozen as I leave my tent this morning. I have about seventeen miles to go to reach the eastern end of the grasslands and I realize that I have overslept. A few miles into the hike I discover that this isn't going to be an easy day.

The snow is deeper out here than it was when I entered the grassland so the snowshoes come out, and the going becomes slow. I also notice that I have a bent trekking pole. I'm not sure how it happened, I haven't taken any major falls yet this trek and the terrain is pretty flat. It sure is disappointing though. These things are supposed to be nearly indestructible and here I have a bent pole only eighteen days into a hike on flat terrain. Hopefully there will be an opportunity to get it replaced in the future.

After a while the snow thins out a little and I'm at the awkward stage again, just like along the McClusky Canal. The snow is too shallow to need snowshoes but too deep to hike normally. The snowshoes come off again and my feet are wet and cold the whole day. Several times I post-hole up to my knees causing great discomfort. I am already getting sick of hiking through this stuff and it's affecting my progress and my mood...and today is definitely not a good day for either of those things.

I don't reach the eastern trailhead until about 5 p.m. and I have a choice to make. From here the rest of the trail in the state is mostly on private land. I can either pitch here for the night or push on to the next campsite, which is more than ten miles away. I decide that stopping here would be too short of a day and I want to get away from this snow-covered slosh bog. So I push on.

I'm still about four miles away when it starts to get dark. I'm hiking along busy ND-18 now so I put on my headlamp to make me more visible, stepping into the ditch every five minutes to dodge passing semis. I've been hiking in the dark for almost an hour when I finally see a trail marker on a fence post to my left. The campsite is beyond the fence across a field, but being so dark and covered with snow there's no way I'll be able to find it. Instead I climb the nearby stile to my right and pitch for the night along the edge of the trees. Today was a long stressful day and I'm definitely ready for bed.

Sunday, April 14
Trail Day 019
Miles hiked 10
Home of Tony and Mary - Colfax, ND

My time camping near the trailhead last night was short lived. I carry a Delorme inReach device with me in case I get into trouble. When I got in my tent last night I received a message that said there was a severe winter storm coming in early tomorrow. I consider my options:

#1- There is a ranch on this property owned by the university that I could seek refuge in as soon as I awoke in the morning.
#2- I could try and alert someone from the local chapter about my plans.

There is one person I know who lives nearby, so I decide to give them a call. I feel guilty because it's now after 11 p.m. and I don't like to ask for things unless it's an emergency. I'm not sure if this situation qualifies, but I'm surprised when someone answers the phone.

I explain my situation and that I wanted to alert someone of my plans in case I got stranded. They decide they won't let me spend the night in the cold and offer to host me for the night. I pack up all my gear and within a few minutes a van pulls up to the trailhead. Hence I meet Tony, a teacher from Colfax who is actively involved with the Dakota Prairie Chapter to develop a six-mile stretch of trail between Walcott and Colfax. We arrive at his home and I meet his wife, Mary, whom I spoke with on the phone. We spend the next hour having a nice chat about my trip, my future plans, and the local trail segments. They offer me a spot on their couch and within minutes I'm out.

I awoke to find that the storm had not occurred. After checking the forecast it appears the storm has been delayed and won't hit until about 1 p.m. today. I decide to avoid making this a zero-mile day and hike as far as I can until the storm hits. Tony drops me off back at the spot I was camped at and I begin my hike.

The short segment of trail I am hiking this morning is on an old ranch that North Dakota State University now maintains and uses as a field research station known as the Ekre Grassland Preserve. The short segment of NCT plus about two miles of loop trails were all built by Eagle Scouts last summer, so I am the first long-distance hiker to use it. From the ranch it is a ten-mile roadwalk along minimum maintenance roads to Walcott. Unfortunately, I only manage to hike about three miles before the storm hits and I have no choice but to push on to Walcott. My hosts won't be back until noon as they have headed up to Fargo to run some errands. After three hours of trekking through raging wind and snow, I arrive in downtown Walcott where a section of newly created trail begins and Tony arrives at the same time to pick me up.

What a relief to be out of the cold. En route to their household we stop for a pancake breakfast at the community center in Colfax and I waste no time devouring several plates of eggs and pancakes. A bunch of local kids hear my story from Tony and Mary and I am surprised when a few of them walk up to me and ask for my autograph. I hope these kids will get out and enjoy this great trail once it warms up later this spring.

The rest of the day is spent resting and planning for the next few days. I make a call to Tom in Fargo to let him know I've connected with Tony and am safe from the storm. Tom is NCTA board president. I met him last year when I volunteered in Minneapolis, and he provided the information on the new segments in this area and the local contact information, which included Tony's information.

I will spend the night here again and keep trekking in the morning, hopefully making it to Abercrombie at the Red River, then cross into Minnesota on Tuesday morning. Tony and Mary have been such wonderful hosts. *Thank you dear friends for sharing your home with me during this horrific winter storm. I am extremely grateful for your hospitality and your kindness, God bless.*

Monday, April 15
Trail Day 020
Miles hiked: 16
Aber Park - Abercrombie, ND

The storm has finally passed this morning. I'm treated to a fine breakfast of toast and fresh fruit, then it's time to say goodbye and hit the trail. Tony drops me off in Walcott and I begin my hike south along the railroad tracks. There is new trail along the edge of the tracks within the ROW all the way into Colfax; making a six-mile long continuous segment. It is still being developed but there are plenty of blazes available to follow, most of them tacked on to the sides of the old telegraph poles.

The snow is deep because of the storm so I need the snowshoes to traverse this segment. About a half mile north of Colfax, I come to a newly built campsite complete with a latrine and picnic table, all the result of hard work by Tony and his FFA crew. *Nice work guys.*

Once I reach downtown, it is a roadwalk to the town of Abercrombie on the Red River, the boundary between North Dakota and Minnesota. I stop in at the Fort Saloon for a few drinks and a hot meal. There are only a few people here quietly conversing. On the television, the tragedy in Boston is all over the news. (*Three were killed and 264 others were injured during the Boston Marathon after a calculated bombing near the finish line.*) A guy at the table across from me sees my gear and has questions about my plans. I tell my story and where I'm headed and he seems very impressed.

After downing my meal, Tammy (the bartender) informs me that my meal has been paid for, and another beer provided by this same guy, a local named Jon. This is incredible! I've known Jon only ten minutes and he wants to pay for my meal.
Thank you very much Jon, for your generosity.

I linger for a few hours watching the news story and making some phone calls. When I go up to the bar to pay for my drinks Tammy informs me that the last one was on her. This is amazing, thanks so much Tammy. I head back outside and walk the few blocks to Fort Abercrombie State Park.

Here is a reconstruction of an important fort that was once on the very frontier of our nation at the time, and marks the boundary between North Dakota and Minnesota. For tonight I pitch at the Aber Park campground across the street, tomorrow I will cross the Red River and enter Minnesota.

A frosty morning along the McClusky Canal.

MINNESOTA

April 16 - May 28, 2013

Tuesday, April 16
Trail Day 021
Miles hiked: 24
Comfort Zone Inn - Rothsay, MN

From Fort Abercrombie it's entirely a roadwalk to Maplewood State Park, the first off-road trail in Minnesota. My target for today is the little town of Rothsay and I'm out at first light.

I cross the river first thing, finally crossing into my home state of Minnesota. As I enter, my mind drifts and briefly struggles with a harsh reality. I've put an entire state behind me and still have well over 4000 miles to go. It's been somewhat of a struggle already to make it here with the lingering winter. New York seems so impossibly far away, I don't know how I'm ever going to manage this.

I shake off the feeling and force myself not to think about the long term, just take it in one day at a time. Think of the thru-hike has a series of day hikes strung together and it wont seem so overwhelming. As I leave the town of Kent behind the roadwalk follows a series of low maintenance roads and brings me past a large drainage ditch with a berm on one side, reminding me of my journey along the McClusky Canal. At first glance it appears that this berm could provide an opportunity for a section of off road trail in the future, it should definitely be investigated as an option.

Today is the first time on this hike I am able to shed some layers and still be comfortable. Around 1 p.m., I take off one of my fleece jackets after stopping for a lunch break on the side of the road. The rest of the day is uneventful as I make my way through mostly open farm country and I get to Rothsay a little after 4 p.m. I check in at the Comfort Zone Inn across the street from the world's largest prairie chicken statue. Nice rooms for an affordable rate...this will do just fine.

Wednesday, April 17
Trail Day XXX
Miles hiked: 00
Comfort Zone Inn - Rothsay, MN

Another snow storm came in early this morning and I woke up exhausted so I decide to take a zero mile day to wait out the storm and get re-energized. It's definitely not a good day to be hiking the roads with the strong wind, the icy road surface and near white-out conditions. The gas station next door has some microwavable meals that I stock up on and I spend the day watching some TV and catching up on journal entries. Hopefully I can continue on tomorrow.

Thursday, April 18
Trail Day 022
Miles hiked: 29
Pelican Motel - Pelican Rapids, MN

I awoke at the crack of dawn to ensure I can make the twenty-nine miles to my destination and I am hiking by 6:30 a.m. As I leave the motel the storm is still raging, the wind trying to again throw me off the road and visibility is poor. Once I reach the little town of Erhard, I take a break under the overhanging roof of the liquor store to have some water and snacks. It's pretty quiet, not many cars on the road.

A few miles further down the road I am at the south entrance to Maplewood State Park. This whole area is a complex of giant hills deposited here by the last glacier, sometimes known locally as the Maplewood Hills or Leaf Hill Moraines. On a clear day you can get some fantastic views across the many lakes and to the bluffs on the far side. Within the park I pick up about four miles of off-road trail, snowshoes needed the whole time. Despite the heavy snowfall I still get some nice (hazy) views of some of the bluffs. Once I leave the north entrance to the park it is a roadwalk along scenic MN-108. The snow has stopped but the wind hasn't relented. Unfortunately, this road has no shoulder and in many places it is a narrow causeway between two lakes. At these places the snow has blown across the road and caused ice to form, additionally visibility is poor. I am forced to move over far into the ditch to give passing cars plenty of room.

Despite being in mortal peril for most of this segment, the scenery is spectacular; many lakes, islands and glacial hills. This scenic highway leads me to the town of Pelican Rapids, home of the world's largest pelican. The little trail town has everything a hiker needs all on the main street. I had planned to stay at the municipal campground in town but I arrive to find that there is still two feet of snow in the campground and the wind is still howling.

After traversing a fancy pedestrian bridge from the campground and stopping to admire the giant pelican statue, I decide to push on the extra half mile and stay warm, cozy, and dry in the Pelican Motel on the north side of town. I check in and am disappointed when there is no hot water, but it is still a better alternative than being out in the howling wind with nowhere to drive a tent stake. This will do.

Friday, April 19
Trail Day: 023
Miles hiked: 24
Motor Side Inn - Frazee, MN

I had intended to get up nice and early to start hiking but I am exhausted and ended up sleeping an extra hour. I don't hit the road until 8 a.m., and yes, today is entirely a roadwalk to the town of Frazee. The route takes me along scenic County Road 4 through more lake country. I pass through the small town of Vergas en route to Frazee and make a quick stop at the convenience store. There's not much here in Vergas for services, but I do snap a picture of the world's largest loon at the city park.

A few miles further along the roadwalk, I get another photo of a giant bird as I cross the US-10 overpass and enter the town of Frazee where I see what has to be the world's largest turkey. I have a food drop in town and I notice that it is almost 4 p.m., the post office closes at 4:30 p.m. I increase my pace hoping that the door will not be closed when I get there. I arrive just in time to pick up my package with fifteen minutes to spare.

Back out on the street I make a phone call. I received an email a few days ago from Hank who asked me to call him when I reached Frazee. A few minutes later, a car pulls up and I meet Hank, the mayor of Frazee. He is an active member of the Laurentian Lakes Chapter and is very enthusiastic about my hike and wants to hear all about it. He has already set me up with a motel room and a hot meal at The Hornet. He drives me the few miles out of town to the Motor Side Inn and tells me he'll be back to pick me up at 6 p.m. for dinner.

I waste no time in unpacking my gear, drying my wet socks, and getting a hot shower. Sure enough, Hank is there to pick me up at 6 p.m., and we head to The Hornet for dinner. Barbie, the editor for the *Frazee Forum*, joins us. She had sent me an email awhile back requesting an interview, and I had spoken to her during my day off in Rothsay. But she wanted to come down to meet me and get a photo, so the three of us have a wonderful chat.

Afterwards it's back to the motel, and Hank says he'll pick me up in the morning for breakfast. I make another call to Matt, Regional Trail Coordinator for North Dakota and Minnesota, NCTA. I've met him many times before and he offered to host me for a day or two as I hike through Tamarac National Wildlife Refuge. We make plans to meet at a road crossing in the refuge tomorrow and then I'd spend tomorrow night under his roof. Plans in place, I spend the rest of the night organizing my food drop and then it's time for bed.

Saturday, April 20
Trail Day 024
Miles hiked: 21
Home of Matt and Stacy - Detroit Lakes, MN

Hank picks me up at the motel and we're off to have breakfast at a cafe. I order the sausage, mushroom, and cheese omelet, with orange juice. I quickly devour them. Several customers stop to wish me luck on my hike, a few of them have been following my journal. After breakfast, Hank makes sure I have some of Frazee's famous turkey jerky and some smoked fish to go. This is unbelievable. *Thank you so much Hank for your generosity and enthusiasm. I had a great time in your friendly town of Frazee.*

From Frazee it is a fourteen-mile roadwalk to the beginning of the certified trail in Minnesota. It also is the beginning of a long continuous segment of trail that stretched from the southern border of Tamarac National Wildlife Refuge all the way to MN-6 just north of the town of Remer (at the edge of the Chippewa National Forest). The roadwalk itself is very scenic.

Before long after leaving Frazee, I can tell I am now in the North Woods. Pine trees are found in great abundance all around. I enjoy the smoked fish and the turkey jerky for lunch on the side of the road just before entering the refuge. I'm glad I stopped there on the side of a little hill free of snow, because where I stand now (at the entrance to Tamarac National Wildlife Refuge), the trail is obstructed by at least two feet of snow. I will definitely need the snowshoes for quite awhile today. After snapping some photos of the entrance and taking a video, I head in. The snow is pretty hard so my pace is not hindered too much. This segment of trail was just built this past year. There are no blazes yet and flagging tape marks the way through the forest. At a road crossing I see a bunch of cars parked and there are many people ice fishing out on Tamarac Lake.

As I cross, a ranger pulls up next to me and rolls down his window. He asks where I'm staying tonight and how long it will take me to get there? "The refuge closes at 10," he says. As soon as he leaves, another ranger on foot comes off the lake and asks me the same questions. These Fish and Wildlife Service guys sure are strict about their "no overnight use" rules. I know the rules though, and I made sure I planned accordingly while doing the research for this hike.

In about an hour, I reach the point where Matt said he would pick me up. The trail doesn't actually cross here but the road is only about 200 feet from it at this spot. I bail off and bushwhack around a beaver pond, up a hill and down the other side, and onto the road just as Matt pulls up in his car. What unbelievable timing!

It's about a half hour drive to Matt's home in Detroit Lakes where I will be spending the night and possibly the following night. When we arrive, he shows me the room they have made ready for me and then I head to the kitchen to cook one of my meals over the stove. I meet Matt's wife Stacy and their four children, who seem fascinated with me and what I'm doing—though also a bit confused about where exactly I live.

I first met Matt two years ago at an informational meeting about the trail at Macalister College in Minneapolis. I was doing research for this hike at the time and went to find out more specific information about the trail in this area. He and Stacy have both hiked the AT and related many of their experiences during dinner. Before too long, it is time for bed as I am overly tired from all the snowshoeing. I'm off to sleep in no time.

Sunday, April 21
Trail day 025
Miles hiked: 12
Home of Matt and Stacy - Detroit Lakes, MN

I awoke fairly early this morning and Matt has me at the trail by 8 a.m. The going is fine at first, the snow is crusty from freezing overnight. After a short time I come to an area I recognize, two bridge crossings followed by a nearly 1,000-foot-long boardwalk through a Tamarac Bog. I helped construct these bridges last October; it's a fine stretch of trail in the fall.

Shortly after the Tamarac bog is a trailhead where I stop to have lunch. Then, just as I am getting ready to continue on a truck drives past, stops, and then pulls in to the trailhead. Two Fish and Wildlife Service officers exit the vehicle, one of them is an officer I had already talked to yesterday.

"Did you spend the night out here last night?" he asked.

Again I tell him where and by whom I got picked up yesterday and what my plans are for today. "Guys, I promise you I am not stealth camping in your refuge. I understand the rules and I intend to follow them. "

After my encounter with the officers I continue on freshly blazed trail and it begins snowing almost immediately. The flakes soon become larger than quarters and it's a total whiteout...in April! Within a few minutes, the trees are completely covered in snow and I can no longer see any blazes. At some point I take a wrong turn and end up at a fence line. This is a wildlife refuge, this fence probably shouldn't be here. I check my GPS and discover that I have walked a half mile in the wrong direction. I find the next waypoint and navigate to it by bush whacking over the fence and through brush. Almost an hour later I have managed to find the trail again and continue on through deepening snow.

Then, the rain starts, softening up the snow. So I sink with every step, even with my snowshoes on. This makes for very slow hiking and I am forced to cut my day significantly shorter than I had planned because it is starting to get late. I am out of the refuge now and had plan to get to Elbow Lake road, but have to bail off at County 35 at the edge of Greenwater Lake SNA. I give Matt a call and he is there to pick me up. Only twelve miles hiked today... this isn't looking good.

Monday, April 22
Trail Day 026
Miles hiked: 14
Home of Ray and Lynette - Bad Medicine Lake

Matt dropped me off this morning at the small pull-off on County Road 35 where I ended my hike yesterday. He and his son William, hike with me for a short distance, then after taking a video, they turn and leave. *Thanks for your hospitality Matt, it was nice to catch up and finally meet your family.*

The hiking is a little better than yesterday but still very slow with the soft snow. The trail in this area is fairly hilly, I get a nice glance of the surrounding area with no leaves blocking the view. After a fairly uneventful day, I make it to the trailhead on MN-113 and make another call. I'm on the phone with Ray, president of the Laurentian Lakes Chapter. He emailed me a few weeks ago saying he would be interested in hosting me for a night. It's supposed to be very cold again tonight so I take him up on his offer.

Within about a half hour, he is there to pick me up and he takes me to his place on Bad Medicine Lake. Here I meet his wife Lynette, and the three of us have dinner. The interior of the house is incredible—Aspen lumber on the ceiling, birch on the floor, complete with a wood stove and a view from the dining room across Bad Medicine Lake. After dinner and a nice conversation about the trail, I retire to the guest bedroom and am asleep in no time.

Tuesday, April 23
Trail Day 027
Miles hiked: 17, +2
Home of Ray and Lynette - Bad Medicine Lake

I got up fairly early this morning and Ray dropped me off at the trailhead on MN-113. I thank him for his hospitality and he says if I run into trouble down the trail I can feel free to give him a call. The snow is crusty again so I'm able to make decent time. Today my goal is to hike eighteen miles to a shelter in Itasca State Park, then to hike to the visitor center in the morning where I have another food drop waiting.

Itasca is significant because it is the headwaters of the mighty Mississippi River. On the north end of the park it begins as a four-foot-wide flowing creek and eventually flows some 2,000 miles to its outflow into the Gulf of Mexico south of New Orleans. The headwaters is a roughly five-mile detour from the trail, and I always wondered why the NCT doesn't go to it. I've been there once (for my seventeenth birthday), and I'm looking forward to a return visit.

Shortly before entering the park, I come to a trailhead with a kiosk and a trail register, half buried in snow. This is the first register I have seen since entering the Sheyenne Grassland in North Dakota. I sign my (trail) name in the book and continue. Soon it becomes obvious that I have entered the park, because the trail is now about twelve-feet wide and shared for some distance with snowmobile trails. At a junction with a major snowmobile trail I have only a few miles to go to reach the shelter I plan to stay in. I continue on, blazes still easy to follow.

The trail here traverses many ridges along lakes and over a causeway with water on all sides. I come to a halt. The trail in front of me does not look like a trail at all. Hundreds of blow downs and thickets of brush block the way. I am standing right next to a blaze so I know I am in the right place, but something isn't right. I am only a mile away from the shelter now and it will be getting dark soon. With the snowshoes still on, I trudge on ahead through the blow downs and brush following somebody's footprints through the snow. My trekking poles become useless and get tangled in the brush. If there ever was a trail here it looks like it's been completely obliterated.

It takes me a half hour to reach the other end of this mess and then more confusion occurs. I appear to be standing at the end of a peninsula, water is visible in front of me indicating that the ice is very thin. The map shows this as solid land, a causeway between two lakes. I don't see a bridge either, and if there is one it is buried under almost three feet of snow. No blazes in sight, no sign of a trail, nothing.

I consult my GPS and it says the next waypoint is straight ahead, but all I see is snow penetrated in spots by water. If I try to cross on snowshoes here I might take a misstep and fall through the ice. I take several minutes to consider my options. I decide to go back and circle around the smaller lake and find the trail on the other side. I nearly lost my balance trying to navigate the blowdowns on snowshoes the first time, so I take them off hoping for more stability. I take my first step and post-hole past my knees. I lose my balance several times and fall on my face. With much struggle, I make it back to the other side of the blowdowns where that last blaze is clearly visible. I get my snowshoes out again to put them back on so I can walk around the lake. I discover that in the last half hour, the temperature has dropped significantly to the point that my snowshoes have frozen solid while they were on my back! They will not fit back on my feet until they thaw.

Panic starts to set in. It's getting dark so I have only a half hour left to get around this lake and find the trail, but without snowshoes it will take much longer. I decide to start heading back the way I came and look for a place to camp. I sink up to my knees with almost every step, losing my balance several times. I take a nose dive and am face down in the snow, trying to get up.

I bring my hand around to brace me, it falls through the snow. I try my other hand, it falls through. Now I try with my knee, no luck. I finally escape by rolling over on my side and using my poles for support. I manage to get back on my feet. I take another step, post-hole and fall again, catching myself with my hands. I lay there for a few seconds, and then a few tears start to form.

Why is this happening? This isn't fair. I've dreamed about this trek for three years and now I have the worst conditions imaginable. Why is there still two and a half feet of snow in late April? I can't take this anymore! All these thoughts run through my head as I struggle to regain my balance. It's almost dark now, the temperature is dropping and I am soaking wet. Hypothermia could become a dangerous reality if I don't get dry. I decide there is only one thing I can do. Luckily I have a cell signal. I give Ray a call.

I tell him my situation and he agrees to pick me up again at a gated access road in the park. It's only two miles from where I am, but it takes me nearly an hour to get there; post-holing most of the way in the dark. I finally reach the road where Ray is waiting and I thank him for bailing me out. Thus, I get to spend another night indoors after a very frustrating experience. *Thanks again Ray, I'm very grateful.*

Wednesday, April 24
Trail Day 028
Miles hiked: 18
Home of Bruce and Linda - Park Rapids, MN

The past four days have been extremely challenging. The huge amount of snow and relentless winter conditions have caused so many problems, and I feel overwhelmed. I've had to use snow-shoes off and on the entire trek so far, almost a month. The continuous use of them the past four days, right on the heels of some long roadwalks, has caused my feet to swell up and the skin on my toes to be scraped off. Every step is painful. I'm tired of being wet, being cold, and being so exhausted at the end of the day from of using twice the amount of energy to go only half the normal distance. I feel betrayed, defeated, lost and alone.

This morning I consider getting off the trail and walking on roads until the snow clears. Ray drops me off at the Itasca State Park visitor center and I go inside to retrieve my package. Here I meet Vicki and Lori. I had been in correspondence with them regarding my package prior to my arrival and now they are here to greet me. Also here to meet me are many other park employees who are busy getting the place ready for the spring season.

After saying goodbye to Ray and meeting and greeting everyone on the park staff, I get started on sorting and packing my food box and I'm treated to a fine cup of hot cocoa. Vicki drops by again and says she wants to make a contribution to my trip and hands

me a $20 dollar bill.
Thank you Vicki, and all the kind folks at Itasca State Park.

With my revised plans there will be no return visit to the head-waters of the Mississippi on this trek. I begin my hike for the day on the park roads and come out the south entrance of the park. From there I head east on MN-200. There is a little gas station/cafe called Itasca Junction close to the park. I have heard good things about their pizza. So naturally, I stop in and order a twelve-inch for myself while having a short chat with a few locals. I enjoy a delicious homemade pizza and manage to eat almost the entire thing and take the rest for a snack later.

I continue the roadwalk and make it to the small village of Lake George where I stop in at a gas station to use their facilities and charge my phone. While here, I check my voicemail and receive a very unexpected call—but the one I needed. I call the number back and within minutes I am talking to none other than Andrew Skurka, the second person to thru-hike the NCT. He had been informed of my situation and thought he might be able to provide some insight.

We spend awhile talking about my situation and he relates his own experience to me from when he did the trail back in '04 and '05 as part of his C2C trek—almost entirely in the winter. I paraphrase a bit, but his advice is simple and necessary. "Just be patient and eventually things will change in your favor. Those moments when you want to give up but stick it out, those are the moments that mean the most afterwards."

We talk for about fifteen minutes. *Thank You Andrew, for your advice and taking the time out of your busy day to call and give me encouragement when I needed it.*

After considering everything he told me, I decide to head back to the trail and face what's left of winter head on. Before leaving Lake George, I make another call. I received a note with my food package at Itasca from Bruce, president of the Itasca Moraine Chapter. He offered assistance and is interested in hosting me for a night. I am calling now to take him up on his offer. We make plans for him to pick me up at County Road 91, about an eleven-mile hike from where I am right now.

I head south out of Lake George and reach the trailhead on County Road 4. I sign the register and trudge in. The sun is out today and the snow is starting to melt, making it really wet and heavy (quite the burden on my poor feet). I need to shed some layers to stay comfortable.

Along the trail today I pass several nice vistas and lake views. About two miles out from County Road 91, I meet Bruce coming down the trail toward me on snowshoes. We enjoy the time hiking back to his truck together talking about the trail and future plans for the area. We arrive at the truck just as the snow starts to fly again. He brings me back to his home near Park Rapids and I meet his wife Linda. I am treated to a fine spaghetti dinner and a beer. After a nice conversation, I'm off to bed, totally exhausted.

Thursday, April 25
Trail Day 029
Miles hiked: 11
Waboose Lake campsite - Paul Bunyan State Forest

I wake up at 7 a.m. to have breakfast. Bruce made some nice French toast. He asks when I would like to get back to the trail and I decide to take half a day and try to get some extra sleep, as I am totally exhausted. I also take some time to inspect my feet. The blisters have long since disappeared, my feet having hardened up pretty well after the first ten days of the trek. My toes on the other hand are in particularly bad shape. The snowshoes were a last-minute purchase for this trek as I wasn't sure I would need them. Everything was looking good until early March, the first major snowfall of the season not coming until well after Valentine's Day. I had been monitoring the weather in North Dakota pretty closely and saw that the northern parts of the trail in the state were right on the edge of most of the snowfall that came in. I decided to buy a pair about a week before leaving just in case conditions got worse...which they absolutely did!

Back at Lake Sakakawea I had high hopes for a smooth beginning. The snow was pretty much gone; less than an inch in the shady places, the rest completely clear. It all changed that final day along the McCluskey Canal when I encountered the first significant snow depth. What I failed to mention before, is that was also the first day it actually snowed on this trek, and it has continued to snow off and on literally every day since. After that day the snowshoes became a daily routine, except on days that were exclusively roadwalk. The snow has just gotten deeper and deeper the further east I have gone.

My feet had no time to adjust to the weight of the snowshoes before this trek. I had to get the heavy-weight ones to support my pack weight as well as my own, so they are quite heavy, a whooping four pounds. When they are not strapped to my feet they are strapped on the back of my pack and made it that much heavier. As I examine my feet now, the toll these monstrous things have taken is apparent. Most of the skin on top of my toes is completely gone, rubbed clean by the friction and pressure of the compression straps. The past few days this has caused a considerable amount of pain in every step, as well as a pair of blood-stained socks. I sure will be happy when (if) I can finally ditch these things and send them home.

I manage to get a little sleep and then Bruce drops me off on the

trail at noon. *Thanks for your hospitality Bruce.*
Today's hike is very strenuous, especially on snowshoes. It takes me until nearly 8 p.m. to make it the short distance to Waboose Lake where I will camp. The lake now has a campsite situated on a peninsula and a spur trail going all the way around it forming a loop from the NCT (hard work accomplished last year by the Itasca Moraine Chapter and an AmeriCorps crew). The tent pads are not yet clear of snow, but I manage to find a fairly dry spot to pitch for the night.

Friday, April 26
Trail Day 030
Miles hiked: 12
Home of Darrel - Walker, MN

I overslept this morning, still tired from the night before. I don't get going until nearly 9 a.m. It would be another strenuous hiking day with many ups and downs. Early on, I spot a set of very large wolf tracks heading down the trail in front of me. Many frustrations also occur today; several clear cuts have popped up on the trail and I have to guess which direction the trail goes. Making matters worse is the fact that the boundary paint the loggers use is the same color as the NCT blazes, which makes spotting the trail across the clearcut impossible.

I make my way across mud and debris to the far side of the clearing where I skirt the edge looking for the trail. To my right, I spot an opening and head on in. There was a blaze not too far down the green tunnel...I'm back on track. Most of the blazes I encounter are faded and hard to see. Some critical intersections with forest roads are not marked and I end up taking a wrong turn at the county line of the Chippewa National Forest boundary.

This leads to a mile-long bushwhack through knee-deep snow to find the trail again. The lakes are still frozen, so getting water is also quite a challenge. And with the strenuous hiking, the warm weather (it got past 60 degrees today) and the extra energy needed to get through the snow on snowshoes, I've been drinking a lot. Luckily, I had arranged to get picked up again today along County Road 12.

At the end of the day I meet Darrel from Walker. Darrel had emailed me earlier saying he would be interested in hosting me for a night and I took him up on his offer. Back at his house, which has been in his family since 1939, I am treated to a fine meal of Salmon, baked potato, salad, and a glass of wine. Afterwards, he invites me downstairs and he pulls this strange looking instrument out of a case. He then tells me his story of how he spends his free time. The strange-looking instrument, is the bassoon that he plays in several orchestras. We spend the rest of the evening talking about the trail and future plans for the local chapter, and then I'm off to bed.

Saturday, April 27
Trail Day 031
Miles hiked: 14
Just north of Woodtick Trail - Chippewa National Forest

I awoke at the crack of dawn and had my pack all ready to go by 6:45 a.m. Darrel said he would treat me to breakfast downtown at a local diner so we are there by 7. I waste no time in gulping down an entire entree of an omelet, pancakes, an orange juice, and a side of sausage. On the way out, I meet the owner of the place who, after hearing my story, gives me some complimentary cookies for my trip. Fine folks here in Walker.

Darrel drops me off at the trailhead and I'm hiking by 7:30. In no time I need to shed layers as it has turned very hot (relatively speaking). The highs for today are in the 70s and I need to drink lots of water to stay hydrated. The snow is starting to melt faster now but it is still incredibly deep, wet and heavy. It is at the point now that even with snowshoes on I posthole down about a foot because the warmth has softened up the snow so much, pushing it to the brink of the slush phase. Hence the second half of the day is very slow, my pace a whopping one mile per hour.

At the crossing of MN-371, there is a van parked and a woman with a camera taking pictures of me as I emerge from the woods. It was Gail, a writer for the *Pilot-Independent* in Walker. We go across the street to a picnic area and sit down for an interview. She asks me some questions about my hike, my thoughts, and feelings so far. Unfortunately, today was a very frustrating day and I fear I may have been a little on the negative side of things.

After the interview, I refill one of my water bottles (thanks Gail) and I'm hiking again. The snow appears to get thinner the further east I travel. Many spots east of 371 have standing water in them rather than snow. According to my map, I passed a few campsites today but was totally unaware of it because they are not marked from the trail. Lucky for me I am now in the Chippewa National Forest where dispersed camping is allowed pretty much anywhere. I find a dry spot just off the trail at the end of the day and pitch for the night.

Sunday, April 28
Trail Day 032
Miles hiked: 21
Crown Lake Campsite - Chippewa National Forest

I awoke this morning and got going right away. I am hoping to make it to the crossing of MN-84 today, but if the snow is deep it will be a longshot. Shortly after hoisting my pack and taking the first few steps, I hear a load crash on the trail behind me. A large tree limb has fallen from above, not more than fifty feet from where I stand now. Wow, if I had left camp about ten seconds later, it would have fallen right on me!

As I am hiking, it is apparent that the snow is melting rapidly; many more puddles to cross today. Eventually, I come to a spot with no snow, the trail is completely clear and dry. I take off the snowshoes to give my feet a break and continue hiking. I am amazed to find that the next half mile of trail is completely clear. When it appears again the snow is only about three inches deep, so I decide to leave the snowshoes off. What a welcome change.

At a road crossing, I spot a plastic bag laying on the trail with my (trail) name on it. Inside are two candy bars, a bottle of water, and a note telling me to leave any trash behind in the bag so I don't need to carry it all the way to the next town. My first care package! Unfortunately, there was no name on the package so, *Thank you to whomever left it there for me, it was much appreciated.*

The snow depth varies throughout the rest of the day but the snowshoes stay off. Pretty much all the south-facing slopes appear to be clear. Toward the end of the day, I come to an area that has had a very recent logging operation and most of the trail has been cut-over, no blazes remaining. Luckily, someone has been through recently and flagged the route, so I am able to find my way through the debris with little trouble.

With little time to spare, I finally make it to the MN-84 crossing. There, at the trailhead, is a note addressed to me and again lays out instructions to retrieve a care package. This one is hanging in a tree by a rope, and when I get it down I am amazed at the contents. Inside are four bottles of water, a soda, some packets of hot cocoa mix, and many types of other goodies. Inside is also a note, signed *Erica from Bemidji*. This is amazing! *Thank you Erica for*

taking the time to deliver this amazing bundle of trail magic!
As I am packing away my new trail food, two police cars pull into the trailhead. They seem suspicious of why I am here and I tell them my story, where I have hiked from, where I am hiking to, and my experiences so far. I also explain the garbage bag that I have just finished attaching a thank you note to, and am currently hanging back in the tree. I explained that someone left it here for me and I am simply saying thanks. The two officers wish me luck and then depart...I wonder if they are looking for someone?

It's almost dark now and it is almost two miles to the next campsite. This particular road crossing is surrounded by private land and is not part of the National Forest so I can't just walk into the woods and pitch anywhere. Also, I'd rather not pitch right here in the trailhead as I am certain those officers will return to see if I have indeed left, so I have no choice but to push on. Right on the other side of the road, I encounter two stretches of trail that are submerged under deep water, so I trudge through and finish the day with wet and cold feet. It's past dark when, under the light of my headlamp, I finally reach the campsite and pitch for the night.

Monday, April 29
Trail Day 033
Miles hiked: 20
Remer Motel - Remer, MN

I awoke fairly early and enjoyed a breakfast from the contents of my care package. A cold soda and a bag of Doritos are hard to come by on the trail. I am in high spirits today because of the generous care packages and the improving weather conditions. The snow is melting rapidly and despite being a foot deep in some places, I do without the snowshoes.

My progress has still become slower because of many blowdowns

I encounter—over thirty of them, many nearly impassable. I cross several forest roads and a few miles north of one of these crossings I come to a halt. There is a very large blowdown across the trail in front of me. I look for a way around and I am discouraged to find that both sides of the trail are also impassable from the deep snow and the debris left behind from the many years of clearing the trail. I am now in a position where I am boxed in with blowdowns on three sides of me and the only direction to go is backwards.

"Well, shit," I say to myself. I take out my map to come up with a plan. I decide to backtrack the last two miles to the last road crossing and follow the forest road all the way to County Road 4 and hike that down to the little town of Remer. I am disappointed because a short distance past this mess of blowdowns is a segment of trail called the Milton Lakes Esker that I was looking forward to hiking. Unfortunately, it is impossible to continue on the trail from this point, so I have to hike this portion as a roadwalk.

I reach the town of Remer before nightfall and check in to the Remer Motel for the night. I get a nice warm shower and head down the street for pizza and a drink at the bar. I am given a warm welcome by the locals, and after finishing my meal I return to my room and crash for the night.

Tuesday, April 30
Trail Day 034
Miles hiked: 27
Itasca County Fairgrounds - Grand Rapids, MN

I was more tired than I thought. I slept in until 9 a.m. I quickly get ready and am out on the road at 10. It's a four-mile roadwalk along MN-6 to the point where the NCT crosses the road. This spot marks the end of the certified trail in Minnesota. There is a ten-mile segment that extends further east, but it dead-ends at the Chippewa National Forest Boundary, not practical for a thru-hike. Once the Arrowhead Reroute gets approved this segment will be abandoned because it goes the wrong direction. I get a quick video of the sign at the crossing and continue on.

Later in the day, I walked along the Tioga Trail, a paved bike trail that parallels the road for much of its route. A car pulls over and a man gets out and walks toward me. I recognize him instantly, Matt from Detroit Lakes. Matt had some business in Grand Rapids and happened to drive by as I was walking the trail. We exchange some short greetings, I gave him a quick update on the trail, and then we part ways again. *It was nice seeing you Matt.

Within an hour, I make it to Grand Rapids where I plan to spend the night at the county fairgrounds. This is where the Mesabi Trail begins; a paved bike trail that is completed in segments between Grand Rapids and Ely. I will be hiking this trail over the next several days as the first of four trails that make up the Arrowhead Reroute. I arrive at the fairgrounds just before dark and pitch for the night beneath a row of pine trees.

Wednesday, May 1
Trail Day 035
Miles hiked: 24
Nashwauk City Campground - Nashwauk, MN

I got a good night's sleep last night so I'm up fairly early. I can tell it is going to be a cold day because the sky is completely overcast. The beginning of the Mesabi Trail is at the opposite end of the fairgrounds a short walk away. I take a video at the golden archway that marks the beginning of the trail. These arches are also present wherever the trail enters a town so I encounter several of them today. Only a few miles after leaving Grand Rapids

I take a slight detour from the Mesabi Trail to hike some off-road trail newly constructed by the Arrowhead Chapter. I know there is a 1.5 mile segment that starts at a power line and rejoins the Mesabi Trail on its northern end somewhere around here. I reach the power line and start walking. According to my map, the trail starts about a mile down the power line, but I'm having trouble locating it.

After a mile and a few hundred yards there is still no sign of a trail, no flagging, no blaze, nothing. I make a phone call to the only person I know who had recently hiked this trail. "Windigo" Doug is a section hiker from Michigan who did the Arrowhead Reroute last fall. We have been in contact the past several months via email about my hike and the trail, so we're talking now about what I should be looking for to locate this trail. Within a few minutes, I find the entrance and feel a bit dumb. I had only needed to walk another hundred feet to see the blue blaze on a tree and the carsonite post marking the trail. It was nice to finally get to talk to Doug though so I have no complaints. *Thanks for your help Doug.*

After hanging up the phone, I head in and expect to encounter more snow but to my relief it has mostly melted, only a few pockets remain. This short segment of trail travels around old mine tailings piles so the terrain is pretty rugged, I am reminded instantly of hiking on the Superior Hiking Trail. Very fine trail constructed here by the Arrowhead chapter.

After rejoining the Mesabi Trail for a half mile and crossing the Prairie River, I see another carsonite post off to the left—another segment of trail that I had no idea existed. I head on in despite having no idea where this trail goes, and find a pleasant hike along the river. This new segment is very short and currently ends at County Road 61,and finding my way back to the Mesabi Trail from here is no problem.

The rest of the day is pretty uneventful as I follow the Mesabi Trail up to Nashwauk where I have a drop box waiting. Unfortunately, I don't arrive until 5 p.m. and the post office closed at 4 p.m. Looks like I'll have to wait until morning to get my package.

I head to the gas station for some supplies then I decide to get my camp set up for the night. I start pitching my tent in the city park when a police officer pulls up. "Am I in the wrong spot?" I ask.

He then explains that the tenting area is across the street and that I can set up over there. He then asks me where I'm headed and I tell my story. He seems interested and wishes me luck as he drives away on patrol, even waives the camping fee. I pitch my tent in the area he pointed out and call it a day.

Thursday, May 2
Trail Day: 036
Miles hiked: 24
McCarthy Beach State Park

It's freezing cold when I wake up this morning so it's hard to get up and moving. I cook a hot breakfast first thing then head on down to the post office to retrieve my package. I arrive to find that they don't open until 9 a.m. I kill some time by organizing my first camera memory card and all the maps I have used so far to send them home. At 9 a.m., I take care of business and am finally able to hit the trail.

More hiking along the Mesabi Trail today. One of the attractions of the day is an overlook into the Hull Rust Mahoning Iron Ore Mine, supposedly one of the largest of its kind in the world. It's a bit hard to see things as the overlook has become somewhat over-grown, but I take a good video nonetheless. A few miles further up the trail is the town of Hibbing where I stop for a quick snack and make a phone call. On the other end of the line is Zach, a fellow SHT volunteer who I met last year while working to install the new bridge over the Encampment River. He lives in Hibbing and wanted me to call when I got close, so we make plans to meet later.

A few miles up the trail I pass underneath US-169 and see a guy walking toward me. Zach had spotted me while driving by so he pulled off the expressway to the nearest trail crossing to intercept me. He stops by to visit for a few minutes and gets a few photos of me on his way home. He offers to take my empty water bottles and fill up at his house and says he'll pick me up in Chisolm and shuttle me to nearby McCarthy Beach State Park for the night, which happens to be one of his favorite spots. *Thanks Zach.*

It's about four miles into Chisolm from where I now stand, so I'm there in about an hour. As soon as I arrive at the trailhead Zach pulls up with a Sammi's pizza in the back seat. "Your dinner," he says. I've never had Sammi's before, it is a small pizza chain that started up here in Hibbing. There are now a handful of them scattered around northern Minnesota, best pizza I've ever had.

We spend the fifteen or so minutes it takes to get to McCarthy Beach State Park talking about various hiking adventures. Zach informs me that the Encampment River Bridge has been washed out once again because of the high meltwater. This is very disappointing to hear, it was a lot of work to get that bridge into place. This would mark the fourth time in half a decade that it has been destroyed.

In a short while we arrive at the park and Zach sets me up at his favorite spot. It appears we have just narrowly missed an amazing sunset as a bright red stripe is visible on the horizon across the lake, quickly giving way to darkness. Zach takes another picture of me at the picnic table as I continue wolfing down my pizza under the light of my headlamp and then he heads out for the night. He'll be back in the morning to pick me up and shuttle me back to the trailhead in Chisolm. *Thanks for your help today Zach, and for the awesome trail magic.*

After stuffing myself with pizza I secure my food safely in the nearby picnic/warming shelter and crawl into bed.

Friday, May 3
Trail Day: 037
Miles hiked: 19
Lakeshore Motor Inn - Virginia, MN

I'm shivering when I wake up this morning. I learned a few things during the many frozen mornings in North Dakota, so last night I brought my boots into my tent and wrapped them in a raincoat underneath my sleeping bag. As hoped for, they didn't freeze solid, only a little ice on the outside. I waste no time in breaking camp and immediately heading over to the warming shelter to cook breakfast and wait for Zach to arrive.

It seems no one else is foolish enough to camp out in this cold weather so I have the place to myself. I haven't been to this park since I was a little kid and have no memory of it, but its main attraction is a large shallow lake, supposedly one of the best swimming beaches around. The NCT will likely pass through here in the future. It is a gorgeous park with typical North Woods scenery, towering pines all around as far as the eye can see.

About ten minutes after I have finished eating and am getting my gear packed Zach arrives. More stories are told as he shuttles me back to Chisolm to pick up where I left off yesterday. He takes a final photo of me to post on the NCTA's Facebook page as a

"Strider Sighting", and then we part ways.
Thanks again Zach for the amazing meal and setting me up for the night at one of your favorite spots. It was great to catch up.

The hike today is pretty uneventful along the Mesabi Trail as I pass through a few small towns and I make it the nineteen miles into Virginia by 4 p.m. I make a phone call to Jean, editor of the *Hometown Focus* newspaper in Virginia. She sent me an email a week ago requesting an interview, so after getting directions to her office I pay her a visit.

I'm treated to some nice snacks as she conducts the interview and even offers to put me up at her place tonight. I politely decline as I have already made plans to stay at the Lakeshore Motor Inn, which happens to be right across the street from her office. I need some time tonight to soak my feet and take a nice hot bath and I will likely be sleeping in tomorrow morning. There is also freezing rain in the forecast for tonight and I decided I didn't want to encourage anyone to drive out in it in order to drop me back on the trail. So, I head across the street to the motel after the interview and relax for the night. *Thank you Jean for your kindness, it was a pleasure meeting you.*

Saturday, May 4
Trail Day: 038
Miles hiked: 25
Mesabi trail at MN-135

Virginia is a quite pleasant hiker-friendly town. There are motels, grocery stores, and restaurants all within a short walk of each other, nestled between two lakes bustling with birds of all sorts. As I leave my motel this morning I am glad I decided to stay inside. There is a coating of ice in the parking lot and on all the cars outside. It is warm enough now that the freezing rain has turned to just rain, but it is still very chilly, and the pavement slippery. Within a few miles of Virginia I pass a familiar spot along the Mesabi Trail. There is a paved access road leading up a mountain via switchbacks to a visitor center. I am curious, so I hike the short detour to the top and am faced with quite a scene. Perched on this little mountaintop with a spectacular view down into the town of Virginia, is a small tourist information center. It included a gift shop surrounded by many relics of Iron Range mining history, chief of which is a giant dump truck parked at the very edge near the entrance. I remember the place instantly, because we stopped here on a family vacation when I was about 7 years old.

By the looks of the place it hasn't changed much since then. I head over to the door, it is unlocked. The kind man at the desk informs me that this is the first day they are open, I am the first visitor of 2013! I sign his guest book and tell my story. He is absolutely thrilled about my hike, and before I leave he takes my picture in front of the giant behemoth outside and wishes me safe travels. I am ashamed I do not remember the name of the man who greeted me at the desk. *I pray our paths will cross again Sir, so I can give you a proper recognition.*

Back on the Mesabi Trail, the rain has intensified and I am cold for most of the remainder of the day. Eventually, I end up at Giants Ridge Resort, a ski resort that was still busy with skiers only a week ago. I stop at the entrance to the lodge to get out of the rain and study my map. The Mesabi Trail ends five miles east of here at MN-135, after that, it is a long roadwalk all the way to Ely with only two places to camp in between that I know of. Unfortunately, the nearest one is about twelve miles away and I know I can't make it there before sundown. I could ask to pitch right here on the campus of the resort, but I feel like that would be too short of a day after just twenty miles.

I decide to push on and at least get to the end of the Mesabi Trail before dark and hope there is somewhere nearby to pitch a tent. Right off the bat after leaving the lodge, I am faced with an obstacle. The new bridge for the trail (across the small lake near the lodge) is flooded with two feet of water blocking the entrance. There is no way around so I have no choice but to plunge in and get my feet wet. I then hike the last five miles of the Mesabi Trail and reach the end shortly before dark. There is nothing here...no kiosk, no bench, nothing. No houses anywhere in sight either.

It is still more than seven miles to the next available campground, and that is several miles off my route. It is getting dark fast and this road has no shoulder, and hiking it in the dark would be extremely dangerous. Reluctantly, I decide to find a place here at the end of the trail to pitch for the night. I find a small patch of trees tucked between a pile of rock on one side and an intersection of two gravel roads on the other. This will have to do.

Sunday, May 5
Trail Day: 039
Miles hiked: 38
Adventure Inn - Ely, MN

I woke up this morning to the sound of traffic on MN-135. I get right out and moving and am hiking before 7:30 a.m. It is fifteen miles to the town of Tower, and I make a quick stop about halfway there at a little rest stop to have breakfast. Afterwards, the day warms up a bit, and once I reach Tower I take a short rest and check the time, it is only noon. I have a choice to make: I could stay here at the last available place to camp before reaching Ely or I could push on all the way there (twenty-three miles away) likely getting there after dark. I'm already nearly eleven days behind schedule because of all the snow, and it is only noon. I can't justify stopping here and taking another full day to reach Ely. I decide to go for it.

I head on in to the gas station to grab a Pop Tart and a Powerade, which I quickly demolish, and then begin my long haul to Ely. Three miles down the road is the small town of Soudan where I look to the north and catch a glimpse of the Soudan Underground Mine facility, now a State Park.

More memories pop up in my head as I think back on the two times I visited this park in the past. The first time was on that same family trip that we visited the Iron Range visitor center when I was about 7. The second time was just last summer when I stopped in while on a weekend trip to visit the new Lake Vermillion State Park right next door, and beautiful Bear Head Lake State Park a little further down the road. Lake Vermillion State Park will likely host a section of North Country Trail in the future, again after the Arrowhead Reroute gets approved. A single-track hiking only trail along the shoreline of Lake Vermillion would be a spectacular addition to the trail.

En route to Ely about halfway, a guy in a pickup pulling a trailer stops and asks if I am hiking on purpose or if I need a ride. I tell him that I am just out for a hike and so he continues on his way. That ride sounded good though, I'm now at mile twenty-eight and my feet hurt. After several hours I am finally able to see the Ely water tower in the distance, only a few miles to go.

Just west of town, a guy with a long beard driving a van pulls over in front of me. He saw me walking along the road and turned around to make sure I have everything I need to get where I need to go. I quickly tell him my story and he wishes me luck and drives away. Only a few moments later I am walking down the main drag of Ely, along MN-1/MN-169.

I don't stop until I reach the far end of town where I have a reservation at the Adventure Inn. I arrive and head in. The woman at the desk instantly knows who me. She gives me the key and informs me that my package has arrived and is waiting in my room. I bring all my gear up to the room and close the door. I made it. It's not quite 8:30 p.m., yet the sun is still out and I am standing in my hotel room in Ely with incredibly sore feet and one fresh blister from the long roadwalk.

I take a few minutes to unpack my gear and then I'm out, exhausted from thirteen hours of continuous hiking a whopping thirty-eight miles today. I will be taking two full days of rest here in Ely so I am fully charged and at 100% when I enter the Boundary Waters Canoe Area Wilderness and tackle the notoriously rugged Kekekabic Trail.

Wednesday, May 8
Trail Day 040
Miles hiked: 24
Kekekabic Trail - south of Snowbank Lake, Superior National Forest

I had a good rest here in Ely. The past few days it has been hovering above 70 degrees, so the deep snow is basically gone except for the far eastern end of the Border Route Trail and the north end of the Superior Hiking Trail where I will be hiking in about a week. Yesterday, I brought my snowshoes to an outfitter here in town and had them shipped on down to Heston's Resort on the BRT, my next resupply point (just in case I need them).

Ely is a great hiker town and I have enjoyed my stay here, but now it is time to move on. The woman at the desk at Adventure Inn told me about a place called Britton's downtown that has a good breakfast menu. I head there first thing and am sitting down at the table by 6:30 a.m. I order an omelet with toast and within a few minutes my meal is in front of me. A very delicious breakfast to start off this day.

Back at the motel it takes awhile for me to gather all my things and pack them away. I'm not out the door until 8:30 a.m. Though my pack is loaded with a little extra food it is much lighter than the previous week. The snowshoes together weigh over four pounds, and it is such a relief to have that weight off.

From Ely it is a twenty-mile roadwalk to the beginning of the Kekekabic Trail, where I will hike for forty-two miles through the Boundary Waters Canoe Area Wilderness to the Gunflint Trail, there to pick up the BRT, followed immediately after by the SHT. Around 400 miles of continuous off-road trail.

Before I get to the beginning of the "Kek" though, only a short distance outside of Ely I make a small detour. A few miles east of the small village of Winton is the Kawishiwi Falls hiking trail. It consists of a loop trail just over a mile long that brings the hiker past an amazing waterfall just downstream from a hydropower dam. I hike the loop trail down to the falls and stand to admire the magnificent view in front of me.

Since I bypassed the small waterfall segment in the Sheyenne State Forest back in North Dakota, this is the first waterfall I have seen on this trek, and the detour sure is worth it. With the recent and rapid snow melt, the water is raging over the falls and is a spectacular sight to behold. There are a few other people out enjoying this trail today as the weather is again pushing 70 degrees.

From here I hammer out the remaining roadwalk to the Kekekabic trailhead off Snowbank Lake Road, just as the rain starts to fall. I get a picture of the sign and then head in. As I hike, the rain constantly changes between drizzle and downpour. I only get about three miles of the trail done before the sun sets and I pitch for the night on a rocky hilltop.

Thursday, May 9
Trail Day: 041
Miles hiked: 09
Kekekabic Trail - south of Alworth Lake, Boundary Waters Ca-
noe Area Wilderness

I awoke this morning several times. Confused? Let me explain.

I first woke up right at day break and decided I wasn't ready to get up yet. As soon as I laid my head back down I was asleep again. This happened four more times until the sun shone brightly through my tent door. At that point it was way past time to get up. It was a very strange feeling. Every time I awoke I wanted to get up and get moving but couldn't muster the energy to do so. It was as if some kind of spell was over me that couldn't be broken until the sun hit the side of my tent.

When I finally do get going, the trail is fairly easy to follow but also makes for very slow hiking. The trail has received more use in recent years and a very faint sign of a tread is visible. However, none of the stream crossings have boardwalks or bridges, and dozens of blowdowns obstruct the trail, causing the painfully slow pace.

Within the first few miles, I come across a group of three hikers out doing the Snowbank Lake Loop Trail, which the Kek shares for a short distance. I am the only person they have seen on their multiple-day adventure, so the guy in front is startled when he sees me. The group is impressed with my hike and wish me well. One point of interest passed along the trail today is an old band saw blade left out in the middle of the woods. It now serves as a marker for a spur trail leading to a campsite. After covering only nine miles it is getting dark so I pull off into the pine and pitch for the night.

Friday, May 10
Trail Day: 042
Miles hiked: 17
Gabimichigami Lake campsite - Kekekabic Trail

Another spell lie over me this morning as I struggled to get going. To my dismay, I discover that my boots have again frozen during the night and it's a struggle to get them on. I thought these mornings were behind me, you would think approaching mid-May that the weather would have turned decent by now.

Today has many more blowdowns and many deep stream crossings to contend with. I get a nice video at a river crossing so dangerous it necessitated the construction of a bridge out here in the middle of the wilderness. Thank goodness the bridge is there, it would not be possible to cross this thing without it. This is Agamok Falls, a highlight of the Kek for sure.

I manage to briefly lose the trail at a beaver pond where the flagging and all signs of a trail suddenly stop. I see faint evidence of a tread leading off to the left, so I follow it around a corner. There, I discover that it gets fainter as it goes up a mountain and the brush and blowdowns get thicker. "This isn't right", I say to myself, and I backtrack to the beaver pond where I was pretty sure I was on the trail. I take a closer look and see evidence of the trail heading straight through the shallow pond. All the fir and spruce trees straight ahead are missing their lower branches on one side, indicating they were trimmed at one point.

I plunge in and wade across to the other side and find where the trail picks up again on dry land. The next section of trail brings me to higher ground that has been completely burned over. It is possible to see for miles in all directions, charred stumps dot the landscape. I see one small island of green trees along a lake that happens to be the location of the campsite I pitch for the night.

Saturday, May 11
Trail Day: 043
Miles hiked: 22
Heston's Resort - Gunflint Lake, BRT

This morning I woke up extremely cold. I have on every piece of clothing I brought with me and still feel uncomfortable. The sun manages to come out for the first part of the day, then less than a mile into my hike, it starts to drizzle—not rain, but little tiny ice pellets. With my rain gear on and the sky temporarily overcast, visibility is somewhat reduced and I lose the trail near where it crosses a portage.

I spend a few minutes poking around the brush nearby and trying a few routes that turn out to be just short animal trails. I need to use my handy GPS to navigate to the next waypoint, bushwhacking up and over a ridge. At the top, I take a glance around looking for any sense of direction on where to go. I look down and spot the trail in the distance below, a narrow light band stretching across the desolate landscape. It turns out I had only been off trail by about 100 feet.

The sun shines in and out the entire day, and it is shining when I come to a trail junction. I have reached the spot where the Centennial Trail diverges from the Kek and heads back on a loop to the Gunflint Trail, the paved road that provides one of the few access points to the Boundary Waters Canoe Area. This means I am only a mile from the eastern trailhead. In no time I arrive at a completely empty parking lot with a kiosk but no trail register. This is it, I've put the Kekekabic behind me.

Just up the road from the Kek is the beginning of the Border Route Trail, which travels for about sixty-five miles along the Canadian Border to the northern end of the Superior Hiking Trail. It's the afternoon now, I take a picture of the sign and head in.

This trail so far is surprisingly well maintained and marked, blue flagging tied on trees every 100 feet or so. Soon I reach another burned area and it is here that the snow starts to fly. Snow, on May 11! It is also at this time that I come to a landmark on the BRT known as Magnetic Rock. This twenty-foot chunk of vertical rock stands alone on a hilltop surrounded by miles of pine saplings trying desperately to repopulate the burned area.

The snow doesn't let up all day as I continue on, the trail eventually connecting to a series of ski trails, making the hiking easier. I'm surprised to see several gravel road crossings along the route today as well as several signs labeling the BRT. I am outside the wilderness boundary at the moment, so these kinds of markings are allowed.

After awhile, I begin to worry that I won't make it to my destination tonight as the sky is turning dark. No sooner have these feelings sunk in than I come to a trail junction. To the right is typical hiking trail tread with a sign saying "BRT, Bridal Falls" and straight ahead is the ski trail with a sign saying: "Hestons .5 miles." Thank goodness I have made it at last.

I follow the ski trail down to a power line and look for the resort. It's almost dark and only one house nearby has its lights on, so I head there and knock on the door. A man opens the door and I ask: "Hi, am I in the right place? I'm looking for Hestons Resort."

"Well, you're kind of in the right place, Barb is here." He opens the door wider and I see a woman coming toward me. Hence, I meet Barb, one of the owners of Hestons Resort. I had spoken to her on the phone a few days earlier in Ely, asking if it would be okay to ship my snowshoes over. Her husband Greg is here too, and their son Paul.

It turns out, I am at their neighbors' house where they are all having dinner. The man that let me in is Dan, and his wife, Carolin, is at the table. They have just finished eating dinner and they invite me in for some leftover pasta and fish. Dan also offers me some red wine, which I gladly accept. Then it's time to tell my story as everyone has questions about my hike.

Greg informs me that I will not need my snowshoes as the past few days have made a huge difference in the snow depth. I am glad to hear this news, this winter has lingered on long enough. After dinner, Barb says she will get one of the lodges ready for me to spend the night in. It happens to be the same one that Nimblewill Nomad stayed in four years ago while on his thru-hike. While Barb is getting things ready, Paul hands me my food package and shows me to the lodge, a very fine establishment indeed. Within only a few minutes it is warm and cozy inside. It has been a very long day on the trail so I am ready for bed, in an actual bed.

Sunday, May 12
Trail Day: 044
Miles hiked: 13
Partridge Lake East campsite - BRT

I slept in this morning; didn't roll out of bed until 9 a.m. I needed the extra rest as I had a long day yesterday and all the blowdowns and stream crossings on the Kek were quite an energy drainer. The first thing on my agenda is to take a shower, the warm water feels good. Next, I spend a good hour cooking, eating and organizing my food drop. This one was a little overloaded and it is not possible to fit it all in my pack. I eat as much of it as I can for breakfast but am still forced to leave a good chunk behind.

I also decide to leave my snowshoes behind as Greg was certain I wont need them. I am relieved. I am tired of lugging around that extra weight. I had a chance to check my feet this morning, my toes have healed from the lack of snowshoes since leaving the Chippewa Forest. It's been nice the past few days, despite the condition of the trail, to not have a sharp pain in my toes with every step I take.

After all is taken care of, I head outside to a bright sunny day, however it is still very chilly. I head over to the house to thank Barb and Greg for their generosity but find that they have left to run some errands. It's almost noon and I've already lingered long enough, so I leave a note for them and attach it to the door. Very fine folks here at Heston's. *Thanks Barb and Greg for your kindness. It was a pleasure meeting you, your family and your neighbors.*

The trail leading out from Heston's brings me past Bridal Veil Falls. The trail is well marked, most intersections have a big sign pointing which way the BRT goes. Also on the trail today are lots of Moose droppings, some of them are very fresh. Whatever left these passed through here no more than a few hours ago. Soon enough as I ascend a rise and come to a brushy area, I come face-to-face with one of these amazing animals. A cow moose stared at me from about thirty feet off the trail. After taking a moment to study me, she quickly scampers off into the brush, no time for a picture.

This is the first time I have seen a moose in the lower forty-eight states (I've been to Alaska where they are plentiful). Not long after this encounter, darkness is approaching and there is a half-mile long spur trail leading to a campsite just ahead. The short trek is surprisingly strenuous, lots of ups and downs. The campsite is worth the extra effort though, as I pitch on a tent pad nestled on a nice lake among great cedars and pines.

Monday, May 13
Trail Day: 045
Miles hiked: 13
North of Clearwater Lake - BRT

I find my shoes frozen again as I get moving this morning, and it remains cold all day. After forcing my shoes on and getting out on the trail a light drizzle begins. The highlight for the day is visiting a place called Stairway Portage Falls. I think the name pretty much speaks for itself. The BRT intersects a portage near a river crossing and the steep contour of the north end of the portage necessitated the construction of stairs.

A splendid waterfall can be seen from these stairs and I stop here to have a snack. The rest of the day is pretty uneventful except for a few patches of remnant snow, some over a foot deep still. I make it through these without issue and soon I'm back on higher ground which is entirely snow free. I pitch for the night in a small clearing and drift off to sleep.

Tuesday, May 14
Trail Day: 046
Miles hiked: 16
Two miles west of McFarland Lake Trailhead - BRT

My campsite last night was bare of any trees large enough to hang a food bag from, so I had to get creative in hiding and securing my food. The best thing I could come up with was to wedge it between a rock and a fallen tree and cover it with branches and leaf litter. I know I was taking a chance burying my food like that as bears have incredibly powerful noses, but I had no choice under the circumstances. Luckily, it was all still there when I awoke this morning and after cooking breakfast I hit the trail.

Progress is slow because of remnant snow over a foot deep in places. I have to inch forward being very careful where I place my feet. The BRT is a very rocky trail and with the tread obstructed by snow it would be very easy to roll an ankle, or even break it. Unfortunately, I fall into this scenario three times during the day despite being very cautious. Luckily, my hiking shoes have some ankle support built in so I was spared from having a severe sprained ankle, but nonetheless I feel great discomfort most of the day.

After making it through the rest of the snow the trail parallels a small stream, marking the border between the US and Canada. The trail along here runs unbelievably straight only a stone's throw away from our friendly neighbor to the north. I have a suspicion this may have been an old railroad at one time. Eventually, the trail heads back to higher ground and I manage to take a wrong turn, twice.

There are several places along the BRT where portages cross, and the junctions I encountered today were not marked in the usual fashion (probably due to the remoteness of this section). It must be hard to get in here to maintain any structures. After taking a moment to study two different maps and consult my GPS, I figure out which way the trail goes and hike the rest of the day without incident. Despite the mishaps encountered today, the scenery is spectacular.

The past few days—and especially today—I passed through several "cathedrals". As I've mentioned before, cedars are my favorite trees, specifically the northern white cedars native to this region. In many places here great stands of these trees are clumped together, shading the ground beneath, not allowing any undergrowth to establish itself. The deep shade allows the sun to seep through only in very narrow rays, the great silver trunks like pillars of a great cathedral, more magnificent than one ever created by man. It is quite a sight to behold. After climbing up and out of one of these cathedrals I pitch for the night on a ridge top, only the trail separating me from a sheer 200-foot dropoff on the other side.

Wednesday, May 15
Trail Day: 047
Miles hiked: 22
Jackson Creek campsite - SHT

I actually got a good early start this morning. Within a few miles I come across two hikers out on the trail for a long weekend. Hence, I meet Matt and Eric. They ask where I was coming from and I tell them my story. They have heard of the NCT and seem impressed that I have made it this far given the conditions I've encountered. They wish me luck and we continue on in opposite directions.

After another half mile I come to the first trailhead since leaving the Gunflint Trail many days ago. This last segment of the BRT brings me to the Pigeon River, the border between the US and Canada. The trail parallels it for a good distance then steers south toward the Swamp River. Soon I come to a bridge and spend a few moments examining it. The approach has been washed out in the recent past and the bridge has listed quite a bit in the middle. No railings are attached and the approach on the far side is a slippery ramp.

I proceed very carefully, arms outstretched for greater balance control. I make it across without incident but have to cross the river again shortly. The second crossing is nearly identical to the first, so I take my time. At this point I now have only a few miles to go before reaching the end of the BRT. The trail is steadily climbing as I hike on, several spectacular overlooks provide a good view over the forest below and across the border into Canada.

Halfway up to the final overlook as I am ascending I turn a corner and am startled to a halt. Lying in the middle of the trail is a fully grown moose. The corpse is fully intact, couldn't have been dead more than a few days. The scavengers haven't even gotten to it yet. I give the animal a wide berth as I continue up the mountain to a trail junction.

To the right is the main trail and to the left is a spur trail to the last overlook, known as 270 overlook. I take the spur to the overlook and am given a great view 270-degrees around. Directly to the north, the Pigeon River can be seen only a few miles away, just a narrow ribbon separating our two great nations. In the distance I can see a cell tower among the peaks of the mountains so I check my phone, I actually have a signal. I make a quick phone call home to make plans for the next week. My family has a cabin along the North Shore of Lake Superior and Roxanne is again going to be my support crew for a few days. I will have another opportunity to slack pack and get some more ground covered.

I am now only a few days out from Grand Marais, where the first pick up will likely happen. As a matter of fact, this overlook I am at now is not only the BRT, but as of this year it is also the northern terminus of the SHT. There are no markings yet, no blazes to indicate that this is the SHT, but I assume that's because trail work has been delayed because of the weather. From this overlook it is only a mile and a half to the end of the BRT. Once the Arrowhead Reroute gets approved this little one and a half miles of tread will be three trails in one! (BRT, SHT, NCT).

In no time I am at the trailhead, where I stop to filter water from the flowing river nearby. The first trailhead for the SHT is less than a quarter mile away and when I arrive there is only one car. The trailhead is marked with the classic wooden signs with blue lettering indicating the mileage to the next few points of interest. There is also a trail register, which I take time to sign and express my joy in finally arriving here. The SHT has a very special place in my heart and many memories were born from it.

Two years ago from this very spot, I took my pack on its first test run over Labor Day weekend. That short trek ended disastrously, as the pack was not rightly fitted. After just three days I could barely walk because my back was so screwed up. I learned a lot that weekend about proper packing and made the necessary changes over the following months. It feels strange now being back here, having walked all the way from the middle of North Dakota, nearly 1,000 miles.

The hike down the SHT starts out fairly flat and very wet. There is standing water in many places. Soon however, the trail winds and climbs up, steeply at first then more gradual. This brings me to the highest point on the SHT at over 1,800 feet, a place known as Rosebush Ridge. Just around the corner from this spot the trees open up at a vista and I can see Lake Superior for the first time on this trek. A smile forms on my face as I look across this vast expanse of water, the largest freshwater lake in the world. "I'm home!"

I get the same feeling that Thorin Oakenshield must have felt during *The Hobbit* when he sees the Lonely Mountain for the first time…that's exactly the scene that popped into my head at this moment. There is a little haze out on the lake but in the distance I can barely see the outline of the Greenstone Ridge, the low mountain range that makes up the spine of Isle Royale.

I spent a week there last summer preparing for this trek, and more memories come pouring in. I remember getting on the boat at 6:30 a.m. for the two-hour ferry ride from Grand Portage to the island. I remember the ranger in Windigo telling me the route I had chosen along the Minong Ridge was the hardest on the entire island and the consequent knee pain I had the second day of my trip. I remember hiking back along the Greenstone Ridge and coming through a large area bare of foliage due to thousands of tent caterpillars. I remember strolling back into Windigo a day earlier than planned and meeting Paul and Jamie, two friends from Lansing who were kind enough to share some of their delicious food and their shelter with me, the first trail magic I ever received.

I linger at this spot for a few minutes then push on the last few miles to the next campsite along Jackson Creek. A large patch of snow is covering one of the tent pads but there is still plenty of room for a tent nearby. I pitch here and call it a night.

Thursday, May 16
Trail Day: 048
Miles hiked: 22
Judge C. R. Magney State Park

An amazing thing happened last night. As I was about to doze off I decided to check my phone and I had a signal in my tent! That has never happened before this far up north. It's even more unusual considering the campsite is down in a valley between two high ridges. A new tower must have been put up recently. I took the opportunity to send a few texts to some friends who are planning to come visit in a few days before I finally dozed off.

When I awoke in the morning the sun was shining. After a hot breakfast I hit the trail and after a few miles I make it to Hellacious Overlook. Isle Royale is clearly visible in the distance and I once again think back on my adventure there last summer. Soon after this the trail becomes dotted with many obstacles; blowdowns and patches of deep snow, some up to two feet deep. At one point right at the base of a hill I encounter a six or seven-foot deep drift and without snowshoes to navigate over it I sink up to my waist. Coming down the other side a bridge over a stream has been washed out and the only way to cross is to carefully pick my way across slippery boulders. I make it across without any trouble and for most of the day trail conditions improve.

After descending some steep steps, the trail comes out onto a dog sled training trail and follows it for several miles allowing for a brisk pace. After this the trail flattens out and emerges onto gravel Camp 20 Road, which the SHT follows for four miles to the boundary of Judge Magney State Park. The trail through the park is fantastic, paralleling the Brule River, allowing access to great views of many waterfalls.

One in particular is known as Devil's Kettle Falls. In the summer months the river forks at the top of a bedrock cliff, one fork flows over it and another plunges down into a large hole in the bedrock never to be seen again. They say scientists still have no idea where the water from the kettle comes out (I would imagine it would be somewhere underneath Lake Superior.) Unfortunately, because of the recent snow melt, the river is raging and the Devil's Kettle is completely submerged, but the raging falls are still impressive.

Leaving this spot the trail climbs several hundred stairs almost straight up to the top of the canyon ridge and there leads to the campground where I will be spending the night. When I arrive I take a look around and many more memories flow over me. The last time I camped at this park I was seven or eight years old. I remember meeting another kid a few years older than me named Mike. He and his family were at the campsite next to us and offered us shelter under their tarp when a thunderstorm came in. I remember Mike joining us for a hike to the kettle and him and his family leaving shortly after. I remember our car dying at Grand Portage the next day and having to get towed back to the campground and then to Grand Marais to await repairs as we were stranded for a few days.

I check my phone again, I got a decent signal so I call home to confirm plans for a pickup tomorrow near Grand Marais to start slack packing for a few days. I also get a call from some friends that are planning on joining me on the trail within the next few days, it'll be a nice change of pace to have some company for awhile. I set up camp and after a quick shower I crawl into bed looking forward to the days to come.

Friday, May 17
Trail Day 049
Miles hiked: 25
Strider's Family Cabin "The Shack" - near Finland, MN

I'm up early this morning and hiking by first light. The scenery today is some of the best the SHT has to offer. For the most part, the trail follows the ridge line of the Sawtooth Mountains overlooking Lake Superior but today for about a mile and a half the trail comes right down to the shore on the "Lakewalk." I stop here to have breakfast as I did not eat before leaving the park this morning, listening to the waves crash against the rocks.

Next, I descend into the Kadunce River Gorge. This is one of my favorite spots on the SHT though I don't come here nearly as often because it's so far north. A spur trail leaves the main trail and follows the rim of the gorge for a mile, allowing a hiker to witness a narrow but incredibly deep canyon. Bypassing this trail and passing by several great campsites I arrive at the next trailhead and see a familiar vehicle.

As soon as I appear, my mother Roxanne, emerges from the driver seat and gives me a big hug. She is overjoyed as she has not seen me since dropping me off near Sibley on Lake Ashtabula almost two months ago. I stop here to take a break as she has some trail magic for me—cold pizza and fresh fruit. I spend the next few minutes recapping my journey through the Boundary Waters. Soon I must push on though as I still have a lot of ground to cover today. We made a plan for me to get picked up outside Grand Marais near Pincushion Mountain. I switch my pack out for a lighter day pack that makes me feel like an astronaut as I continue down the trail.

The trail immediately plunges down to the banks of Kimball Creek and then back up again as it takes to the ridge top. I encounter a large group of hikers on a weekend escapade, about ten people, most of whom have too much gear. I pass them by and keep bounding down the trail with my astronaut pack making good time through gorgeous trail. I pass through a patch of nice mature pines along the rim of the Devil's Track River Gorge before descending into the gorge and stopping on the bridge spanning the sheer canyon walls.

I take a good video and then cross the bridge past a group of campers and out the other side toward Pincushion mountain. I'm surprised when I get close that the entire area is a maze of multiple use trails so I have to keep a careful eye out for blazes. A spur trail leads out to a bald rock outcrop overlooking Grand Marais where I take a few minutes to rest before finishing the final stretch along a ski trail. It is here that I hear something scampering quickly down a tree and I get just enough of a glimpse of it to tell that it is a pine martin trying to avoid detection.

Roxanne is waiting for me in the parking lot overlooking the town and we head down to Grand Marais for a good Subway dinner, which I have been craving since leaving Ely. Then it's an hour drive down scenic MN-61 to our family cabin, which has come to be known as "The Shack." For the next week this will be base camp as I slack pack most of the SHT and hopefully make up for some lost time.

Saturday, May 18
Trail Day 050
Miles hiked: 17.5
Cascade River State Park, then on to "The Shack"

It was nice to wake up inside a heated room this morning. It's drizzling when I get back to the trailhead in Grand Marais and it continues to rain all day. I'm hiking along the North Shore State Snowmobile Trail for a good distance and it's here that I encounter the first distance-hikers of the season. Bob and Mike are out finishing the entire SHT after hiking half of it last year. I tell them where I'm headed and they seem very enthusiastic about the concept of the NCT. We exchange greetings, talk for a few minutes about gear and planning and then part ways.

The rest of the day is pretty uneventful until I reach Cascade River State Park. Like most of the parks along the North Shore, the main attraction is a big river gorge with the SHT running parallel to it for many miles. The sides are incredibly steep in places and the trail is very narrow. At one of these points I encounter a very large ice flow across the trail dropping off into the canyon. I stop and take several minutes to study it as there appears to be no way around. With closer examination I find a route that is possible using tree branches as handles to climb around the inside edge of the canyon. I make it around without incident and continue on without further issues.

I arrive at the trailhead quite early in the afternoon and I would like to go further, but the next road crossing is ten miles away so I probably can't make it there with this terrain before dark so I call it a day.

Back at The Shack: After having some dinner I hear a car horn outside. My good friends Tony and Ashley have arrived to hike with me tomorrow. This is the first time I have seen them in two months and I am overjoyed to be with them again. I've known them both for many years and we even ended up as roommates in college. In fact, I met Ashley the very first day of college and we've pretty much been friends ever since. She was also kind enough to write me a letter specifically for this hike, to carry with me to get me through the hard times. I've held off on reading it so far, determined to at least make it through Minnesota before even considering bailing out on this journey.

We've all gone hiking together as a larger group several times over the years, mostly on the SHT. At this point I've actually hiked half the trail in sections but I never get tired of this area, so I have no complaints about re-hiking some sections. They've been to The Shack many times but haven't yet seen it in its current state. Small additions have been made to it over the years that took place in four stages. Tony and Ashley are among the few people to have seen it at every stage of its existence.

The three of us spend the rest of the night catching up on events back home, having a few drinks, and planning the hike tomorrow. It's going to be a good day.

Sunday, May 19
Trail Day 051
Miles hiked: 21.5
Oberg Mountain - SHT, then on to "The Shack"

Everyone is up fairly early this morning and we are excited for the day. Last night we decided to drop Tony and Ashley's car at Lutsen, which means they will be hiking with me for about fifteen miles today. Everyone packs rain gear, as it is drizzling when we depart. After dropping of the first car we all hop in Roxanne's car and head for Cascade River State Park where I left off yesterday. After taking a group picture at the first waterfall we depart, making our way up and out of the gorge. After only a short distance the rain intensifies and thunder starts rolling in. As we are ascending one of the higher peaks a bolt of lightning crashes across the sky near us as an instantaneous flash and horrendous boom is heard overhead. We all cower down for a few seconds in terror and then cautiously continue on our way. That last bolt of lightning struck the top of the peak we are currently climbing. Before long however, the thunder rolls away and the rain stops allowing for a more comfortable hike.

The trail is now following the ridge again and a fog has rolled in obscuring most of the view of the valley below but also provides a unique opportunity for good pictures. Eventually the sky clears and it's good hiking the rest of the day as we chat, joke and occasionally sing. Later, we reach a gorgeous section along Lake Agnes complete with a multi group campsite, where we pause for awhile to take in the scenery and beauty of the place. After a few more miles we arrive at the trailhead where their car is parked and it's time for another goodbye, as I will be pushing on another seven miles to Oberg Mountain alone.

Alas, I am saddened that I had such a short time to spend with these friends before they had to return to their lives. But I'm grateful they were able to make it up here, even if only for a day. *Take care dear friends, you will be missed.*

After parting ways, I make my way through Lutsen ski resort, up Moose Mountain, and down the other side (no doubt one of the steepest sections of the SHT). I end the day at the Oberg Mountain trailhead where Roxanne awaits. Then it's back to The Shack to rest up for another day on the trail.

Monday, May 20
Trail Day 052
Miles hiked: 24
Sugar Loaf Road - SHT, then on to "The Shack"

The next two days I'll be hiking trail that I've already hiked in the past. There is a loop around Oberg Mountain that I have hiked multiple times with several different groups of people. I've hiked all the sections of the SHT between here and Tettegouche State Park in their entirety. Never the less, it will still be a very enjoyable hike. I never get tired of hiking the trail up here, it's like my home.

The trail today brings me over Leveaux Mountain, Britton Peak, and Carlton Peak before heading into the Temperance River Gorge. I pass a few people out for a day hike despite the wet and chilly weather. Once I'm down in the gorge I'm not surprised to find the place fairly busy with people. This park is very popular with tourists with easy access off Highway 61. The trail here parallels the gorge on both sides of the river with old stone walls built by the CCC between the drop off into the gorge and the trail.

After leaving the gorge the trail meets up with the Cross River and follows it for several miles displaying gorgeous river-front scenery. The trail eventually leaves the river and wanders southwestward and this section is very wet from the recent snow melt. There is standing water is most places and this slows my pace down somewhat. As a result I don't reach the trailhead on Sugarloaf Road until much later than I anticipated. I decide to bail off here instead of push on to Caribou Falls where I originally intended to end the day. It's nice to get inside The Shack at the end up the day and stay warm and dry after a very wet and chilly hike.

Tuesday, May 21
Trail Day 053
Miles hiked: 26
"The Shack"

It's raining again this morning as I begin my hike and it continues to rain all day. I make the few miles from Sugar Loaf Road to Caribou Falls pretty quickly and take a few moments to enjoy the view of the falls. A spur trail leads to a large winding staircase that leads to the base of a wide river gorge where the falls pour over a tall cliff. It's a very impressive site especially from the fresh snow melt.

As I continue on I am displeased to find most of the trail in this area is completely flooded. Most of the boardwalk I encounter today is either floating or completely submerged depending on how it was constructed. This makes for a very treacherous journey as everything is extremely slippery. I don't even bother to try to keep my feet dry because it's not possible; much of the trail is under a foot of water.

Most of the hike today takes me through George Crosby Manitou State Park, which has some very steep climbs now slushy with mud. Even the larger bridges here are flooded, separated from land by a few feet of water on both sides. I don't think I've ever seen this much flooding up here. It's a slow crawl up the mountain on a slippery muddy trail until I reach the parking lot for the state park.

The rest of the day is a pretty relaxing hike with rolling terrain, nothing too steep. I pass a dilapidated fur trapper's cabin and several nice campsites, including one right across from Lilly's Island. This is a unique feature of the SHT, simply a small island connected to the main trail by a narrow boardwalk. On it can be found several stone platforms to allow access to the lake for swimming or filtering water and there is also a trail register, which I make sure to sign before moving on.

After a few more miles the trail starts to go uphill again and the trail finally dries out somewhat. I pass a familiar spot, where I first encountered a black bear on my first solo hike. Being a 14-year-old kid at the time I wasn't quite sure how to react. It was a smaller bear, so I was a little worried that Momma Bear might be around somewhere. It took it's sweet time leaving the area, but once it was out of sight I continued on and made it back to the cabin soon after, where, along the way I tripped on a boulder and fell, cutting my hand in the process.

With this memory still running through my head I emerge from the woods onto a gravel road, turn, and take a short walk down the road to the very doorstep of my cabin. A perfect place to end the day.

Wednesday, May 22
Trail Day 054
Miles hiked: 23
County Road 5 (Silver Bay), then on to "The Shack"

Today I get an earlier start as I don't have to drive anywhere; I just walk out the door and begin my hike. Today, I'm on a portion of the trail known as Section 13, the first section of SHT that I ever hiked. When my family purchased the land back in 2003 and we built our little cabin, the first thing we did after finishing was take a day hike on this section of trail. Now, ten years later, I'm finally hiking the whole trail in its entirety, a goal I've had since I first discovered it. Section 13 has a lot of highlights. There is an old logging site, a large beaver dam with a boardwalk built over it, a large glacial erratic the size of backhoe, and several cool mountain peaks with no names.

This section also passes through Wolf Ridge Environmental Learning Center. To add even more personal history to this trail, every year the sixth graders from the middle school I attended come to this very environmental center for a week in February to learn about different aspects of the outdoors. They taught us how to rock climb, how to rig a shelter, and how to start a fire among other things.

I was here in 2002 as a sixth grader for a week with my teachers and classmates, and then a year later my family bought land literally across the street. We discovered this fantastic gem of a trail, and now exactly ten years later I'm hiking the whole thing end to end. How does that happen?

The section through Wolf Ridge is fairly rugged, but the real challenge today comes in Tettegouche State Park. The trail crosses the Baptism River on a large metal suspension bridge and then climbs steeply up a gully known as the drain pipe, and it is aptly named as there is water trickling down it as I climb. After this, the trail climbs directly over Mt. Trudee and Round Mountain before skirting along a cliff edge looking out across Bean and Bear Lakes.

I pause here for a few moments to take in the beauty before continuing a general downhill descent toward County Road 5 where I am being picked up today. I'm about a mile and a half away from the trailhead when I pass a spur trail to a campsite and see a sign tacked to a tree. The cardboard sign reads "Strider NCT Party", with an arrow pointing down the spur. I take the trail and arrive at the campsite and see a familiar face. Hence, I meet for the fourth time Dave, aka "Diablo."

He is a fellow SHT volunteer who also was on the Encampment River Bridge project last year. He hiked the AT in 2007 and the SHT in 2011. He is now maintains this section, and was hoping to meet up with me when I came through this area...it turns out he timed it pretty well. We share stories of both our long hikes while having a few beers. He's a funny guy and tells a lot of amazing stories in his southeastern accent. Diablo is from Ohio originally, is very aware of the Buckeye Trail that I will (hopefully) be hiking a few months from now if I make it that far. He's spent quite a bit of time on the East Coast and decided to tackle the AT in 2007.

When I first met him he had brought along a scrapbook he made of his hike, and I spent quite a long time paging through it, inspired by the fantastic views. After about an hour or so in good company, I decide to push on as I don't want to be rude and keep Roxanne waiting. We shake hands as Diablo wishes me luck and then I head back down the trail, taking the cardboard sign with me as a souvenir. I'm exhausted when I finally reach the trailhead as today was probably the toughest section along the entire trail.

Thursday, May 23
Trail Day 055
Miles hiked: 26
Gooseberry Falls State Park, then on to "The Shack"

I'm very excited this morning because soon I will have another friend joining me for a few days. On top of that, the weather has improved and it looks like it's going to be a very nice day. The hike begins at the trailhead on County Road 5 where I ended yesterday. Just as I am about to begin, Diablo emerges from the woods on the way back to his car after a night on the trail. He informs me that we forgot to take a picture yesterday. Luckily, there is a guy in the parking lot ready to go for a ride on one of the nearby ATV trails; he takes our photo. After shaking hands with Diablo again I start off down (actually, up) the trail.

After a few miles I am hiking along the Beaver River, which has some nice rapids and several fantastic campsites. I pass a few day-hikers on this stretch who were out enjoying the nice weather. Soon the trail climbs uphill to Fault Line Ridge where I get a view a few hundred feet down into a wide canyon. There are quite a few blow downs along the ridge and I pass a trail steward with the orange chaps on and a chain saw in hand doing maintenance clearing the fallen trees. *Thank you sir for your hard work.

I take a rest once I reach the ridge above the Split Rock River and I have a grand view all around. I can see the famous Split Rock Lighthouse off to the northeast, the mouth of the river to the east, and of course the grand view of the Lake fading out into the distance. I continue on and the trail descends into the Split Rock River gorge, crossing a bridge over the raging river.

On the west bank I come face to face with The Split Rock, the landform that gives the river and the surrounding area its name. It's basically a large slab of rock that has somehow been cloven right down the middle. Littering the forest floor nearby are hundreds of pieces of loose rock, but unlike ballast they are flat and smooth and are not nearly as treacherous to walk on. After clearing this area I have a few more miles to go to reach Gooseberry Falls, which is my destination for today.

This park was always my favorite as a kid until I got older and the park became too crowded and too surfaced with pavement. At that point my favorite park became Tettegouche, specifically the hike out to Shovel Point. I still enjoy coming to this spot by the falls though, time after time every year. I get a good video of the falls and then head to the visitor center to await my friend who should be arriving soon. No sooner do I sit down on the bench outside than I get a text message, she has just arrived and is on her way down. Impeccable timing!

Within a few moments I stand up, she comes around the corner, and I am face to face with Karlee, a great friend from college. She has decided to come and hike with me the next few days and it will be so nice to have company again.

We decide to catch up a little before heading to the cabin, so we decide to hike the short loop around the falls. The trail loops around on both sides of the canyon with great views of the many waterfalls along the way. A few patches of snow and ice are still clinging to the steep walls of the shaded ravines. Then, on the way up to Karee's car, we pass two women coming down the trail and I recognize one of them as Gayle, executive director of the Superior Hiking Trail Association.

I greet her and she recognizes me from the time I volunteered on the trail construction crews during the past few summers. We have a short chat and she asks me how the trail has been so far. I make sure to specifically talk about the washed-out bridges and the flooded trail north of here. After the quick overview she wishes me luck and then we part ways.

Arriving at The Shack, I show Karlee around and introduce her to Roxanne who has dinner ready to go in the oven. We spend the next couple hours enjoying dinner, catching up on events back home, and then planning the hike for tomorrow. Karlee is a marathon runner and did the 100-mile ultra marathon on the SHT last year. We met in chemistry class in college during the semester I had decided to quit the cross country team. We found we had a mutual interest in the sport and ended up running together every week. We decide to do a solid twenty-one miles tomorrow. I have no doubt she will do fine.

Friday, May 24
Trail Day 056
Miles hiked: 21.5
Reeves Road – SHT, then on to "The Shack"

Today is going to be a very eventful day. It is Memorial Day week-end so my entire family will be up at the cabin to visit me and work on a few additions to improve the place. The forecast calls for another nice sunny day, perfect to finally dry everything out. Roxanne has prepared some sandwiches and some fruit for Karlee and I to bring along on the hike today. How nice it is to get some relief from the same old granola bars, trail mix, and dehydrated meals.

We shuttle Karlee's car to the Reeves Road trailhead and then get dropped off at Gooseberry Falls where we will begin our hike. Coincidentally, this is where the 100-mile ultra marathon starts, so everything we see will be new for her. The trail heads north out of the park and follows the Gooseberry River for a long ways before finally breaking off and heading southwest. Early on we encounter a porcupine right on the trail out for a morning stroll. He takes his sweet time as he waddles down the trail, totally oblivious to our presence. I've never seen one this close before so it is a fun start to the day.

After leaving the river the trail climbs gradually uphill and provides some nice views of Lake Superior near a place known as Wolf Rock. Shortly after this we need to take a detour. The next segment of trail includes the Encampment River Bridge, which got washed out a few weeks ago. A temporary roadwalk has been designated to take hikers around this segment and join the trail again on the other side. It adds maybe a little more than a mile to the hike so it doesn't add that much distance, plus there is not much traffic on that road so it makes for a nice leisurely hike. We encounter another backpacker along this stretch who, after we exchange greetings. He indicates he is going "all the way" to the end of the SHT near the Pigeon River. *Good luck dude, I hope you make it.*

Several places along this roadwalk also have a foul lingering smell, which we soon discover are several deer carcasses finally decaying after the warm up. Luckily, we don't have to be exposed to it for long. We soon find a nice shaded spot at a fork in the road among several large boulders to have lunch before rejoining the trail a short distance down the road. The trail from here follows Silver Creek most of the way between here and Reeves Road, and includes a very nice campsite.

We stop here to take a break before pushing on up one final climb that includes some interesting rock art. The end of this section is incredibly straight, likely falling on property boundaries and is densely shaded with evergreens. Eventually the trail emerges out onto the snowmobile trail, which it follows the last half mile down to the road across from Dixie's Bar, and then to the trailhead. We enjoy some homemade monster cookies that Karlee made and brought with her on the drive back to the cabin.

When we arrive, there are many vehicles parked out front. As I emerge from the car, a shady-looking dude comes walking toward me from the cabin. My friend Trevor, has come up with my father Jim, and brother, Matt, to help install a new refrigerator in the cabin—and of course to see me. We embrace and he comments that I look strong for having walked for so long, and indeed I do feel strong.

Inside the cabin everyone else is moving about, they seem to not have realized that I have arrived. When I open the door, "Luke!" is the first thing I hear as my family sees me for the first time in almost two months. They can tell that I have lost some weight, but that I do look strong and healthy. They want to know about the Kek first and foremost, because that's the section of trail they were most worried about me getting lost. I give a brief description of my hike since leaving Ely, and they seem amazed that I made it through with such little difficulty. Afterwards, I introduce Karlee to the family and am relieved that they get along well.

We spend the rest of the night having dinner, talking about things on the trail and things back home, and then sit around a camp fire with a few drinks. Karlee's poor feet have a few blisters on them (she did not have the break-in period for her sneakers that I did). Luckily I have learned much about foot care on this trek so I am able to work my magic and relieve much of the discomfort. When everyone is finally ready to retire for the night Karlee and I make plans for tomorrow's hike and then get some rest.

Saturday, May 25
Trail Day 057
Miles hiked: 24
Fox Farm Road – SHT, then on to "The Shack"

I'm not surprised to find that I am the first one up this morning. Almost everybody had quite a bit to drink last night—even before the two of us got back from our hike—and so this morning everyone else is sleeping in. I have some time to myself to catch up on journal entries before Roxanne wakes up and again prepares lunches for the hike today. Shortly afterwards, Karlee wakes up and we have breakfast before gearing up. It's going to be a longer hike than yesterday so I'm hoping to start a little earlier.

We decided last night to drop her car at Fox Farm Road and hike there from Reeves Road where we finished yesterday, making a good twenty-four mile hike. At the Fox Farm trailhead we snap a few photos and then Roxanne shuttles us to Reeves Road to start off the day. Our hike takes us through Lake County Demonstration Forest where the forest environment changes frequently providing some interesting diversity. In some places the majority of trees are evergreens, in others they are primarily oaks with open grassy spaces underneath the canopy. The eastern hardwoods provide the majority of the foliage and there are plenty of rocks on the forest floor in this section. There are many places where the trail passes near several open areas where the beavers have been at work.

After awhile, I realize that something is off. Despite feeling strong and healthy the day before, today I feel somewhat sluggish and very tired. I'm intrigued when I find out that Karlee feels the same thing, and for a long stretch neither of us says anything, we just focus on not tripping on rocks and falling on our faces. After awhile though, we get a chance to rest at a large fallen tree we use as a sofa. After eating a nice healthy lunch we feel somewhat re-energized and the rest of the day is much more lively.

We pass a small waterfall where we stop for a break and I notice several small fish trying to clamber up to the other side. We watch for a good five minutes as none of them have the strength yet to make it. Later on we pass a large group campsite where several tents are set up and people are wading in the stream nearby. Soon we come to a bridge where I am shocked to see a large sheet of ice on the far side, still clinging to life in the constant shade. After crossing this obstacle we have only a few miles to go to finish out this hike and we are provided with one last view of the Lake before reaching the trailhead.

Back in the car we have a few snacks, more of the fantastic monster cookies that Karlee made, and I find out that she has never actually been to the shore of the Lake. I convince her to stop at Flood Bay Wayside on the way back so she can experience why I come up here so often. We hang around for a few minutes despite it being frigidly cold this close to the Lake, and then finish the

journey back up to the cabin. Once back, we enjoy another fine
dinner and more camp fire chats before again retiring to bed.

Sunday, May 26
Trail Day 058
Miles hiked: 27
Martin Road (Duluth), then on to "The Shack"

My heart is a little heavier as I wake up this morning. The company I have had the past few days will be completely gone by the
end of the day. Everyone is up fairly early and we head down the
road to our favorite local restaurant bar for breakfast. The place
is called Our Place right on the main drag in Finland. I have had
many enjoyable meals here with friends and family over the years.
I down an entire omelet with pancakes on the side.

After breakfast, it is time to say goodbye to the men of the family
as they will soon pack up and head back home. I take a few moments to address each of them separately and say goodbye. This is
the last time I will see them until I complete my hike in October.
Then I climb into Karlee's car as I watch the other vehicle drive
away.

Karlee drives me to the Fox Farm Road trailhead where we ended
yesterday and then it is time to say goodbye to her. I've enjoyed
her companionship for the past few days and I am very sad to see
her go. After a hug and a goodbye, I enter the woods with a heavy
heart and teary eyes as I hear the car pull away behind me.

The trail I am hiking today has particular significance, as I helped
construct part of it. In fact, the first section today from Fox Farm
to the Sucker River is the very first section I ever worked on as a
volunteer, and is what I was working on when I first heard about
the NCT. All day long I pass familiar landmarks; a set of stairs I

helped build, a stretch of trail I remember benching into the side of a hill, a section of boardwalk I helped lay out, and a large boulder I remember working around with my mattock. There even was the trailhead off Lismore Road that I helped clear so the loader could get in with gravel and actually construct the parking pad.

This section of the thru-hike had its foundation three years ago. It was just completed last year, finally filling in the final gap to make the trail complete from Jay Cooke State Park near the Wisconsin border up to Canada. It was fairly difficult because of mostly private land the trail needed to cross and in some places it still hasn't been completely resolved, as a lot of the trail towards the end of the day is superimposed onto ATV and snowmobile trails.

At one spot I encounter several young kids on ATV's and dirt bikes going faster than they should. In another spot the trail wanders through an archery range where a few people happen to be out practicing. I manage to make decent time and arrive at the trailhead at Martin Road just on the outskirts of Duluth where Roxanne is waiting. I can tell she is heavy-hearted, as this is the last time she will be picking me up at the end of the day. She too is heading home tomorrow, which also means tonight is my last night at The Shack.

The air somehow seems darker as we make our long trip back to the cabin. We even have the opportunity to see the beacon at Split Rock Lighthouse shining for unknown reasons. I've managed to witness quite a few of these "chance sightings" over the years. As we leave it behind, I realize that today was the first time I have felt truly alone on this hike since my rough patch in Itasca State Park over a month ago.

Monday, May 27 - Memorial Day
Trail Day 059
Miles hiked: 22
Willard Munger Inn - Duluth, MN

I can tell that Roxanne is upset as I am getting ready this morning. She seems very gloomy, of course because in a few hours she will have to leave me once again and watch me hike away into the distance, not to be seen again for many months. My pack also feels unbearably heavy this morning. Of course I've been slack-packing for the last nine days so that is to be expected. From here on out I will be on my own until the very end, totally unsupported.

I got a text yesterday from another friend I met in college who recently moved up to Duluth saying she was available today and wanted to hike with me for a good distance. We made arrangements to meet at the trailhead on Martin Road.

It takes us about an hour to get there as Martin Road is on the very outskirts of the city of Duluth. We arrive a few minutes early and have some last moments alone in the car before another vehicle arrives. I get out and start unpacking my gear as my friend Kelsey, walks over ready to go hiking. It is a bit chilly today so we need to bundle up. I make some last-minute adjustments to my pack, and am dismayed when one of the buckles snaps and flies off. Luckily, it wasn't vital to the functionality of the pack so I don't have to get an immediate fix. I'll have to remember to get that checked later.

We take a few pictures in front of the sign at the trailhead, then it's time to say goodbye. With a last hug from Roxanne I turn and begin hiking. *Thanks Mom, for everything you've done for me so far on this hike.*

The hike starts out in some pretty developed areas and the hiking is fairly easy. Kelsey and I catch up as we hike along, discussing my adventures on the trail so far, how things are going for her and her husband in Duluth, and what my plans are after this. After passing through the developed areas, the trail passes through Hartley Nature Center before reaching the University of Minnesota Duluth campus. After a short roadwalk the trail descends into the gorge of Chester Creek, which is quite impressive. If it were not for the houses visible on the ridge above you would think you were in the backcountry again.

In the gorge we stop for a snack break near a waterfall and talk more about college and some of our favorite professors. We share a mutual friend in Tony, as they both were in the same degree field. I met Kelsey in a geography field course two years ago, and it was by far the best class I ever took. We got to spend eight days in the Boundary Waters learning about various concepts relating to the outdoors (including the history of the Wilderness Act and the formation of the U.S. Forest Service), and the key players that had part in those accomplishments.

We had class sessions several times a day and at some point during the course we all had to give a presentation. At the end of it all we needed to take a final exam, write a final report, and were awarded with three credits for the course. It was only a few days after that class that I decided to commit to thru-hiking the NCT, and inherited my trail name the very next day.

We soon continue on down into the gorge and eventually emerge out the other end onto city streets. From here the SHT follows sidewalks down the hill to the Rose Garden and the beginning of the Lakewalk trail which it then follows all the way through Canal Park. Shortly before reaching the Lakewalk we take a short detour and stop in at the Portland Malte Shoppe right on Superior Street. I first heard about this place four years ago from a member of the college cross country team who lives up here and I have been coming here ever since. To date, it is probably some of the best ice cream I have had. The cute red-haired girl at the window is shocked when she sees my pack and her eyes light up as she starts asking questions and finds out I've traveled almost 1,200 miles come on this journey.

After getting my malt, we continue down the Lakewalk into Canal Park. This park is the heart of tourism in Duluth, located right on the waterfront with many restaurants, shops, and hotels in the immediate area. The biggest attraction is the aerial lift bridge, which allows large ocean and lake freighters to pass underneath into the harbor. Being Memorial Day I am amazed at how few people are out and about, the place is basically a ghost town.

I get rather annoyed at the few people who are around feeding the seagulls, even though there are signs everywhere that say "Don't feed the birds." That is blatant ignorance of the rules and it displeases me, especially now that there are thousands of birds swooping around putting other people in harm's way. We make it past the mob of birds and follow sidewalks around the canal museum, the aquarium, and the DECC arena and after taking a pedestrian overpass across I-35 we begin on more off-road trail to climb towards Enger Park.

This park is quite popular among tourists, there are many gardens, lots of overlooks, and of course the six-story stone Enger Tower. The trail passes right by here but we don't climb it as we have both been here many times already. The trail passes behind some residential areas with some surprisingly great views that overlook the city and the harbor below. After reaching a place called Piedmont Knob, we take a few pictures and then it's time to say goodbye to Kelsey.

There is a spur trail leading away from here to another parking lot where she has another car stashed. *Thanks for coming out to hike with me Kelsey, it was great catching up.*

After leaving Piedmont knob the trail descends again into a valley and I come to a road crossing and a sign that says "trail closed." I am now at Haines Road, where everything has been torn up for an improvement project and the plans include putting in a culvert for the trail so hikers no longer have to cross the road. With all the destruction I am unable to see where the trail picks up on the other side of the road, so I make my best guess and pick my way across slowly. It is Memorial Day so there are no workers around to keep me out. I am pleased to discover that I correctly guessed where the trail picked up and continue on with no trouble.

I end the day hiking down into the Kingsbury Creek gorge where evidence of last year's terrible flooding is visible. I take the spur trail down to the trailhead and hike the extra quarter mile to the Willard Munger Inn where I plan to stay tonight. Andrew Skurka and Nimblewill Nomad both stayed here on their thru-hikes so I figure I should keep the tradition going. I check in and head to the room to update my Facebook status, thank all the friends who came to hike with me this week, and also note that today marks exactly two months since I began my hike way back in North Dakota. With that thought running through my head I drift off to sleep.

Tuesday, May 28
Trail Day 060
Miles hiked: 22.5
Jay Cooke State Park

I woke up this morning and headed straight to the lobby for breakfast. I haven't had cold cereal in quite awhile so I enjoy devouring several bowls of it before I feel content. Afterwards, I head back to the room and get all my gear packed up and ready to go before check out. Also in the lobby at this time are Bill and Sally, Bill being a direct descendent of Willard Munger himself whom the Inn and nearby Munger Trail are named. They see my pack and ask the usual questions and we spend quite a good deal of time talking before I finally hit the trail around 9:30 a.m.

Along the trail today is more evidence of last year's terrible floods. I should expand on this a little more. In 2012 the Duluth area had the flood of the century—literally. Most of the ground up here is a thin layer of topsoil on top of solid basalt bedrock, and after several days of constant pouring rain the water had nowhere to go but sideways. The rivers had enough power to alter their own courses, entire roads were destroyed, bridges washed out, sinkholes appeared in the middle of major city streets. The entire city of Duluth was declared a disaster zone. It was a terrible natural event. The city itself has more or less recovered, but the surrounding countryside is another story entirely.

Some of the trail on higher ground is still intact and I hike past Spirit Mountain to Magney Snively Park where I get one last look back towards Duluth. Spirit Mountain has the only camping spot between Duluth and Jay Cooke State Park, but hiking through Magney Snively makes me think that this would be a great place for a future campsite, or even a shelter. There is very little underbrush most of the way and the floor is covered by soft grasses, making for a very pleasant hike. Eventually, the trail reaches the base of Ely's Peak and a spur trail leads to the top, providing a great view almost 360 degrees around.

After Ely's Peak the trail descends into the Mission Creek Gorge where some of the trail has been repaired since the flooding. There is an old historic bridge on the creek that the trail uses and right at this point there is a sign that says "trail closed." I dare not go any further after this sign because at some point I know it will dead-end. The trail beyond here leading into Jay Cooke State Park is completely obliterated, mud slides having wreaked havoc on it last spring.

At this point I turn and follow the nearby ATV trail to the paved Munger Trail and follow it into the park. Along this stretch of trail is (former) Forbay Lake, which is now completely drained after the dam burst and released all the water into the countryside. Even the paved trail has entire sections missing, only recently filled back in with gravel.

Right after this the trail enters Jay Cooke State Park, my destination for tonight. I follow the Munger Trail spur to the park headquarters and get a campsite for the night. After setting up, I head over to the site of the famous "Swinging Bridge", which was certified NCT. It was originally built by the CCC in 1935 and had been washed out only once before in the 50s, where it was raised a few feet to its current height. It is a very iconic and historic structure, being considered the gateway to the North Shore. The bridge is gone now because of the flooding and it is the only crossing of the St. Louis River for several miles so tomorrow, I will need to take a large detour to get around the park and cross the river.

As I stand at the former approach, I can see that work has already begun to repair and replace the bridge. The north side of the bridge has been completely removed and the horribly mangled metal frame is lying there. The south side of the bridge is still mostly intact and has been stabilized by cables. Seeing all the damage done to this historic structure brings tears to my eyes, as this park was always one of my favorites and I have many childhood memories here. To think that water had enough power to completely destroy a stone and metal structure is just incredible.

Despite being a very sad moment, this is also somewhat of a proud moment for me. This bridge also marks the southern terminus of the SHT, which means today I finally accomplished a goal I've had since I first set foot on the trail ten years ago. Back then our family cabin was newly built, the trail crossed our road only 400 feet away, and I made a goal to hike the entire trail within ten years.

As of today, mission accomplished!

After taking several photos of the mangled bridge remains and grabbing a soda at the vending machine, I head back to my camp and drift off to sleep with a heavy heart. This is my last night in Minnesota.

Glacial Erratic along Section 13, Superior Hiking Trail.

WISCONSIN

May 29 - June 7, 2013

Wednesday, May 29
Trail Day 061
Miles hiked: 31
Pattison State Park

I'm up fairly early this morning and get a good breakfast cooking before finally packing up and heading down the trail. Today's detour adds about eight miles to my hike but I have no choice, as this is the only off-road option with the bridge being destroyed. I follow the Munger Trail out of the park and through the towns of Carlton and Wrenshall before it finally starts heading southeast.

It has turned out to be a very nice day, more typical for this time of year. I am hiking in only a T-shirt and shorts and it grows quite hot. The scenery is very pleasant along this paved trail, nice views of wetlands, a few cool rock outcroppings, and some nicely constructed benches to sit and have a rest once in awhile.

After a few hours, I reach the point where the trail reaches MN-23 and the trail forks—one fork going uphill to join the road and one fork heading straight to pass underneath the highway. To reach the Wisconsin border I need to take the straight fork, which at this point is no longer paved, but a grassy two-track with a ballast surface. Luckily, because of the long winter, the grass is not long so I am able to navigate the last few miles with no difficulty.

Soon the trail comes out to a service road paralleling a railroad track and I follow this south for a half mile before hitting paved County Road 4 and crossing the railroad tracks into Wisconsin. After snapping a picture I take a last look back at my home state, then turn and continue hiking. The rest of the day is completely a roadwalk to reach Pattison State Park where I plan to spend the night. After a few miles at a road intersection a county vehicle pulls up with two county workers inside. They stop and ask me where I'm headed and we spend a few minutes talking about where the trail passes through this area. At this moment we happen to be right across the railroad from a future segment of NCT in the Macquarrie Wetland Preserve, owned by the University of Wisconsin Superior. I had heard about the construction of this segment before leaving to begin my hike but it is not slated to be completed until next year so I am not able to hike it at this time. After explaining where the trail goes in this area, the two workers wish me luck as they pull away and I continue down the road.

The next several miles are on back-country gravel roads, I when I finally reach the last paved road that will bring me into the park, I come to a trail crossing. I am now standing on the Gandy Dancer State Trail, which is the same trail where I encountered Nimblewill Nomad last year when I crossed paths with him on the last day of his Ice Age Trail thru-hike. The trail down there was a crushed limestone surface on an old rail grade and was very nice hiking. But up here, this far north, it has deteriorated into an overgrown and rutted two-track, with signs indicating the trail is closed until further notice. I stand here for a moment as the memories of that day last August when I finally met the guy that inspired me to do this hike come flowing in.

I remember camping on the shore of the St. Croix River the night before and beginning my hike on the Gandy Dancer Trail north toward the place where my car was parked. I remember running into a familiar face at a road crossing and discovering that it was a fellow SHT volunteer I had met earlier that year that was also there to try and intercept Nimblewill. His name was Gray Ghost and is a very experienced hiker, having completed the PCT a short time earlier.

After catching up for a few minutes I remember seeing three hikers coming toward us and knew that I was in fact going to meet the legendary hiker. The three hikers stopped to talk to us and I was surprised to find that Nimblewill already knew who Gray

Ghost was. The two other hikers were Nate and Paul, who had already thru-hiked the Ice Age Trail and came to accompany Nimblewill on his last day. I remember Nimblewill himself turning to face me and I introduced myself and told him what an inspiration he was to me.

We spent probably fifteen minutes talking about my plans for the NCT, and his future plans for that year to complete the New England Trail after the Ice Age Trail. He gave me several pointers about planning (specifically about the long mile days) and about not letting the long roadwalks discourage me. It was a great experience, one that will live long in my memory.

I continue hiking down the road, and shortly before entering the park I come over a rise and look to the north and am surprised at what I can see. Way in the distance, almost on the horizon line, I can see the city of Duluth and a faint glimpse of the Lake, allowing me one last look at my favorite place back home. Just around a bend in the road from this point I see the state park boundary sign and a trailhead comes into view. I turn left onto the park trail system and hike down to Big Manitou Falls where I stop to take in the view. These falls are pretty impressive as they fall over a sheer cliff and into a large valley with sweeping views to the west. After enjoying the view I pass through a hiker culvert under WI-35 and enter the park campground where I make camp.

I made better time than I expected and so I take the opportunity to see all of the NCT within the park. The section through Pattison is currently a dead-end segment as it is surrounded by private land so a thru-hiker would normally see only a small portion of it before turning right past Little Manitou Falls and back out to the road. But now since I have some extra time I decide to hike all the NCT within the park, about four miles round trip. Most of it follows closely to the river making for a very pleasant hike. On the way back I am startled by a porcupine running across the trail right in front of me and quickly scampering up a tree to escape me. I snap a quick picture and continue on, giving the porcupine a wide berth. Right after this, I hear a high-pitched screeching noise and look around wondering what in the world it is. Suddenly, a large bird comes into view right in front of me as it bursts from canopy above and I duck as it flies right past me, screeching angrily. It gets so close I can feel the wind from its feathers graze the back of my neck. I get a good enough glimpse of it to identify it as a goshawk.

I keep moving down the trail hoping to avoid another fly by, but the bird seems intent on hurting me as it continues to fly up into the canopy and then swoop down angrily at me. It does this eight times. I run, dodging between trees as I go to avoid being hit. Luckily, I escape unscathed and hike back to the campground wondering what I did to provoke it. Goshawks are somewhat territorial birds and I come to the conclusion that it must have had a nest somewhere nearby and didn't like that I was that close. It's kind of strange, many people fear and almost expect to be attacked by anything else; a bear, a mountain lion, a rattlesnake, but a bird is a much less common and overlooked threat.

Back at the campground and after getting a soda from the park vending machine, I cook a meal and sit down to take a good look at my maps for tomorrow. After making a plan I read some more pages of Tolkien before settling into bed. I have a long day ahead tomorrow.

Thursday, May 30
Trail Day 062
Miles hiked: 33, +3
West Mail Road Trailhead - St. Croix National Scenic Riverway

I'm up at first light, and after a quick breakfast I'm heading out of the park. I hike the first mile or so of trail within the park again and peel off at the intersection to Little Manitou Falls. I snap several pictures of the magnificent waterfall before bailing out onto WI-35 and hiking south. The rest of the day is entirely a roadwalk and last night I made a decision to put the pair of sneakers I brought with me to good use.

So far I have had these with me as a spare pair of footwear for walking around in camp or in town after a day on the trail to keep my feet dry. Since today is entirely a roadwalk, I decided to wear the sneakers to take some weight off my feet. By the end of the day I would regret this decision. My feet are used to the hiking shoes but not the sneakers.

Today also is my first day of summer. It's at least 75 degrees and the bugs are out. After awhile, the trail leaves the paved roads and heads into the woods along some logging roads. I wish this segment of the trail route was blazed because toward the end of the logged segment I make a wrong turn and hike over a mile in the wrong direction, ending up at a landing for the logging trucks. Realizing my mistake I backtrack to where I made the turn and continue on east.

Soon I come to another turn that is the right one. I had simply turned one intersection too soon, as the turn I originally took was not on the map. Back on track now I still have many miles to go before reaching my destination for today at the entrance of the St. Croix National Scenic Riverway. Besides some of the heavily logged areas on the county forest land, there is no easily identifiable public land between Pattison State Park and the Riverway, meaning I have to make thirty-four miles today to reach a legal camping place.

Along the gravel road up ahead some movement catches my eye. I look up quick enough to catch a small black bear scurrying across the road as fast as it can run about fifty yards ahead of me. This is my first bear encounter on this hike, but not my first ever. Seeing this bear brings back the memory of my first solo hike on the SHT when I was 14 years old, and hiking the section just north of my cabin. I had only two miles to go to make it back and as I came over a rise there was a small black bear foraging for some food about thirty feet ahead of me.

I remember how scared I was at the time, being only a young kid and having this animal only a stone's throw away. I remember my concern as it wasn't a very big bear, meaning its mother could still be around. I waited for ten minutes as it slowly wandered off down the next rise and I quickly made my way down the trail away from the bear in case its mother happened to be around. Shortly after I made it back to the cabin, our neighbor down the road from us stopped over for a visit. When I told him the story of my encounter he didn't believe me, saying encounters like that right on the trail are extremely rare.

Right after the wildlife sighting, it starts to rain and continues to rain the rest of the day. At the same time, out of nowhere I get swarmed by a small horde of mosquitoes. On goes my headnet. Shortly before dark, I come to a large yellow gate with the unmistakable National Park Service logo, and right next to it the NCT logo. I have arrived at the entrance to the newly constructed segment of trail through the St. Croix National Scenic Riverway.

I pitch my tent on the other side of the gate and head into my tent. To say that I regretted wearing those sneakers today is an understatement. Both of my feet have larger blisters than all those early days in North Dakota from the continuous pounding of the roads and the towpaths. This is surely going to hurt for awhile. I won't make this mistake again.

Friday, May 31
Trail Day 063
Miles hiked: 14
Swanson's Motel - Solon Springs, WI

I could hear the swarming of the mosquitoes outside my tent all night. Summer has definitely arrived. The first thing I do after getting up is put on my bug shirt and my head net to prepare for the buzzers today. Then, after a quick breakfast at the bridge, I am off down the newly constructed trail along the scenic St. Croix River.

After a few miles I come to the Gibson Cabin, an old structure that is currently due for rehabilitation. This would be a great asset for hikers and paddlers on the river if the National Park Service fixed it up and put some bunk beds inside, like a two story hiker shelter. Then a fire pit outside in the clearing and an outhouse is all you would need to make this one of the best campsites on the entire trail.

It's a pretty thick jungle along the riverbank, but once the trail veers away the forest starts to open up and soon I'm standing on the edge of a prairie-like pine barrens. At this point, a nice breeze comes up and allows enough relief from the buzzers that I'm able to take off the long sleeves and the head net. As I am stopped under a grove of a few dozen pine trees, I notice dozens of ticks climbing all over me...half of them the infamous Lyme-disease carrying deer tick! By the end of the day I will have picked off more than fifty of the little buggers, stopping every twenty minutes to check myself and pick off the ones I can find.

Today is another warm humid day—but the ticks aside—this section of trail is quite enjoyable. The soil here is quite sandy so my feet get some relief on the soft tread. I pass three campsites along this section with trail registers made from ammo boxes. I take time to sign each one, the last site having a large group of people currently staying in it. If I had to guess I'd say they are a trail crew out building new trail somewhere nearby.

At the crossing of US-53, I'm at the outskirts of Solon Springs and I take a break at the bench outside of the Laundromat on the edge of town. Once I decide to get going again I stop in at the DQ across the street from Lucius Woods Park for a Blizzard (it seems like forever since I've had one of these). With my ice cream in hand I hike through Lucius Woods and am surprised when I meet a couple coming down the trail toward me. The man asks, "Are you Strider?"

This floored me. This is the first time someone has recognized me on the trail. It turned out these two have been following along with my progress since the beginning. They snap a quick picture of me and then continue on their way.

Once I have consumed my Blizzard, I make a quick detour to the post office to pick up my next food drop. Across the street is a restaurant with a small patio so I head over there to empty my box and transfer all the goods to my pack. I am still hungry after that Blizzard, so I decide to stop in at the grocery store for some fresh fruit before leaving town. I am only in there for a few minutes and pick out a nice box of strawberries. When I get to the register to pay, I suddenly hear a loud tapping noise at the glass door. Golfball-sized hail came out of nowhere and was now falling from the sky at an incredible rate. Lucky for me, I just happened to be inside when it hit. With nowhere to go I find a spot in the corner of the store and crack open my box of strawberries. The storm only lasts a few minutes so I am out the door in no time.

The pavement outside is steaming from the earlier heat of the day and before long most of the water has evaporated. Still hungry, I decide to head in to the restaurant, KD's Diner, for lunch. The server/bartender Taylor, comes and takes my order. After downing my first glass of soda while I'm waiting for my food, I answer several voicemails on my phone regarding National Trails Day tomorrow.

The Brule St. Croix Chapter of the NCTA is having a hiking event at the DNR fish hatchery in Brule, and they have invited me to come by for a few hours and talk about the trail. I get in touch with Peter, the chapter president, and let him know that I am not sure where I will be staying tonight, so I will get back to him later once I know for sure.

Soon my food comes and I chow down on the delicious burger. After awhile, as I am starting to slow down, Taylor comes over and sits at the table with me. She tells me that when she saw me walk in she had a feeling that I had a story to tell, and she wanted to hear all about it. I find out that she has never heard of the NCT, even though it crosses the road literally one block down the street. I tell her about my travels so far, about the horrible winter conditions in Minnesota, and the amounts of ticks I had just this morning.

I give her the link to my website so she can follow along and find out more about the trail in the process. "This is awesome, Thanks!" she says before a few customers show up and she heads back behind the counter.

Eventually I finish my meal and shoulder my pack to head out again. "Be safe out there", Taylor shouts to me as I pass through the door. The sky has really darkened since I went into the restaurant and I only make it a few blocks down the road when it starts to pour. "Well this sucks," I say to myself. I decide that it's not worth it to head out into a storm and get all muddy and soaked when I have an event to be at tomorrow, so I turn around and head back. Within a few minutes I'm back in KD's Diner soaking wet.

"Do you have a phone book?" I ask.

I walk back over to my table and Taylor brings me the book. One of the voicemails I received earlier was from a couple here in town that knew about me and that I was close to Solon Springs. It turns out, the trail actually crosses their property south of town and they were hoping for a chance to meet me and hear more about the trail west of here, or just to wish me luck if they didn't get the chance. I call the number back and am on the phone with Debra. Her husband Thomas, is the one that left the message and unfortunately he is not home right now.

I tell her my situation, that I was basically calling to say that I have some time now if they wanted to meet me and also ask if there is any place to stay in town. She recommends a famous place, Swanson's Motel on the edge of town. I thank Debra for her help and after getting off the phone with her I look up the number for Swanson's Motel. A few rings later and I am on the phone with Charlie, the owner. I tell him I am hiking the NCT and looking for a room tonight. He says they have plenty available and even offers to pick me up right here at the diner in about a half hour. *Wow, this is amazing, thanks Charlie!*

I kill some time in the diner waiting for the half hour to pass. Many more locals are here now for an early dinner. Soon Charlie arrives so I load my gear into his car and we head for the motel. When we arrive I am surprised to find that it is not so much a motel than a group of individual cabins. Yes, this will do nicely. When I get to the office to check in I meet Jan, the co-owner. I explain that I am hiking the whole NCT end-to-end, and because of the storm I decided to stay in town tonight.

As soon as the words came out of my mouth she tells me about another fellow who had come through a few years ago doing the same thing. Yes, I have stumbled upon yet another establishment that Nimblewill Nomad visited on his epic journey in 2009. They give me a cabin all to myself near the main building for a hiker trash rate, and request a photo in front of their office before I turn in. Fine folks here at Swanson's Motel.

The first thing I do when I get inside is take a nice shower and then enjoy some time watching TV and catching up on a few journal entries before finally drifting off to sleep.

Saturday, June 1 - National Trails Day
Trail Day 064
Miles hiked: 14
Highland Campsite

Last night, I reached Peter. He said Tim, another local chapter member, would be coming to pick me up this morning and shuttle me to the fish hatchery for National Trails Day. I cook myself breakfast before heading out this morning and no sooner have I checked out and thanked Charlie and Jan for letting me stay at their wonderful establishment, than a truck pulls up and I meet Tim. I load my gear into his truck and we head for the hatchery.

Just outside Solon Springs, we spot an NCT tool trailer belonging to the Brule-St. Croix roving crew lead by Bill, the Wisconsin Regional Trail coordinator. His crew must be out building some new trail. Hopefully, I will get a chance to meet some of them after I begin hiking today. Tim fills me in on what I can expect the next few days until reaching the Chequamegon National Forest. It sounds like I can expect well-marked and maintained trail.

Soon we arrive at the Brule fish hatchery and I bring my gear over to the NCTA booth. The goal of today is to educate locals about the NCT and hopefully recruit some new members. I'm here to share my story with them and mingle with the local chapter members. Later on there will be some guided hikes on the trail but I will be gone and back on my own before that occurs.

At the booth I meet volunteers Chuck and Phil, both active members. There is a spur trail behind the booth leading to the main trail about a quarter mile away, so after a little mingling Chuck and I decide to take a scouting mission to make sure it is in decent enough shape for the hike. We manage to stay on course but the DNR has not mowed it this year so it has almost disappeared. The only visible markings are little blue circles painted on some of the trees. It's a good thing we went ahead and checked it out, the chapter brought their trailer with them so they can mow the trail before the hike with their DR mower.

I decide to stay for lunch and head over to the grill for some brats. One of the volunteers warns me about some of the trail coming up in the UP of Michigan. Some of the trail in the Porcupine Mountains is apparently in bad condition and hasn't been cleared in awhile. I'm glad for the heads up, though it'll be hard to tell exactly where on the trail he is talking about. The Porkies are a pretty expansive area with lots of trails.

After lunch Tim shuttles me back to Solon Springs and I begin my hike for the day. I have a short roadwalk to reach the first section of trail through the Brule Bog. This section is a very impressive example of boardwalk construction. Over the past four years the chapter has built a two-mile-long boardwalk through a remote cedar and tamarack swamp. This must have taken major funding and a dedicated crew to get it completed in such a fashion. After coming out the other side it becomes apparent that the new trail being built must not be connected to the existing trail yet. I never saw the tool trailer again, nor the spot near the railroad tracks that it was sitting on. *Sorry I missed you Bill.*

The next section of trail is another fantastic section along the Brule-St. Croix portage. This specific section of trail has been used for hundreds of years by Native Americans, voyageurs, fur trappers, and many others before now being incorporated into the nation's longest scenic hiking trail. All along the portage there are large boulders with plaques honoring some of the famous travelers to the area. There are a few names I recognize: Henry Schoolcraft, Johnathan Carver, Greysolon DuLhut. What an impressive and inspiring piece of trail.

Despite my break this morning I feel exhausted, so I decide to take a short day and pitch at the next campsite near the Highland Township Hall.

Sunday, June 2
Trail Day 065
Miles hiked: 25.5
About two miles east of County Road A - Chequamegon National Forest

It was a chilly one last night, I had to put on everything I have with me to stay warm. For whatever reason, I was extremely tired and slept in until 9 a.m. The first order of business is to get some water from the town hall nearby. When I get there I find the water has not been turned on yet, so I will have to ration what I have... so no hot meal today.

As soon I start hiking the weather warms up fairly quickly and before too long the buzzers are out in force. I need to wear my bug net all day to keep the blood-thirsty mosquitoes away. A few miles out I come to a large sign that is the first I've seen of its kind along the trail. It has the usual mileage features of a directional sign but at the top there is an arrow pointing to the left with an ND and an arrow pointing right with an NY. A very neat sign.

The rest of the day is pretty uneventful; a few good overlooks along the way as I head toward the Chequamegon National Forest and more ticks by the dozen to pick off as I hike through some grassy areas. Once inside the national forest boundary, I find a spot and pitch for the night. Getting to sleep proves a little difficult as I happen to pitch my tent near two screech owls. I saw one fly over as I was setting up but now that it's dark and I'm in my tent, there are two of them hollering back and forth to each other. My tent is right between them and it feels a bit creepy as their screeching noise continues for what seems like hours as I try to sleep.

Monday, June 3
Trail Day 066
Miles hiked: 23
Lake Owen picnic area - Chequamegon National Forest

After the owls stopped screeching, I managed to get some sleep and woke up this morning earlier than I expected. Within a few hours I'm standing at the edge of the Rainbow Lakes Wilderness. Being a designated wilderness area it has the same rules as if you were in the Boundary Waters in Minnesota: no blazes, no markings, no permanent structures. It's a small area but one unique enough to be worth protecting. The trail tread is fairly well traveled so it's quite easy to stay on track. There are many gorgeous lakes all around and I stop at many of them to take in the view.

I was short on water yesterday and so wasn't able to eat any of my dehydrated meals. There is a town up ahead a few miles off the trail where I plan to get stocked up and rehydrated. I reach the first paved road and head on down to Drummond, a little berg in the middle of the forest. At the gas station I fill up on water and use their WiFi to check my email. I make a few phone calls and then head across the street to the Bear Country Inn for a meal. I'm the first person here this morning as the place has just opened. Inside I'm greeted by Tiffany, who sits me down at the bar and hands me a menu. I order soda with water to keep well hydrated. While the cooks are working to prepare my burger Tiffany asks the usual questions. She is familiar with the trail but has only hiked a few miles on it. She also warns me there may be some bad thunderstorms tonight, possibly tornadoes.

After awhile some of the locals come in and the bar is pretty busy. Many of the folks notice my pack and ask the usual questions. A few of them have heard of the trail and think it's neat that someone is hiking all the way through. Fine folks here at Bear Country Inn.

Back on the trail I try to get as far as possible before the storm hits. The section leading out of Drummond has been completely obliterated by recent logging. No evidence of the trail exists anywhere, but luckily someone has come out recently and painted some key blazes to navigate through the mess. I reach the picnic area on Lake Owen and decide to stay here for the night. There is a small stone shelter here that I could get to quickly if it started to hail, or worse. I filter some water from the lake to keep fully stocked and read a few pages of Tolkien before drifting off to sleep.

Tuesday, June 4
Trail Day 067
Miles hiked: 25
Beaver Lake Campground - Chequamegon National Forest

The storm last night wasn't as bad as they said it would be; just a good soaking. I begin my day hiking through the Porcupine Lakes Wilderness, another small but incredibly pristine area. Many more lakes and rocky outcrops abound. It is also fitting that I should see a porcupine while in the Porcupine Lakes Wilderness, waddling off the trail and up into one of the rocky ravines.

Outside the wilderness boundary I'm in some of the weathered-down remains of the ancient Penokee Mountains. The topography and visual quality is very similar to the Sawtooths along the North Shore in Minnesota, and they should because the two are actually closely related.

Back in college I did a term paper on the geology of the North Shore and discovered that an ancient mountain range once stretched across the continent where the Great Lakes are located now. Over millennia they have been weathered down by fire, wind, and ice to a fraction of what they once were. These mountains stretched from the edge of North Dakota all the way to eastern New York. Remnants of this ancient mountain range include: the Sawtooths and Misqua Hills in Minnesota, the Penokees in Wisconsin, the Porkies in Michigan, the Laurentians in Quebec, and the Adirondacks in New York.

Many people who hear about the NCT assume it's not very scenic because it doesn't follow a mountain range like the Triple Crown does. Well, the NCT actually does follow a mountain range, just one that mostly doesn't exist anymore, but the parts that are still around are spectacular. Nothing too high elevation wise, but still a tough climb. I am looking forward to the end of this hike—if I should ever make it that far—to the finale through the wild Adirondack Mountains of New York, a true representation of what these ancient Penokees must have once been like.

Located within one these ancient mountain valleys are the remains of an old Swedish settlement and an Adirondack Shelter located nearby. Their is the typical three-sided design with a fire pit and latrine. These shelters are everywhere along the Appalachian Trail, about every 10–12 miles from what I've heard. At this point, I am roughly 1,500 miles into this trek, and this is the first one I have seen. They get more common the further east you go on this trail and I should like the opportunity to stay in a few of them to get the full experience.

After a few strenuous uphill climbs I reach the campground on Beaver Lake and pitch for the night.

Wednesday, June 5
Trail Day 068
Miles hiked: 20
Copper Falls State Park

It rained most of the night and it continues to rain off and on the whole day...the icy cold kind. I need my rain jacket to keep myself warm and dry. Along the trail in a pine grove I see a note tacked to a tree. It's from a guy named Mike, addressed to me. It says there is a side trail leading to his house and I should feel free to stop by if I need anything or want to spend the night.

I decide I should at least head over and thank him for the offer if he's home. I follow the spur trail and end up at Mike's front door. I knock, and soon the door opens and I am greeted by Mike, who is the vice president of the Chequamegon Chapter. He invites me in for a cup of hot chocolate, which I gladly accept.

At the kitchen table we make conversation, talking about the trail, what's going on in the local area, and a recap of my adventure so far. It turns out, the folks in Mellen were trying to reach me, and wanted to know my approximate ETA so they could get an interview for the paper, and maybe take me out for lunch. It just so happens that I will be reaching Mellen today within about an hour or two.

Mike says that he was planning on going into town anyway so he will let everybody know that I am close and try to get something organized. With plans in place I take my leave of Mike and head on down the trail again headed for Mellen.

I continue through the Chequamegon National Forest and within a few hours I make it to the road and head on down into Mellen. I'm a little behind schedule because of the rain, but I made it. Mike is there at the intersection where the trail follows main street through town.

Our first stop is the local paper for an interview. At the office to conduct the interview is Jim of the *Mellen Weekly – Record*. Soon his wife Sandy arrives along with many members of the chamber of commerce, city council, and a few NCTA volunteers. Hence, I got a chance to meet Carol, Linda, Betty, Thom and his two kids Tommy and Elizabeth. We snap a photo in front of City Hall and then head across the street for dinner, courtesy of the kind folks here in Mellen.

I order a large pizza and then sit at the table in good company and tell the story of my experience so far and answer the usual questions. The food comes and I down most of the pizza before taking the rest with me in a box before hitting the trail again. I plan on staying in Copper Falls State Park tonight, and in order to save time Mike has offered to reserve a spot for me while I hike the last few miles there in the pouring rain. Mike also takes my pack so I can travel lighter and hopefully save some of my gear from getting completely drenched.

I hammer out the last few miles in no time and meet Mike at the entrance to the campground. It turns out that the park rangers, after they had heard my story, gave me a spot in the campground free of charge. Wow, what an incredible day of trail magic this has turned out to be! Mike shuttles me to my site and I quickly set up my tent doing my best to keep things dry. Afterwards, Mike brings out a small cooler and asks me to pick out one of the unique flavors of beer he has. We enjoy a cold one together before it's time to say goodbye. I try and get some sleep. *Thanks for everything you've done today Mike, it was a pleasure meeting you.*

Thursday, June 6
Trail Day 069
Miles hiked: 22
Iron County Forest north of Upson, WI

The rain stopped in the middle of the night but everything is soaked when I emerge from my tent early in the morning. The first thing I do is retrieve my leftover pizza and consume it for breakfast before changing back into my wet clothes to begin the day.

I got a message from Beth at NCTA a few days ago about an interview with Dave Carlson, from the Northland Adventures TV Series in Wisconsin. I called Dave back last night and set up an interview for today so he will be here at my campsite first thing for an interview. As soon as I am all changed back into my wet clothes, I hear a truck pull up and I meet Dave in person. He asks me a few basic questions as I start packing my gear and then pulls out the video camera to film the process I use when packing.

Afterwards, he says he wants some action shots with a scenic background so we make plans for him to meet me at the bridge a short distance down the trail. Sure enough, when I arrive there is Dave all ready to go with his big camera in hand. We hike to the bridge overlooking the Falls and take a few action shots and a few stills before he wishes me luck. I continue down the trail. *Thanks for taking the time to come out here Dave.*

The trail through the park is well marked, well maintained, and is a very popular section. I'd have to say it's one of the favorite places I've hiked through in Wisconsin; reminding me a bit of the North

Shore in Minnesota. The section of NCT through the park used to be a dead-end until last year when the Wisconsin DNR acquired a substantial chunk of land adjacent to the park specifically for the trail. In the future it will become part of Copper Falls State Park. In the meantime the Heritage Chapter has gone out to the new addition, flagged a route for the trail, and started building a good portion of it. It still is technically a dead-end, but now there is at least a flagged route through the woods to get over to near Wren Falls.

I follow some newly-constructed tread for about a mile until it ends. Here the trail has been blazed for a good distance and cleared but no tread has been built yet. I need to watch my step for roots and stumps but it's not too difficult to navigate through. It does become difficult where the trail crosses a steep gorge over a river and with no tread, no bridge has been built. I spend a few minutes eyeing up the flag line down one side of the gorge and up the other side, trying to figure out how I can best navigate through this. It's not as difficult going down, but climbing up out of the gorge is a real challenge with a full pack on.

I takes me about twenty minutes to scramble up the side of the gorge using tree trunks as handles. I make it out safely and continue to follow the flagged trail through the thick forest. Soon I emerge onto what appears to be an abandoned logging road. The trail follows this for a short distance and heads back into the woods.

Along this old road I come around a corner and stop dead in my tracks. Not twenty-five feet in front of me is a giant black bear, the biggest I've ever seen! I would not be surprised if it weighed in more than 500 pounds. It turned with its side facing me and its head down in the grass looking for grubs. After about ten seconds it sees me and turns in my direction. We both stand motionless, not sure of what the other will do. This staring contest continues for what seems like forever, but probably was not more than twenty seconds. Finally, the bear puts his head down as if taking a defensive posture, and at that moment I wave my arms in the air has high as I can. I shout as loud as I can and the bear turns and runs off the trail into the woods. Boy am I glad there were no cubs around; it could have been a much different story.

After the encounter with the "Great Bear", I continued to follow the flag line until it disappeared. I spend the better part of a half hour walking in a general circle looking for the next flag, but I am unable to locate it. I continued walking in what I thought was the proper direction and ended up getting lost in a maze of field roads. After following one of the roads and ending up close to a posted private parcel, I decide to get off the path and bushwhack to the east until I hit a road. After a half mile bushwhack I emerge onto the road and get out the GPS to figure out where exactly I am. I am pretty close to where I should be so I continue on down the designated road walk.

From here, there is one more certified section of trail leading to Wren Falls, but it's currently a dead-end. And afterward, the trail follows some ski trails and some abandoned logging roads almost all the way to Michigan. I did a lot of research about this area before my hike and found out this is one of those trouble spots. I decide to follow the road instead of backtracking to follow the ski trail and end up walking WI-77 to Upson.

I'm totally exhausted, and it will be dark soon. From here I head north back to the connector trail and find a spot to camp just as darkness descends and a thunderstorm rolls in.

Friday, June 7
Trail Day 070
Miles hiked: 14
Advance Motel - Ironwood, MI

I'm not sure why, but I'm up and at it early this morning (perhaps from the excitement of putting another state under my belt). It's about fourteen miles to Ironwood, MI where I have my next food drop. I'm there before noon and head to the post office first thing. I actually have two packages coming here to Ironwood, both really important. The first is my regular food drop with all the maps I will need for Michigan, and the second is another GPS unit from NCTA to use to navigate through Michigan.

The GPS I have been using to this point only had enough data for the first three states so I will be sending this unit back to them and exchanging it for the next one. When I arrive, I am nervous when they only bring out one package. The GPS hasn't made it here yet. I hope it arrives by tomorrow, otherwise I will have to burn two whole days as tomorrow is Saturday.

With nothing left to do, I head to the north end of town along US-2 and check in to the Advance Motel and spend the rest of the day relaxing, sorting through all the supplies in my box, and catching up on journal entries.

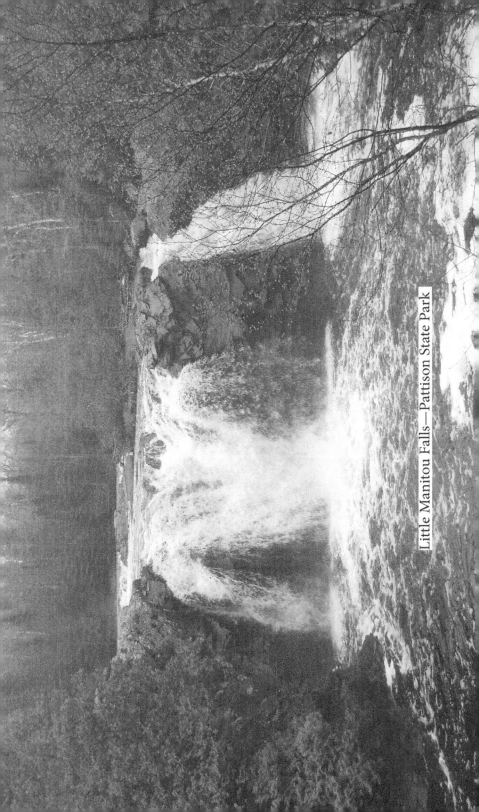

Little Manitou Falls—Pattison State Park

MICHIGAN:
UPPER PENINSULA

June 8 - July 1, 2013

Saturday, June 8
Trail Day 071
Miles hiked: 21
Black River Harbor Recreation Area - Ottawa National Forest

The post office doesn't open until 10 a.m. and I need to spend some time organizing afterwards. The package I didn't receive yesterday contains all the maps I will need for getting through Michigan, but there are too many to carry at once so I have to sort them out and send some home. I am relieved when I arrive at the post office and the second package is there.

I keep the maps that will get me through Marquette and will send the rest home to be used later. I spend the next several minutes splitting the maps into groups, labeling them, and sealing them back up in a box along with the first GPS to send home. I don't get hiking until after 11 a.m.

My route out of Ironwood begins on the Iron Horse ATV trail for the first few miles and then takes to the roads. It's about a fifteen-mile roadwalk to get to the beginning of the certified trail in Michigan just north of the Copper Peak ski hill. The ski hill is pretty massive in its own right, I bet this place is just packed in the winter time.

It's a nice day for hiking but the bugs are out in great profusion, requiring the use of my bug net. The trail leads through a small chunk of the Ottawa National Forest passing several spectacular waterfalls; Conglomerate Falls, Nawadaha Falls, Potawotami Falls, and Sandstone Falls. I take hundreds of photos and dozens of videos at this fantastic spot and continue on.

I end the day at the campground near the mouth of the Black River where it empties into Lake Superior and take a campsite with a great view of the lake. I am the only camper here tonight, even the host is gone. I have the sunset over the lake all to myself.

Sunday, June 9
Trail Day 072
Miles hiked: 24.5
Greenstone Falls campsite - Porcupine Mountains Wilderness State Park

I woke up fairly early this morning and broke camp right away. I decided to take advantage of the location and eat my breakfast at the picnic area at the river mouth, only a quarter mile hike from my campsite. There is a small safe harbor, a fancy picnic shelter and a fine suspension bridge (certified NCT) across the river.

After breakfast the hike begins across the bridge and takes me past Rainbow Falls, probably the most spectacular waterfall I've seen yet in Michigan. Also along the trail today, a little piece of trail magic occurs en route to the falls in the form of free beer! As I am hiking, I come across four cold unopened cans laying near the trail. Clearly someone was out for a fun night on the river and dropped some of their goods en route to their camp. I take one for the road and leave the rest.

After passing the falls the quality of the trail decreases quite a bit. It follows what appears to be an overgrown abandoned logging road all the way to the boundary of Porcupine Mountain Wilderness State Park. The tread is a narrow strip of mud clay through tall grass and brush. In several places the trail is crossed by deep narrow gullies, not bridged and too wide to jump over, not the best hiking.

Before long however, I emerge onto a paved road that brings me to the entrance of the state park where finely groomed and maintained trail picks up again. The scenery is spectacular, the Presque Isle river flows below, cascading through narrow canyons and over falls. It reminds me very much of the North Shore where I was hiking only two weeks ago. The terrain is pretty rugged, but then they wouldn't call them mountains without a reason.

I pass by several cabins today and I was hoping they would be first-come first-serve like the Adirondack shelters, but I discover that they are all locked and a reservation is required ahead of time. I am disappointed that the cabins are not accessible but I end up finding a nice campsite right by a small waterfall. Several other campers are already there when I arrive and I pitch my tent near theirs. They seem to be having a good time as a group so I let them be as I enjoy my snickers bar and my magic beer before I head to bed.

Monday, June 10
Trail Day 073
Miles hiked: 25
Lake Gogebic Motel - Bergland, MI

I awoke this morning to the sound of other campers leaving with their dog. I decide that now is as good of time as any to get up and start the day. There is still one other tent pitched nearby, which means the group I saw last night were in fact two separate groups. *Darn, I wish I would have joined them.* It would have been nice to have some campfire talk. I head on over to the fire pit to cook breakfast and study my maps for the day's hike.

About halfway through my breakfast, a woman gets out of the other tent and walks over for a morning chat. Hence, I meet Sarah from Indiana who was out on a trip with her friend, Tom. I tell her my story and about the trail and she is very interested. She leaves for a little while but comes back with Tom after their gear is all packed away. We finish our breakfasts together with more questions as Tom is filled in on what I have been up to the past few months and where I am headed. It turns out they are heading back home today, so they offer me two bananas, some dried fruit, and a Clif bar for the road. *Thank you dear new friends for your trail magic.*

After saying goodbye to Sarah and Tom, it only takes me about fifteen minutes to finish my usual business, and then I'm off. I pass another cabin on the way out of the park. It is occupied, a fire is burning in the pit, and there are some matches and a hatchet nearby. But I don't see anyone. Soon I am at a trailhead where I stop for a quick rest before heading back in. After a short distance, I am out of the Porcupine Mountains Wilderness State Park and again in the Ottawa National Forest.

The bugs are terrible, just stopping for a few seconds results in being covered head to toe with the little buzzers. Unfortunately, the bugs are not my worst problem today. After only about three miles from the state park boundary I lose the trail. The faint tread and the blazes simply disappear into the brush. I take out my GPS and make for the next waypoint. This leads me to a shallow and narrow river. The water is just up to my knees so I decide to jump on in and follow it for awhile as it seems to be heading in roughly the direction I need to go.

After awhile the river turns the wrong direction so I climb out and try an overland route to find the trail again...no success. I manage to cross the trail twice and find no sign of it. The rest of the day turns into a very long, frustrating bushwhack through the forest totaling about thirteen miles. The thick brush and blowdowns make the going very slow and painful, literally. I stumble several times, and on the last one I manage to flat out trip myself and smash my head against the trunk of the tree in front of me. Amazingly, no blood, but my head pounds the rest of the day.

More difficulty emerges as I manage to get as lost I have ever been on a trail. Finally, deciding to quit fighting against nature, I decide to take the path of least resistance and just make my way toward the road in the most direct way possible. The most direct route ends up not being direct at all. The many beaver ponds combined with the rough terrain keep pushing me further south than I want to be, eventually onto some private land holdings.

I pass a private residence on a seemingly abandoned logging road (I guess it's really the guy's driveway). He doesn't appear to be home but I speed up to avoid spending more time trespassing than I need to. After a creek crossing the brush thins out a little bit and I am able to plunge back into the woods and toward the road.

After an entire day of bush whacking, I finally emerge onto MI-64...in the wrong place! I have managed to steer myself way south of where the trail crosses the road because of the terrain and specifically a very large beaver pond right at the end. I look at my map to try and figure out how far I am from the trailhead and I discover that there is actually a little town at the end of this road. The hike there would only be a few miles longer than hiking back north to the trailhead. So, not knowing what kind of condition the next segment of trail is in, and with barely any energy left at all, I decide to head south toward the little town of Bergland and get out of this mess for a night.

I arrive late. Luckily, there is a grocery store still open and a motel to spend the night. My head seems okay except for a large bump where it hit the tree, but it's still pounding when I check in. After a nice hot shower and a cold can of Arizona Tea, I go to bed totally exhausted.

Tuesday, June 11
Trail Day 074
Miles hiked: 34
Old Victoria Shelter

I slept in late this morning, which is very unfortunate because I have a very long roadwalk to get back to the trail; about nineteen miles. Along the way, a car pulls up alongside me and a young woman asks if I need a ride. I explain that I'm just out walking, so she just smiles and waves as she drives away.

Once I arrive, the trail is easy to follow with none of that frustration from yesterday. It is however very strenuous, the most strenuous section I think on this entire trail so far. I have to stop to catch my breath several times. You would think in hind sight I would have picked up on the fact that a section known as the Trap Hills would probably have some climbing involved.

After nearly ten hours of walking thirty-four miles, I finally reach my destination, the hiker shelter at Old Victoria. This is the site of the original town of Victoria, a few historical buildings remain and act as a museum and historic site now. It is closed this year because of construction on the Victoria reservoir nearby, lots of truck traffic going in and out. However, behind the old buildings back in the woods about 100 feet is a shelter built for hikers right on the trail. This is a blessing as the shelter has a screened front, the bugs were bad again today so I don't have to set up my tent in misery.

I eat a few more snacks on the floor of the shelter and suddenly become very uncomfortable from a painful cramp in my leg, likely from the strenuous hike of the day. I set up my sleeping pad and sleeping bag on one of the bunk beds and as soon as my head hits the pillow I'm asleep, totally exhausted.

Wednesday, June 12
Trail Day 075
Miles hiked: 14.5
O Kun de Kun Falls - Ottawa National Forest

I had a very comfortable sleep in the shelter and I'm up at 8:30 a.m. The hike today begins on another mile of trail until it crosses the road, then the trail splits in two different routes. The first route continues straight across the road back into the woods, however, there is a bridgeless river crossing that can be dangerous to cross in the spring time. The second route turns left onto roads for eleven miles and returns to the trail on the other side of the river. This is the high-water route and it passes through the little town of Rockland where I have a food drop waiting.

I make it into town by 10 a.m., retrieve my package, then head over to Henry's Inn for a hot meal. I'm a little early, they don't serve food until 11 a.m. Here I meet Sally, who is Henry's wife and today's cook. She is very interested in what I'm doing and asks many questions about my adventures. She takes my order: 1/2 pound ground round burger with fries, a plate of garlic bread, a soda and a milkshake, all homemade. I find out from her, that Nimblewill Nomad actually took a day off in the apartment upstairs when he came through four years ago. She requests that I also sign the guest book like all the other travelers who have stopped in at the Inn over the years.

Soon my order is ready, and I am in heaven as I bite into the best burger I have ever had in my life. *Thank you Sally, you are a great cook.* After my fantastic meal at Henry's, I take a quick trip over to the little grocery store for a Powerade and a box of fresh raspberries. On this trek, I have developed a craving for fresh fruit so I get some any chance I can.

I linger in town for awhile organizing my food drop and looking over my maps. The day has grown very hot, folks in town say it's pushing 90. I only have seven miles to go via roadwalk to get back to the trail but the heat proves to be a big obstacle. I am worn out pretty quickly. I take a break about halfway at a little rest stop. I fill up my water and take a short nap on a shaded picnic table before continuing on again. Within an hour I have reached the trail where I have a short hike to reach O Kun de Kun Falls, and the last reliable water source for some time. I decide to pitch here for the night and call it a short day as I am totally exhausted.

Thursday, June 13
Trail Day 076
Miles hiked: 22
About a mile east of forest road 1500 - Ottawa National Forest

I regret not pushing a little further yesterday, but at the time I felt a shorter day could be good for me. My muscles were tired and needed to relax a little. What I really need is a day off. I am far over-due for one. However, the next suitable location is Marquette, still at least five days away. I have no choice but to push on.

The trail leading out from O Kun de Kun Falls is harder to follow than the trail the day before, and it gets worse. Soon I come to a road crossing, which is also the high water route as the river on this next section is not bridged. It's a "cross at your own risk" kind of deal. I stay to the trail and after a mile I hit the river. The water is dark brown because of the mud-clay soil in this region so it's impossible to see the bottom. I try the crossing and after two steps I'm already past my knees. There's no way I can make this crossing safely, so back up the trail I go.

Once I hit the road again I follow it around to the other side of the river to pick up an ATV trail back to the NCT. The mosquitoes are out in huge numbers now, I can hear the constant buzzing all day long as they try to keep up and get a bite out of me. Once I find the trail again it's less than a mile before I lose it. It's the same crap as before: no markings, no tread, no maintenance to speak of. I get out my GPS again to try and find the trail and my path leads me down into a shallow bog, thick pine trees on all sides. I can't see any way through, and to my surprise I can't seem to find the way I came either.

Somehow, after wedging my way through the thick wall of conifers, I ended up in a small clearing completely surrounded with no visible way out. "This is impossible!" I am trapped in a small enclosed space, the mosquitoes descending on me relentlessly as I struggle to find a way through. I begin to lose hope. If the rest of Michigan is in this kind of condition there is no way I will have the time or the energy to finish. For the first time on this hike, the thought of failure seems like a good possibility; that I will be defeated by the trail and never make it to Vermont.

Tears start to well up as this bitter reality sinks in and takes hold. In hindsight, these feelings were probably amplified by the unpleasant experience of bushwhacking an entire day and being overheated and exhausted (which can be a powerful force on the trail). While aimlessly looking around for a way out, I manage to find a small gap in the foliage where I am able to wedge my pack through and then crawl after it to the much thinner brush on the other side.

Eventually, I manage to find the trail again, but this next segment is nothing but relentless blowdowns. It makes the going incredibly slow and dangerous, and I fall several times. I am generally a very positive person but this is a time where I truly have to complain. These Ottawa National Forest segments are brutal. There is little maintenance, insufficient blazing, incomplete or missing boardwalk and puncheon, no markings at road or trail crossings, and completely overgrown tread with impassable blowdowns. This is not what a National Scenic Trail is supposed to be, and no hiker should have to experience this for days at a time. I am very disappointed, annoyed and a little angry at the lack of care this trail has been given here. In hind sight, this section is probably just too remote for the volunteers to keep open every year; and likely not their fault. Perhaps a mobile trail crew could come in handy to help keep this segment open?

Toward the end of the day I come to a trail junction. There is a spur trail to a forest campground, which I decide to visit because I am low on water. It is a bit of a detour, a mile and a half one way to the campground. When I arrive the place is deserted. Of course it's pretty obvious why no one is here at this time of year, the mosquitoes here are the worst I have ever encountered. (Growing up in Minnesota as I did, that's saying a lot.) It's made worse by the fact that my bug net is compromised. That long bushwhack two days ago really did some damage to it. The thick foliage tore many holes in the netting and the frame is bent from my unfortunate head-butt with the tree. It's not bug proof anymore.

After quickly filling up my water at the hand pump I head for the outhouse for shelter. Once inside, I drop all my gear and spend the next few minutes squashing all the buzzers that made it inside with me. Then, I settle in a corner and finish my rations for the day in a place I had hoped would not be necessary to take shelter in ever again. I think back on the night I spent in a bathroom in North Dakota because the weather was bad, and now here I am again taking shelter in a bathroom, this time to escape the armies of mosquitoes. I can hear them outside the walls, so many the sound of my own chewing is drowned out. It takes all the courage I have to open the door and head out again.

I hike on for only a few more miles with great frustration as more blowdowns have covered the trail, some almost impassable. What little energy I have left is quickly depleted, so I stop for the night and find a place to camp. Then it happens, the last straw.

In the process of hanging my food, my bear bag hanger gets snagged on a branch and I try with all my strength to get it down. It won't budge. There are no rocks, no large sticks, nothing around to use as an anchor to get my rope up in a tree. I have no choice but to cut the rope, leaving the anchor trapped up in the tree, and once again bury my food in hopes a bear doesn't get it. I go to bed totally overwhelmed by defeat. "That's it, I'm done. I can't take any more of this shit!"

Snuggled in my sleeping bag I open a small Ziploc I have carried with me this entire trek. Inside is a hand-written letter from my friend, Ashley for: "when you need your friends" and the going gets tough. I told myself I would avoid opening it for as long as possible, but it appears tonight may be the time. I never thought it would happen this soon. In the midst of all the frustration, a tiny smile manages to find its way to the surface. Her letter reminds me that my friends back home are all rooting for me and that I have people thinking about me every day, supporting me. Afterwards, with the realization that I may actually be ready to quit and disappoint myself, I'm painfully reminded that to do so I would be letting them all down.

Friday, June 14
Trail Day 077
Miles hiked: 27.5
Big Lake Campground - Copper Country State Forest

I had a dream last night that helped lift some of the grief and frustration from my mind. I saw a green mound with stone wall ruins nestled on the edge of a gorgeous lake. The shadow of a great suspension bridge is seen in the background crossing over the lake. Three men are standing in front, the sunset streaming across the sky behind them. One of the men steps forward out of the shadows and I recognize him as Andrew Skurka. "We're waiting for you Strider," he says to me.

And in that moment, Nimblewill Nomad is revealed to be one of the other men. "You were meant to do this," Nomad says to me.

The third man is Ed Talone, the first NCT thru-hiker, whom I have not met before. "You're almost there."

The wall ruins I determine have to be Crown Point, the old British fort at the official terminus of the North Country Trail, and the bridge must be the Lake Champlain bridge crossing into Vermont. As much as I wish this scene was real, it becomes obvious that it's a dream because the bridge from Crown Point faces the east so seeing the sunset where it appeared is impossible in real life. I'm over a third of the way through this hike, so I guess Ed isn't that far off on his claim that I'm almost there.

I awake in my tent to the sound of hundreds of mosquitoes buzzing around outside trying to get in (a few stuck inside filled with my own blood). I suddenly feel a surge of new energy, a drive to get going, a desire to chase down the dream I just had and be the fourth person to hike the NCT. I eat breakfast in my tent and get going right away. The mosquitoes are horrible at first but thin out over the course of the day. To my relief the trail is easy to follow today and I experience a change in the environment around me. Soon the soil becomes very sandy and tree cover becomes thinner and thinner. I have now entered a region known as the Baraga Plains and it is somewhat desert-like.

The day has turned very hot and I need to stop in the shade several times to rest. My water is already getting low, but I know there is a campground at the end of the day where I can fill up again.

Eventually, the Ottawa National Forest comes to an end and I am hiking on State land for the rest of the day. Unfortunately, there was a wild fire here several years ago and all the trees have been burned and wind thrown; there is no shade to speak of for many miles. At about 4 p.m.—the hottest part of the day—I realize that I am getting very tired, thirsty, and a slight head ache is developing. Heat exhaustion is starting to affect my body and if I don't get to some shade soon I may be in trouble.

Luckily, there is a shelter nearby in a shaded cove along the Sturgeon River where I stop to take a rest. This shelter is also screened so I have relief from the bugs. The mosquitoes aren't bad here but in their absence in these arid parts the black flies have taken over. I take out my food, take off my clothes, have a quick snack, drink some water, and take a nap. I awake two hours later feeling refreshed, and push on the last six miles, past Tibbets Falls, to the campground where I stop for the day. After setting up camp, I down an entire liter of water and within minutes of crawling into my tent I am asleep, totally exhausted.

Saturday, June 15
Trail Day 078
Miles hiked: 34
Craig Lake State Park

I awoke early this morning, cameled up on water, and got going right away. The bugs are out, but it is a nice hike through the remainder of the Baraga Plains. Eventually, the trail enters the woods again and follows the Sturgeon River for many miles through fairly rough terrain. Many little waterfalls start popping up along the river. I pass a very large rock cairn right on the river. Whoever built this had lots of time on their hands.

Immediately after this the terrain gets very steep and the riverbed morphed into a deep canyon. Many stone fences have been built along overlooks near the largest of the cascading waterfalls. Canyon Falls is the name of this place and it is quite spectacular.

From here the trail ends at a rest stop off US-41, and it's a long road walk into Craig Lake State Park. As soon as I begin the rain comes...and it pours! I put on my rain gear and my head lamp to make me more visible to the oncoming traffic. In a matter of minutes I am totally soaked, but the rain eventually quits. After a few hours I arrive at a place called Nestoria, where I heard there is a great burger joint called Cozy Inn that I plan on eating at.

To my dismay, I arrive to find that it has closed down. This is very unfortunate because I have not eaten all day in anticipation for this meal. Right across the street is the access road to Craig Lake State Park and I begin the hike in. But I am so hungry and the bugs are so bad I dare not stop or they will overwhelm me. I decide to turn around and try to hitch a ride into Michigamme, about eight miles further east to get my hot meal before hiking into Craig Lake.

I stick out my thumb and the third car that passes me stops. Hence, I meet Josh, a young guy no more than a few years older than me who is on his way home from a backpacking trip himself. His loaded pack is in the back along with many homemade bottles of wine. He drops me off at Mt. Shasta Restaurant and gives me one of his bottles of wine for the road. *Thanks for the ride Josh, and for the wine.*

Once inside the restaurant I order a chocolate milk, and then a beer as I wait for my burger. Within a half hour I have consumed everything, including a fantastic piece of chocolate cake (it is my birthday tomorrow). I head across the street to a candy shop to get some extra trail rations and then head toward downtown to try and hitch a ride back to the trail where I left off. After passing the second house on my right I hear a voice: "Where are you hiking to?" I turn and see a man and a woman in their backyard enjoying a few beers.

"Vermont" I say. They seem very interested and invite me over to chat for awhile. Hence, I meet Charlie Brown (no really, that's his name) and his wife Melanie. I tell them my story, where I'm headed, where I've been so far. Charlie offers me a beer, which I gladly accept. During our conversation another man comes out of the house, and I meet Sean (I'm still not sure if he's a relative or a friend).

It turns out, that Charlie's family owned the Cozy Inn until last winter when it closed. What a strange turn of events this has turned out to be. After having another beer (or two) with these nice people, they offer to give me a ride back to the trail in their van. It's not a long drive and we are at the edge of the park in no time. They wish me well as I shoulder my pack and head on in. After walking the gravel roads to get to the trailhead the trail within the park is well marked and easy to follow.

In no time I arrive at the first campsite where I had planned to spend the night. However, with the recent turn of events today, I am in high spirits and feel energized so I push on the few extra miles to the next campsite. When I arrive the place is bustling with people. A church group from the Grand Rapids area has come here for a long weekend of canoeing and fishing in the park; this is their base camp. I let them know that I will be pitching nearby for the night and soon I am telling a few of the trip leaders my story.

I spend a good half hour talking to Jeff, an attorney that spends a lot of time doing business in Chicago. He's hiked a lot of the NCT in the Lower Peninsula and in Pennsylvania and is very interested in my hike. He gives me his business card after hearing that my plans to return home involve a train ride with several hours of waiting in Chicago for a connector train. He tells me to call when I arrive. *I will certainly do that Jeff, it was nice meeting you.*

After talking to the trip leaders it is pretty late so I hang my food and call it a day, glad to be in my tent away from the buzzers.

Sunday, June 16
Trail Day 079
Miles hiked: 24.5
Silver Lake Basin

I slept in a little this morning as yesterday turned out to be such a long day. I can hear the camp bustling outside so I get up and retrieve my food bag. The bugs are not too bad this morning so I decide to take the time to cook a hot meal. As I am doing so, one of the group leaders offers me some coffee, which I decline because I don't drink the stuff. They also offered some leftover food from breakfast, including some sausages and some dried apricots. These I do accept, thanks for the energy boost guys.

After cleaning up and packing away my gear, I emerge from the pines where I had pitched my tent and find that everyone has gone out on the lake for the day. I leave the camp quietly and without a trace.

The trail is easy to follow as it winds through the park around Craig Lake and eventually leaves the park and heads east. Soon afterwards I come to a trailhead with a sign posted "Wilderness." I have arrived at the McCormick Wilderness, an isolated unit of the Ottawa National Forest. I am very nervous, almost reluctant to enter this wilderness given my previous experience in this forest. However, I find out later that this segment is used fairly heavily and I have no problem finding my way through. I do get off track once but find my way back with no problem.

I emerge on the other side of the wilderness to more blazes that eventually lead me to a maze of logging roads. I lose the trail here once by missing a turn but manage to find my way back eventually by sheer dumb luck. Eventually, the trail enters the woods again and is well marked as it reaches the edge of the Silver Lake Basin where it suddenly stops. The trail has not been completed here yet and a short bushwhack is needed to get around to the other side. I was prepared for this one however, and I find my way around easily enough. The flagged route is visible at times but many of the flags have been destroyed. I make it over the ridge and have almost made it to the beginning of the roadwalk on the other side when it gets dark and I decide to call it a day.

Monday, June 17
Trail Day 080
Miles hiked: 28
Home of Lorana - Marquette, MI

It was very chilly when I woke up this morning, I needed to bundle up to start the day. The first thing I had to do was finish the short bushwhack to the beginning of the roadwalk along the Red Road. According to the GPS, I am only a few hundred yards away from it, but it ends up turning into a frustrating two miles. After much struggling and frustration over mountains of logging debris, I finally arrive at a road and discover that the way points on the GPS are too far south and that I have been walking parallel to the road by several hundred feet.

From here it is a long roadwalk using this logging road, which transitions into a wide sandy gravel road past some summer homes and many tree farms for the next 15 miles or so. After that, the certified trail picks up again at a narrow two-track. After a short distance, the trail leaves the track and goes back into the woods where I find a care package sitting on a stump. Two cans of Keewenaw beer are sitting in the shade with a note attached: *Courtesy of Dana.* The day has grown fairly hot, so I decide to take a break here and enjoy one of the beers. *Thank you Dana for your care package, it was very refreshing.*

This section of trail I am on now was newly constructed and newly mapped. This segment isn't even open to the public yet, but I have permission and the information necessary to get through. For a few miles the blazes stop and open up onto a narrow two-track where only flagging is used for awhile. I manage to stay on track just fine, and make it to older single track trail on the other side along the banks of the Little Garlic River. The trail follows the river for a good distance before terminating at a trailhead where a short roadwalk is needed to connect to the next segment.

The next segment is spectacular as it follows along the shoreline of Lake Superior. This is the first time the trail has come right down to the lakeshore since the Lakewalk in Duluth. There is a nice cool breeze coming off the lake and I am able to take off my bug net for the first time since crossing into Michigan. The trail here winds through tall pines in Presque Isle Park on finely groomed sandy tread for several miles. I linger here for awhile, taking some good video footage and many photos.

Near the south end of the park I decide to call it a day. I give Lorana a call, the president of the NCT Hikers Chapter. I had been in touch with her before entering Michigan and she offered to host me for a few nights once I reached Marquette. I let her know that I am still about eight miles north of town but that I am extremely tired and would like to take tomorrow and the next day off to rest. She agrees to come pick me up at Wetmore Landing, just a mile or so up the trail.

After hanging up the phone, I begin to get suspicious as I hike on for over a half hour without seeing any sign for a trailhead. Soon I arrive at a trail junction for Hogback Mountain, which is south of where I want to be! Somehow I went past the point where I was supposed to turn off to get to the trailhead. I turn around and head back as quickly as I can, find the turn, and head up to the trailhead where I find Lorana's car in the parking lot. Crap, she hiked up the trail to meet me, but I was in the wrong place.

I drop my pack and start running back down the trail, hoping she didn't get too far. As soon as I reach the lakeshore I see a woman walking toward me and recognize her as Lorana. I explain what happened and she tells me that someone had stolen the sign marking the turn to the trailhead. What a fiasco that caused!

Back at Lorana's car, she informs me that she has already taken care of dinner: two hot pasties in the back seat. Pasties are a special item unique to the UP and I have been anxious to try one. When we get to her home she shows me my room first—the same room that Nimblewill Nomad and Andrew Skurka stayed in, among others. There is a loft and a bunk bed in the room so I have my choice of comfort. I choose the bottom bunk for simplicity.

Afterwards I chow down on my pasties and get the scoop on the activities of the local chapter. They have been very busy with new trail construction and outreach events. Now, it's time for bed as I am almost completely out of energy. Hopefully two days of rest will be enough to re-energize me.

Wednesday, June 19
Trail Day XXX
Miles hiked: 00
Home of Lorana - Marquette, MI

Lorana has a spectacular house. It is built into the side of a hill so that all but the southeast wall is underground. Being the Tolkien fan that I am, I can't help but make a comparison to Bag End.

Yesterday, after waking up, Lorana treated me to a late breakfast at a spectacular Mexican restaurant (chicken quesadillas are hard to come by on the trail). Afterwards we stop at the grocery store so I can get myself some provisions for the next two days of rest. Soon afterward, I have a TV interview with *ABC10* that goes fairly well.

I'm informed that another hiker "Wolverine" is only ten miles out of town and will also be spending the night at Lorana's house. He is hiking Governor Snider's proposed trail from Belle Isle to Ironwood, which follows the NCT through the UP. I've known about Wolverine for awhile and it's good to know that we will be crossing paths in Marquette. It'll be nice to talk to another long distance hiker and find out what is in store for me as I head east.

Soon I decide to take a nap to regain my energy, and when I wake up I can hear people entering the house. I go into the living room and meet Chris Hillier, aka "Wolverine". He has thru-hiked the AT and the PCT and is considering attempting the CDT next year. As we are greeting each other, the reporter from *ABC10* comes in with his equipment. It was time for Chris' interview. Afterwards, we spend some time talking trail and then Lorana took us out to dinner to meet some of her chapter members.

We arrive at an Italian restaurant called Casa Calabria where we meet John and Marge, Dana, his two sons, and Jan. I thank Dana for leaving me the beer along the side of the trail and answer many questions about my trip so far. Chris tells many stories about his AT and PCT hikes, a very enjoyable evening.

Back at Lorana's, Chris and I both have a tall PBR and discuss troubling spots on the trail that we encountered. For me, the bushwhacks back in the Porkies, and for Chris, some flooding caused by pesky beavers. Then, it's off to bed for a second day of rest.

This morning I was up fairly early. Right away we have an 8 a.m. breakfast at a place called Jeffrey's where we meet Jeff and Sarah, Roger, Cliff, and Eric. It turns out that Jeff and Sarah had come looking for me at Craig Lake a few days ago and I had only missed them by about two hours. We have a nice meal talking about the trail, other trips, and many other things.

Next on the agenda, we head to Walmart to get a few supplies before heading back to Lorana's house for another interview. Soon Jennifer from *Channel 6* arrives and interviews me first, then Chris, then does a segment on both of us together talking about the trail and discussing our gear. Unfortunately, I will not be able to see the result live tonight because we have yet another dinner reservation; but I'm sure it will be posted online.

Before our dinner however, a writer for the *Mining Journal* comes to conduct an interview via tape recorder. It lasts about a half hour and soon afterwards we head to dinner at The Vierling. There we meet Jim and Norma, Jane and Rich. The usual routine commences as we are asked many questions about our travels. Everyone is very enthused and are thrilled that we are out here using the trail.

After saying goodbye to everyone, we take a quick drive to see the ore dock in town and then head back to the house for a last comfortable night of rest. I'll be hitting the trail again in the morning. *Thank you Lorana for being such a wonderful host and trail angel.*

Thursday, June 20
Trail Day 081
Miles hiked: 24
Lakenenland Sculpture Park Shelter

Chris and I awoke at almost the exact same time this morning. It's time for both of us to hit the trail again. By 8 a.m. we are already on our way to drop Chris off at the Michigan Welcome Center, a few miles south of town where he had been picked up by Lorana on Tuesday. We take a photo at the NCT sign with Lorana and then Wolverine is off down the trail. Next, Lorana drives me to Wetmore Landing a few miles north of town where she picked me up Monday evening. I thank her for being such a wonderful trail angel. Few people would go out of their way to make hikers feel at home the way she has. I say goodbye, and after a hug, I too am off down the trail.

It's only about eight miles to downtown Marquette from Wetmore Landing so I'm there in a short time. Once close to the lake again the trail connects to a paved bike path that travels many miles right along the lakefront all the way to the welcome center where Wolverine started today. I have to send some things home, including my camera memory card, which I haven't yet gone through and divided up into albums.

I decide to find a place to sit down and go through my photos. I check my phone and there is a text from Chris who is only a few blocks from me at The Ore Dock Brewery. I head over there and we have another chat, mainly about trail stuff. Before I know it, over an hour has gone by and I need to get hiking again. I say goodbye to Chris and wish him luck on finishing the rest of his hike.

I make my way to the post office and send a package home with my photo card and all the maps I no longer need. Then, I'm back on the bike path leading out of town. Once at the Welcome Center the paved bike path ends and a crushed limestone surface bike/snowmobile trail begins, which still makes for easy hiking. The NCT follows this for a good ten miles or more before heading back into woods and onto a narrow sandy two track.

Soon I come to a trail junction with a fire pit and a hiker shelter. Pointing off to the north is a sign that says "Lakenenland". I have reached my destination for the day. Lakenenland is a sculpture park created by a man named Tom to share his vision with the world. All the sculptures were made by his own hand and he charges no fee for visiting his park. He allowed the NCT access across his property and he built the hiker shelter (complete with a patio door!) just last year, all out of the goodness of his heart.

I follow the sign to a spur trail that brings me to the entrance of Lakenenland. I take the tour and snap photos of the most interesting masterpieces Tom has created. At the end of the trail is a parking lot and there is a guy forming up a slab to be filled with concrete very soon. Hence, I meet Tom himself. I tell him my story about my hike and thank him for building the shelter along the trail. I find out that he is building a pavilion, hopefully to be finished this year. *Thank you for your hard work Tom, and for supporting the NCT. It was a pleasure meeting you.*

Afterward, I head back to the shelter and make a spot for myself on the floor. It's such a relief to have a glass door between me and the buzzers. *Thanks again, Tom.* I read a few pages of Tolkien as I hear a few guys drive by on dirt-bikes shortly before nightfall and then I drift off to sleep.

Friday, June 21
Trail Day 082
Miles hiked: 29.5
South of Au Train Lake - Hiawatha National Forest

I slept in really late this morning, courtesy of a restless sleep. It is raining outside, and as I am making breakfast several lightning strikes make contact very close by, extremely loud thunder following after. I am a little nervous about hiking in these conditions but I go out anyway, there's nothing I can do about it in the end except delay my departure. After a few miles, the thunder and lightning pass, but it rains for awhile longer before quitting.

The trail today is easy to follow and brings me near Laughing Whitefish Falls and into the Hiawatha National Forest where it winds its way first southeast, then northeast again toward Munising. I pass a few campsites not marked on the map, and I call it a day shortly after a road crossing south of Au Train Lake.

Saturday, June 22
Trail Day 083
Miles hiked: 21
Cliffs Campsites - Pictured Rocks National Lakeshore

It rained most of last night and it is already humid as I begin my hike this morning. The trail is pretty easy to follow until I come to a trailhead at the Valley Spur ski lodge. Here I am faced with three different trails going in three different directions...all marked with blue diamonds. Oh, what a mess this is!

With no indication of which way to go, I try the most travelled route which turns out to be a loop trail. I decide to backtrack to a turn in the trail and then bushwhack to the nearest road, MI-94, which the trail does eventually come out to and then terminates.

From here it is a roadwalk into the town of Munising. En route, I pass by Wagner and Alger Falls, right off the road.

Munising is a great little trail town with lots of restaurants, cheap motels, and a nice Marina. I decide to stop by subway for lunch and treat myself to dessert at the DQ. Afterward, I head down to the Marina to restock my fuel and water. I also make a phone call to Tim, president of the Superior Shoreline Chapter. He sent me a message with a request to meet up with me and within a few minutes he arrives with his wife Ellen.

I tell them about my trip so far and then they spend the next several minutes warning me about what is to come on the far side of Pictured Rocks. There was a large fire last year and apparently there are a lot of trees still standing that could fall at any moment. Tim warns me to watch out for the ones with the roots burned away, which could fall at any moment since they are no longer anchored to the ground. *Thanks for the warning, Tim.*

I say goodbye to Tim and Ellen, and then head to the ranger station to get a permit to enter Pictured Rocks. Everyone at the station already knew I would be passing through today and they are all excited when I walked in. I briefly tell the kind ladies at the desk about my trip so far and they fill out the permit for a hiker trash rate.

There is a visitor center a few miles east of town at Munising Falls and this is where the certified trail picks up again and enters Pictured Rocks. There are lots of people at the trailhead but once I get past the falls I don't see a single person. Soon a fog roles in and I am robbed of some good views over the lake. I still get some fine scenery though as there are a few stream crossings and I see beech trees for the first time on this trek. Their smooth silver bark reminds me of the description of the Mallorn trees of Lothlorien in Tolkien's stories.

After seven miles of hiking through Pictured Rocks I call it a day at the Cliffs Campsite. I have the place to myself for a nice quiet night of sleep.

Sunday, June 23
Trail Day 084
Miles hiked: 21.5
Sevenmile Creek Campsites - Pictured Rocks National Lakeshore

The rain came again last night and it gets more intense as I hike this morning. It's only about a mile to the first major landmark, Miner's Castle, and when I arrive it is bustling with people. This quickly changes as the rain intensifies into a thunderstorm. I hang out briefly at the visitor center waiting for the worst of the rain and thunder to pass, then keep hiking through it. Luckily, after about an hour the rain ceases and the sky clears. I can finally see the great scenery this park is known for. Unfortunately, it also turns very hot and I need to take several breaks during the day.

During one of my breaks I meet a group of four hikers at Grand Portal Point while also on a break. They are interested in my travels when they see my bigger than average pack and they seem impressed when I tell them my story. One of them, Lisa, takes my picture standing on a rock outcrop. I shoulder my pack again and they wish me well as I continue on towards Chapel Rock.

I have been looking forward to returning to Chapel Rock ever since I camped there last year, when I came up to do the Mackinac Bridge Walk on Labor Day. Chapel Rock is an amazing formation, when looking at a picture of it you find it hard to believe that such a place could exist. Yet here it is, a "chapel" carved out of the rocks by the forces of nature. The place is crowded with people and I miss an opportunity to take any decent photos. Luckily, I had taken plenty when I was here last so I decide not to worry about it and push on. My mind drifts back to that weekend last summer when myself, my brother, and my mother camped at this spot. On our second night of the trip, we were so completely blown away by the sight of it we didn't want to leave. Such a fun weekend with the family.

The last landmark I pass today is Spray Falls. It's not a large waterfall by any means, but from a distance it is still quite a sight, a narrow spout of water shooting out of the face of the rock, and plummeting down into Lake Superior below. Before long I arrive at the seven-mile creek campsite, my destination for tonight. There are three other campers enjoying a fire to smoke out the mosquitoes and the black flies. After quickly setting up my tent, I decide to head down to the beach instead. There are a few flies but the mosquitoes are nowhere to be found. I enjoy reading an entire chapter of Tolkien while watching the sunset over the Great Lake.

Monday, June 24
Trail Day 085
Miles hiked: 19
Backyard of Ed and Karla - Grand Marais, MI

The buzzers are out again when I wake up, and I need to start the day in my "bug suit". After a few miles however, an opportunity arrives to visit the beach again where I stop to have my breakfast. There are no mosquitoes down here and it is really hot today, so I decide to walk the beach to avoid the bugs for as long as possible. I'm in an area known as Twelve Mile Beach, which is exactly what it sounds like, a twelve-mile long sandy beach. Along the sandy shore I pass by many remains of shipwrecks that became beached long ago, only the ribs remain.

After walking for several hours in the blazing sun, I decide to stop and take a swim in the lake's icy cold waters to cool off. I've

151

had a tradition of swimming in Lake Superior at least once every year, despite the water never being warmer than 50 degrees. After about five minutes in I feel satisfied and refreshed.

Continuing on, I reach Au Sable Lighthouse, the point where the beach ends and the shoreline again changes into steep sided cliffs. There is a staircase that leads up to the light station where I take a video. In the distance, the Grand Sable Dunes can be seen stretching to the east almost as far as one can see. The trail heads back to the woods away from the shoreline and towards the buzzers.

With it being so hot, I would rather not put my long sleeves back on. Instead I decide to grab a snack for the road and not stop hiking until I reach the Grand Sable Visitor Center, more than eight miles away. Before long though, I arrive and head inside to get some respite from the heat and eat my lunch. Here I meet Judy, the ranger working at the desk today. She knows a lot about the NCT and is thrilled that I am hiking the whole thing. After dealing with some visitors she comes over and hands me an apple and a piece of chocolate. *Thank you Judy for your trail magic and your enthusiasm. It was a pleasure meeting you.*

A short hike from the visitor center is Grand Sable Falls, and indeed grand it is. It is a fitting send off from this National Park. Shortly after this, the trail heads back down to the sandy lakeshore where I spend a few minutes talking with a guy on my way to into the little town of Grand Marais. I stop in at Grand Marais outfitters first thing and meet Dennis and Kim, the owners. They have been expecting me and are happy to see that I made it here in good time. They also happen to be two of the nicest people I have ever met.

I got into town less than an hour after the post office closed and I have a package waiting. Before I can say anything Kim calls in to the post office to see if they would let me get my package while

Dennis takes some time to do a few small repairs on my pack. One of the straps has been frayed for most of my hike and I didn't think it would hold up for the rest of my journey. Dennis stitched the strap back together by hand to reinforce it. While this is all going on, a man and his wife walk in. Hence, I meet Ed and Karla of the Superior Shoreline Chapter.

Ed has a place right on the harbor and he offers me a place to pitch my tent for the night. He did the same thing for Wolverine a few weeks back and I gladly accept his offer. Just then Kim walks in with my package from the post office, and Dennis hands me a T-shirt with a blue blaze on the front and the NCT logo on the back. Wow, this is unbelievable trail magic happening all at once! *Thank you Dennis and Kim for your generosity, and thank you Ed for letting me camp in your yard tonight.*

After meeting everybody at Grand Marais Outfitters I head across the street to a picnic pavilion where I work on organizing my food box. I have a brief conversation with a guy from downstate who was up here on an ATV camping trip with his son. I never would have thought to attempt camping in that manner, but it sounds kind of fun after hearing him talk about it for a few minutes.

I head back across the street to the pub where I heard they had excellent homemade pizza. Boy did I hear right! It was possibly the best pizza I've ever had. Dennis sat with me, and soon I met Erin, the bar owner. (There are some kind folks here in Grand Marais.) Soon Dennis informs me that he has to take off and I find out from the server that he has covered my meal. *Thank you so much Dennis, for everything you have done here today.*

On a full stomach, I walk the half mile to Ed's house and Karla answers the door. She directs me to the backyard where I pitch near the harbor. While composing today's journal, I realize that today is the first day on this entire trek that I haven't seen a deer.

153

Tuesday, June 25
Trail Day 086
Miles hiked: 24.5
Muskallonge Lake State Park

I woke up to the sound of Mosquitoes buzzing around my tent (gotta put the bug clothes on before going into town). It only takes me a few minutes to break camp and hit the road to head back to downtown Grand Marais. I need to mail a few things home, including my first pair of shoes, which are very tattered, and my thick fleece pullover. I need to stay until the post office opens. I'm there a few hours early so I eat my breakfast at the picnic pavilion on the harbor. No bugs around here.

As I am getting some of my things in order and taking a look at my maps, a guy walks by with a cup of coffee and stops once he sees my gear. Hence, I meet Mark, a visitor to Grand Marais for a few days. He asks about my gear, the food box operation, and where I'm headed. I tell him the story of my hike so far and he is very impressed. He wishes me luck as he returns to his motel across the street.

About ten minutes later as I am still sorting through some things to send home, Mark appears again. First, he shows me a brochure of the trail that he picked up yesterday. He wants me to confirm that it is in fact that same trail I am hiking. I tell him yes, and point out a few highlights I've encountered so far on the brochure's overview map. He then hands me a brand new bandana to add to my gear list. I accept it gladly as mine is getting pretty worn out. He wishes me luck again and walks away.

After a few minutes, Mark returns a third time with a laptop in his hand. He first apologizes for interrupting me again (it's okay Mark, I'm just killing time) and then he says that he found me on the internet. He shows me the screen and displayed on it is the home page of my website. I then explain why I created the sight, to allow others to follow along and hopefully increase awareness and interest in the trail. He is thoroughly interested and absolutely impressed with my journey. Mark says he will be following my progress from now on, and that he will try and get out and hike some segments of the NCT. He shakes my hand and disappears for the third and final time.

Almost immediately afterward, a car drives down the street and stops right next to the pavilion. The window rolls down and I recognize Judy, the park ranger from the Grand Sable Visitor Center. She asks if I need anything and tells me to take care as she continued on to work.

The town has finally started to wake up and businesses are opening for the day, so I head over to Grand Marais Outfitters to thank Dennis for paying for my meal last night. Afterward, he lets me fill up my water from his sink and then it is time to hit the post office and then the trail. The trail leading out of Grand Marais is well marked, and after awhile heads back to the lakeshore.

My feet hurt today as I am now wearing my second pair of shoes. Additionally, the day has turned quite hot so I need to take more frequent breaks to ease the pain and discomfort. Toward the end of the day I reach Muskallonge Lake State Park. The trail here has been rerouted as the old trail (and part of the visitor center) has eroded away and fallen into the lake. I have the energy and the time to push on, but my feet are on fire. I am worried about pushing too hard the first few days with new shoes. A picnic table and shower would be nice, so I decide to end the day a little early and camp in the park.

As I arrive at my site and set up camp, several people ask where I'm headed and where I've been; including two ladies on bicycles and the guy camping next to me with his family. After brief introductions and storytelling, I get in a nice hot shower, cook dinner at the picnic table, read a chapter of Tolkien at a tiny campfire, and call it a night.

Wednesday, June 26
Trail Day 087
Miles hiked: 28
About a mile west of forest road 500 - Lake Superior State Forest

I lingered too long in camp this morning. I decided to cook a meal for breakfast to take advantage of the picnic table, and so didn't get hiking until well into the morning. The guy next door wishes me luck as I finally depart.

By 10 a.m. it has already turned hot and the sun is out in full force. I noticed last night at my camp that I miscalculated the last food drop and I am actually a day short on provisions and won't have enough to make it to St. Ignace. Luckily, there is a little convenience store a few miles from the park in the Deer Park Township. I head there first thing to get the provisions I need, and to take a break from the blistering hot sun. I enjoy an ice cream bar and stock up on a few sports drinks.

Soon I am back on the trail and the going is incredibly slow. Most of the tread is nothing but sand. The trail zigzags back and forth from the lakeshore back to Coast Guard Road, nothing but a sandy two track several times before finally staying fairly close to the lakeshore. It is at this point that the area Tim warned me about back in Munising comes into view. As far as the eye can see the ground, the trees, everything is scorched black. Luckily, the Superior Shoreline Chapter has been out and attached some plastic blazes to some of the trees so I can find a route through.

Of course there is also no shade, so this stretch of trail is unbearably hot. I heed Tim's advice and watch the roots of the trees as I approach, but there is no wind today and none of the trees seem to be in immediate danger of falling over.

After several hours I finally get a chance to stop as I approach a campground at the mouth of the Two Hearted River. A great suspension bridge straddles the river from the beach of Lake Superior and brings the hiker into the campground on the other side. At the end of the bridge a man is standing admiring the view of the river and he sees me coming across. He asks about the condition of the trail between here and Muskallonge Lake, and I inform him about the vast burn area. He then proceeds to ask me how far I have hiked. When I tell him my story he invites me to his campsite for a beer, which I gladly accept. Hence, I meet Art who was out on a week-long camping trip with his son (who was taking a nap in the van).

We have a nice chat about previous trips we've both had and a little of what I'll encounter as I head south. Art has hiked a portion of the trail in the Manistee National Forest and is here to hike to Muskallonge Lake and back with his son. After I finish my beer, I thank Art for his kindness and continued on.

I'm finally clear of the burned area and I'm in the woods for the next several miles, but I take another break at the next campground on Culhane Lake to cool off and camel up. After this the trail heads south away from the Lake and the mosquitoes are out in full force. Within minutes they become so thick that I am swimming through a cloud of them. My bug clothes and head net are back on, but because of all the bush whacking I had to do earlier in the UP, my net has holes in it so it no longer prevents the buzzers from getting in.

My hands are the only thing exposed and there are so many mosquitoes that I shove my hands in my pockets to spare them some of the torment. This doesn't last long, as I need my hands to swat the ones that have penetrated the bug net. Of all my years hiking in the north woods of Minnesota, these are by far the worst mosquitoes I have ever encountered. It takes every ounce of what little energy I have left to keep from screaming in agony.

I am exhausted and need to stop for the day, but the bugs are such a torment I push on until dark without rest, hoping to find a place where they aren't so bad...but there just isn't one. Finally, I have no choice but to stop and I pitch my tent as quickly as possible and jump inside. I haven't eaten or drank anything in the past several hours and I am starving, so I eat my remaining rations for the day in my tent to avoid the horrendous mosquitoes.

My hands are completely covered in blood and it looks as if I have just given surgery. My clothes, my tent, everything is stained. I have been bitten so many times that my body could no longer handle it and an allergic reaction occurred as a result of mosquito overdose. My hands are covered in swollen bites, which has never happened to me before. I got a pretty good sunburn today as well from the lack of forest cover at the beginning of the day, and I can feel the effects of early dehydration taking hold. I am definitely overheated and over-exerted.

After stashing (throwing) my food pack away, I lie down in my tent and get what rest I can; the heat making it difficult to sleep. Another hard day on the trail—one of those days that makes you question why you're out here.

Thursday, June 27
Trail Day 088
Miles hiked: 26
Rivermouth Campground - Tahquamenon Falls State Park

The sound of thousands of buzzers outside my tent is the first thing I hear as I wake up this morning. There's no describing how badly I do not want to get up out of this tent. I have to get going sometime though, and I'm only a few miles from the boundary of Tahquamenon Falls State Park, where hopefully the mosquitoes will be thinner. I pack up as quickly as possible and head out.

After a few miles, I come to a trail junction with a sign of a park map. I've made it to the park but still have many miles to go to reach the visitor center where I can get some respite from these mosquitoes. After a few hours I come to a road crossing, MI-123, so I know I am close. Sure enough, about a mile further south, the trail emerges from the woods and comes out to a wide paved trail and the stairway to the Upper Falls of the Tahquamenon.

I skip the falls for now as the visitor center is only a quarter mile further and I need something to eat. When I arrive I am amazed at what I see. This place is more than just a visitor center, it is also a gift shop, concession stand, and a brewery which is actually a full-blown restaurant! I waste no time going inside and trying one of their four specialty brews before they start serving food. As soon as the kitchen opens, the server takes my order. It isn't too long before she comes out with my appetizer, a whole plate full of nachos. No sooner have I downed these than my burger arrives and I enjoy it. I get several refills of soda to quench my thirst and after I've finished gorging myself, I head outside to the large patio to see what else is going on...and to let my stomach settle a bit.

Lots of people outside see my pack and want to know my story, including a guy named Tyler. He thru-hiked the American Discovery Trail (ADT) in 2011 with a friend. I will actually be on that same trail for some distance in Ohio where the ADT coincides with the Buckeye Trail. He is particularly fascinated with my trip and wishes me luck.

Here I also meet Shannon, one of the servers at the brewery. She remembers Wolverine stopping in here about two weeks prior and I explain to her how we crossed paths in Marquette and ended up at the same place for two nights. I'm having a hard time tearing myself away from this fine establishment, but alas it is time to hit the trail again. I drop my pack at the trail junction and head to the Upper Falls with only my camera. The view is spectacular and several people have flocked here to see it. After taking some good photos and a video I head back to the trail and hike the seven miles to the Lower Falls, encountering relatively few people along the way.

The day has grown really hot and humid and it starts to drizzle several times. At the Lower Falls I encounter many of the same people I saw at the Upper Falls. Many of them commented that they wished they could have hiked the whole way between the two. I told them all it was only seven miles, but I guess to them that was a long way to go in the heat. At the lower falls there is a gift shop and a concession stand where I decide to have a late lunch; a hot dog and an ice cream cone. By the time I'm ready to get going again the rain has intensified and the thunder rolls in. I have no choice but to go out in it. One fairly close strike directly overhead freaks me out a bit, but there are no more close calls.

After about an hour the storm ends and the sun is out again, making it hot and humid. Also the bugs emerge once again and I scramble to get my bug net on as quickly as possible. After many miles of rolling terrain the trail emerges onto a gravel road and heads east towards the lake passing many summer cabins. A van pulls up next to me and a woman opens the window.

"Are you hiking the North Country Trail?"

I'm totally surprised that she even knew this roadwalk was part of the trail. She then asks if I need anything as she is heading up the road to Paradise. I'm all good on supplies so she wishes me luck and continues driving. The road I am now hiking on ends at Lake Superior at a day-use picnic area, and when I arrive the van that pulled over earlier is parked there. Hence, I meet Doug and Sarah, and their kids who have just finished swimming.

We talk for awhile about the trail and about my hike so far—especially about the horrendous mosquitoes in this area. They say they may have something to help with the mosquitoes and they hand me a tin container with contents that look like a bar of soap. It's a type of bug repellent that you rub on your skin. "Whatever it is, they hate it," says Doug. I thank them for their donation, and as they prepare to leave they leave me their phone numbers in case I run into trouble. *Thank you dear friends for your generosity, it was a pleasure meeting you.*

Afterward, a young couple who overheard our conversation, asked me a few questions about my adventure. They seem impressed and tell me that they are staying at the River Mouth Campground just down the street. Unfortunately, they came to this picnic area to escape the bugs at the campground. It's getting dark though and there is nowhere else to camp for at least ten miles, so reluctantly I head over and get a spot at the campground right next to the shower house, which I happily take advantage of before hitting the hay.

Friday, June 28
Trail Day 089
Miles hiked: 20, +12
IGA Apartment - Trout Lake, MI

I awaken early and leave the campground by first light. I hike the few remaining miles of roadwalk to connect to the next certified segment of trail, which heads back into the woods and to the Lake Superior shoreline for a short distance before heading south. This is the last time I will see The Lake on this hike. I stop here at an overlook for a brief moment before heading south.

I don't make it very far however, as the mosquitoes are horrendous once again. I've been in these horrid conditions for several days now and they only seem to be getting worse. I decide to bring my hike to the roads for the rest of the day to get some relief from the buzzers. It helps a little but it is also very hot today, the hottest day so far this trek, and the road provides little shade.

I drink plenty of water but I feel dehydrated and extremely tired. I can tell that I am not feeling well and that heat exhaustion is definitely taking its toll. I have to get inside out of the heat and the bugs for awhile or I could end up getting sick, or worse. Reluctantly, I stick out my thumb, intending to hitch a ride into the next town. To my dismay nobody stops, after five hours of hiking along the road with my thumb out, more than 200 cars drive by and not a single one stops. At one point I pass a nicely-shaded driveway where I decide to stop and take a nap, physically unable to hike any further.

I awaken two hours later and continue my attempt to hitch a ride...no luck! I have to admit, when I went to sleep the night before last—in my tent surrounded by thousands of mosquitoes, dehydrated and exhausted after an intense reaction to bites that felt like a small seizure—I considered packing it in for the second time. I was shaking in my tent as my body tried to fight off the insect juice circulating through my body and I lost hope. I knew Tahquamenon Falls was about seven miles away, and told myself I would re-evaluate my situation once I arrived. I had not known about the brewery in the parking lot however, honestly it may have saved the hike. I was reminded of that same feeling today as I began this long roadwalk in the heat, but the two-hour nap gave me the little burst of energy to at least see today through.

Eventually, I reach the intersection of MI-123 and MI-28 where I was hoping to find a gas station or something. I arrive to find only a small engine repair shop. They have a picnic table out front where I decide to stop and rest. An attractive blonde woman walks by and asks how I'm doing. I tell her about my day so far, and by the look on her face I can tell she seems concerned. She offers me a nice cold bottle of water, which I gladly accept, as well as a nice cozy armchair to sit on inside the shop to rest for a bit. After a few minutes she comes out and says she will give me a ride to Trout Lake about twelve miles down the road.

Hence, I officially meet Becca, co-owner of the machine shop. She leaves her daughter in charge of the shop as we climb into her van and she shuttles me into town. We have a nice chat along the way (among the topics is how disappointing it is that nobody stops anymore to pick up people in need). She tells me that when I stumbled up to her door she felt a sense of deja-vu, like I was familiar somehow, and she felt the urge to help. Perhaps our paths were destined to cross, and perhaps her feeling was telling her that she was destined to help me.

Soon we arrive in Trout Lake, not much here, a motel and restaurant, an IGA, and an ice cream shop. We head for the IGA, Becca knows a woman there who rents an apartment above the store. The woman is not here today but Becca shows me the right person to talk to in order for me to get a room for the night. I thank her for everything she has done today and after a firm hand shake she is gone.

I talk to the woman behind the counter about spending the night and she talks me through the process. She hands me two keys, each opens a different bedroom, and I get to pick which one I want. I head upstairs to see what the place is like. I am pleasantly surprised to find a three-bedroom apartment complete with a kitchen and a living room with satellite TV. Only one of the rooms has a window in it, so naturally I choose that one.

After settling in I bring the unwanted key downstairs and pick out something for dinner before heading back upstairs. There are currently no other tenants so I have the place to myself. After a shower and gorging myself with as fine of a meal as can be had from a convenience store, I jump in my bed and instantly crash from heat exhaustion and fatigue.

Saturday, June 29
Trail Day 090
Miles hiked: 28
Carp River Campsite - Hiawatha National Forest

I slept for more than twelve hours; waking up at mid-morning. The first thing I do is make breakfast before settling on the couch to watch some TV and rehydrate with lots of water. I'm in no rush to get going this morning as I want to make sure I am fully energized before heading back out into the heat.

I get going at 11 a.m., and head east along County Road H40 to get back to the trail. The most direct and time-efficient route would be to head south on MI-123 and pick up the trail there. Instead, I choose the longest way back to the trail without backtracking to add mileage to make up for the section I skipped yesterday.

After a few hours, I finally reach the trail and head on in. I still need my bug clothes but the buzzers are not as bad as the past few days; maybe because the new bug repellent from Doug and Sarah is working. After a short distance, blazes become scarce and I lose the trail. I spend the next few minutes walking around in a circle and backtracking to find the trail. I manage to find it again without too much trouble, and before long the trail opens up a little more and becomes easier to follow.

The rest of the day is a fairly pleasant hike through the Hiawatha National Forest as the trail heads through some damp areas and skirts along the edge of the Mackinaw Wilderness. I encounter lots of puncheon through this section as well as the first raspberries of the season growing right alongside. I end the day after crossing the Carp River and discovering the campsite that has been built there. After setting up my tent I roll inside and fall fast asleep.

Sunday, June 30
Trail Day 091
Miles hiked: 25
A few miles northwest of St. Ignace, MI-Hiawatha National Forest

I slept well last night, considering the turmoil my body has been through since leaving Grand Marais. I eat a small breakfast before hitting the trail early. Today's hike has lots of ups and downs through some more sandy dry areas.

At the campground at Brevoort Lake I stop at the picnic area to cook lunch and refill my water from the lake. I pick a table right on the lake shore to eat and take a nice long rest as I read a few pages of Tolkien. The lake is bustling with people, lots of tubing, water skiing, and sailing going on. I consider going for a swim myself, but eventually decide not to just as a large family comes barreling down from the parking lot and takes up almost the entire beach area where I am sitting, being loud and obnoxious. I decide to move on and make my way back to the trail.

More ups and downs as I head east now toward St. Ignace, some of the hills being very steep. At the top of one particular uphill climb I can see the top of the mighty Mackinac Bridge and a glimpse of Lake Michigan way in the distance. Tomorrow I will be in St. Ignace. There I can pick up my next food drop and get another respite from the mosquitoes. Feeling a sudden spurt of energy I hike the rest of the day without any difficulty and pass by two campers a short distance in from the upcoming trailhead. They ask how far I've come and cheer me on as I breeze by after I tell them I'm attempting the whole thing.

I arrive at the trailhead and the end of the certified trail in the Hiawatha National Forest, where it intersects with an ATV trail. I still have about an hour of daylight left and most of the ATV trail is still within the Hiawatha National Forest, so I continue on until nightfall. About a mile from the I-75 freeway overpass I find a nice flat spot between the trail and the road just large enough for a tent to squeeze into. Looks like this is home tonight.

Monday, July 1
Trail Day 092
Miles hiked: 06, +5
Vindel Motel - Mackinaw City, MI

Last night was a restless night of sleep. I don't know if it was from excitement of finally reaching the Mackinac Bridge and crossing into the Lower Peninsula, or what. But as a result, I am up at 5 a.m. and reach St. Ignace before 6. The place is like a ghost town; a stark contrast from when I was here last Labor Day. Only one place is open for business, a little diner, so I head on in for breakfast. A few of the locals are in for coffee but otherwise it's a nice quiet morning in the diner on Lake Huron.

After enjoying my meal I make a call back home to plan the next couple food drops. Then I just sit and wait for the post office to open so I can get my next package. After taking care of business I hike the remaining two miles of trail in the UP, passing through Straits State Park where I camped last year while preparing for the Bridge Walk. As I reach the bridge, I head to the toll booth for the Bridge Authority, where I pay three dollars for a ride across the bridge. I wait about five minutes until an Authority vehicle pulls up and I hop in.

The trip over the bridge in a vehicle is a vastly different feel than walking it on foot. My mind drifts back to last year when I came up here to do the Bridge Walk. A new policy went into effect in January of 2012 stating, that thru-hikers were required to hike the Mackinac Bridge on Labor Day for it to qualify as a true thru-hike. At the time I was lucky that I lived close enough to make a weekend trip out of it. However, most people do not have that luxury, and for most potential thru-hikers to complete it they would need to spend lots of money and time to get out here.

The task is made even more complicated by the fact that the bridge is only open to pedestrians one day a year, that being Labor Day. I didn't have any plans last year so I decided to come out and do it, and Roxanne and my brother Matt decided to join me. Luckily, as of September 2015 the official policy has been changed and thru-hikers are no longer required to hike the Mackinac Bridge.

I had actually made a nice trip out of that long weekend. We drove from our home in central Minnesota and spent the first night at Copper Falls State Park. We took a little hike down to the falls early the next morning before hitting the road again to get to Pictured Rocks. We had a reservation at 2 p.m. for a boat tour of the park—surely a highlight of the trip. That night we camped at the Chapel Beach campground right on the NCT. The next day we left Pictured Rocks and headed for Whitefish Point to check out the Shipwreck Museum at the old light station before heading down to Straits State Park. We got a stayed two nights, Sunday was kind of a relax day but I took the opportunity to do some scouting.

The bridge walk starts at 7 a.m. every year from St. Ignace in the Upper Peninsula to Mackinaw City in the Lower Peninsula. We were there right on time, it was only a fifteen-minute walk to the bridge from our campsite via the NCT. I documented the experience with video and photos, even managed to get a video of me crossing the finish line. The place is mobbed with people on that day, the scene being similar to that of a marathon. The north bound lane of I-75 across the bridge closes to permit walkers (and one hiker) to cross safely. All along the way National Guard troops are stationed to ensure the safe passage of the walkers.

We completed the five-mile walk in less than two hours' time and received our certificates that we did in fact complete the challenge. To get back to St. Ignace costs six bucks for a trolley ride, which we gladly paid to avoid waiting in an extremely long line for a bus. So we promptly said goodbye to the Straits and completed the long journey ride home, about nine hours. Our family trip to the "Mighty Mack" was short, but it was fun.

Now, on the other side of the bridge, I decide to take the rest of the day off, but not before seeing the historic Fort Michilimackinaw. I have always enjoyed places like this, old historic forts, some re-built and some in their original state. I spend over an hour walking around inside amongst the buildings and along the palisade wall before finally heading to the south end of town where I check in at the Vindel Motel. This will be my first nero day (near-zero mileage) for this hike. I'm not complaining, as I feel taking the rest of the day off to rest will do wonders for me considering the shape I was in not two days ago. It's a good thing too, as today is again very hot, probably the hottest day of this entire trek.

As I get everything settled in my room I realize I am very hungry, and an idea strikes me. A tradition began on the AT long ago that somewhere around the half-way point of the trail hikers will attempt the "Half Gallon Challenge." The idea is to eat a half gallon of ice cream in one sitting. I'm not halfway yet, but it's close enough and I don't know when I will get another day off like this, so to the gas station I go to find some ice cream.

I find that they only sell it here in pint containers, meaning I will need four of them to get the half gallon. Basic flavors tend to be easier for the challenge but they only have three chocolates (I guess the fourth will have to be Cookies n' Cream).

Back in my motel room, I turn on the TV and start chowing down. In less than forty minutes I have all four containers empty. My stomach is not happy, but I did it! I ate a half gallon of ice cream in one sitting (without throwing any of it up afterwards). Now I can say I did it...and never have to do it again.

After my "lunch", I lie down and take a nice long nap, catching up on journal entries and much needed rest.

On the brink at Tahquamenon Falls.

MICHIGAN:
LOWER PENINSULA

July 2 - July 23, 2013

Tuesday, July 2
Trail Day 093
Miles hiked: 32
Mackinaw State Forest

I'm well rested as I get up this morning. After spending a few minutes packing my gear, I check out of the motel and head down the street to Burger King for breakfast. After downing two breakfast burritos I pick up the trail across the street where it follows a paved bike path for a good two miles or so.

After walking a quarter mile or so without seeing any more blazes, I stop and check my map. The NCT makes a sharp right turn off of this paved trail so it would be easy to miss. Just to be sure I backtrack and sure enough there it is, a newly-built single-track trail leading off to the west. I follow this and it leads me to a nice scenic stretch along French Farm Lake with many drive-in campsites right next. From here the trail heads west toward and into Wilderness State Park. Looking around I need to be careful where I put my feet along this stretch as there is lots of poison ivy growing on both sides of the trail.

Before too long, I reach the park access road and take a detour to the campground to use the facilities and hopefully find a place to cook a meal. I find the bathhouse and as I am at the water pump filling up my bottles I am dismayed to find not a single camp site open to use. This shouldn't surprise me as it is only two days from July 4th weekend.

As I am preparing to leave, a guy comes out of the shower house and stops as he sees my gear. Hence, I meet Greg with his girlfriend Courtney. He asks me where I'm headed and after I tell a brief version of my story he invites me over to his camp for lunch. I can't pass this up so I accept and he directs me over to his site.

As I am unpacking my food and cooking supplies near the picnic table, Courtney emerges from their tent and Greg introduces me. They both watch in amazement as I cook an entire serving of homemade quinoa chili in less than ten minutes on my tiny "supercat" stove. As the chili is cooking, Greg hands me one of his recently-cooked homemade pork chops to tide me over. *Well done Greg, this is delicious.*

They ask many questions about my journey so far, why I am doing this, where my final destination is, etc. They seem amazed that I have walked this far and I'm not even halfway through. Then they tell me a little about out their experiences in the outdoors. Greg is a hunter and fisherman, has been his whole life. It turns out he and Courtney are from northern Ohio, only about twenty miles east of Defiance where the Buckeye Trail passes. I will be in their area in a little under a month if all goes well.

Halfway through dinner a nearby camper notices my gear and stops over for a quick chat. The usual questions ensue, and he gives me a gear tip regarding knives. On this hike all I am carrying is a small pocket knife and it has served my needs so far. The friendly camper gives me the pitch on Moraknives from Sweden. They come in varying lengths, they're lightweight and durable. This guy recommends I get one. Thanks for the tip sir, I may have to invest in one of those someday.

Before I know it, over an hour has gone by and I need to get going if I am to make my goal. My next food drop is in Kalkaska and by taking yesterday off I will arrive on Sunday morning and have to wait an entire day to get my package. To avoid this I'm going to try and hike 30+ mile days for the whole week to cut out an entire day and make it to the post office before they close on Saturday. I shake hands with Greg and Courtney and with my pack shouldered again I head back to the trail. **Thanks for your hospitality new friends, enjoy the rest of your trip.*

On the south end of the park there is a large parking area with a boat ramp right on Lake Michigan. I stop here for a short break as I take in the view across the lake toward some of the small islands and see a few kayakers heading in from a paddling trip. The man is the first one up on shore, and as he helps his girlfriend get hers up he turns and heads for the car to back it down to the landing to load their kayaks. As I am sitting there on the beach the woman turns to me and sees my gear. I meet Jessica, we have a brief conversation about my hike before I load up once more and head south into the Mackinaw State Forest.

At the next road crossing I have a decision to make. It's more than six miles to the next section of trail and the area in between is a roadwalk through private land. I have to decide whether to pitch here for the night on the edge of the forest, or push and try and make it to the next section before nightfall and risk getting thrown off track. Deciding that I need to hike as far as I can to make it to Kalkaska in time, I push on. Not stopping for the entire six and a half mile stretch I make it back into the Mackinaw Forest and pitch my tent a few hundred yards from the road.

Wednesday, July 3
Trail Day 094
Miles hiked: 28.5
Home of John and Dove - Petoskey, MI

I am up at first light and head out after a cold and quick breakfast. I have many miles to hike through the Mackinaw State Forest before taking to the roads a few times for short roadwalks. First, I pass through the tiny berg of Pleasant View, stopping at the township hall for water from their garden hose, then again through Conway as I prepare to pick up the paved bike trail to Petoskey. As I arrive into Conway, I spot the trail behind a nice little diner and cross the street toward it. As I reach the other side I look over and see a table with two women sitting at it—one of them is waving trying to get my attention. I head over and meet Karen and Nancy, who have just met up at the diner before heading off to a bike ride. Nancy tells me that when she saw me she knew I had a story to tell, so at the request of her and Karen I spend the next several minutes telling them the story of my trip, specifically over the last few days.

As I am handed a glass of water, Karen asks if I am hungry, to which I reply, "Yes." She gets up and heads into the diner. They stopped cooking about ten minutes ago (as this is a breakfast-only joint), but when she comes out she says the chef has agreed to cook me an omelet. Wow, this is amazing! I order one with everything on it and continue telling my story to the two nice ladies. Before too long, my omelet has arrived—complete with a side of hash-browns and an ice cold lemonade. I tell the waitress to thank the chef immensely for going out of their way to serve me. On top of that, Karen has covered the cost. *Thank you Karen, I greatly appreciate it.*

As we continue talking, Nancy gets a phone call from a friend. When she hangs up she relates the conversation to us. As it turns out, her friend Peg has been following my hike online since I started, and happened to call right as I was sitting with here with Nancy. It sounds like she was quite jealous that Nancy happened to run into me. (Talk about small world.)

Soon we are joined at the table by a guy on a bike. Hence, I meet Mark, Nancy's husband. We spend a few minutes getting him caught up on what has transpired. Then Karen makes a call. She knows a family in Petoskey and requests that they give me a cold beer when I pass through town, as it has been pretty hot the past few days and will continue through the weekend. I realize again that I have been here more than an hour, I need to get moving again. With much reluctance, I inform these kind people that I have to get moving on or I will never reach my goal. Before leaving I take a picture with each of them on the street corner, and after a few hugs and a handshake I turn and head town the trail toward Petoskey. *Thank you dear new friends for making this a great day.*

I follow the paved trail for the better part of two hours, hiking right along the shore of Lake Michigan before arriving right in downtown Petoskey. First thing I do is get a smoothie at the ice cream shop on the corner before continuing on. Karen gave me a description of the house where her friend Patti lives. I spot the house right from the trail and call the number I was given. Patti answers and comes out to her back patio when I tell her I am down on the trail and looking for a way up the steep bank to her house. She waves down to me and gives instructions for the quickest way up and around to her front door.

After hanging up, I am at the door in minutes. She invites me in with much enthusiasm and introduces me to her family as I enter. First I meet Dillon, Patti's son. He is particularly interested in my hike and has many questions for me. I am offered a spot at the bar in their kitchen where Patti opens a beer for me. Next, Patti's husband Andy comes in and has many questions for me. It turns out Andy is a former professional soccer player, both in the US and the UK. A few minutes later Dillon's girlfriend Becky walks in, just back from a trip to LA. They all gather round as I tell my story so far and that I hope to make it to Kalkaska by Saturday.

As I am sitting, enjoying a rest and another cold beer, Patti asks me where I plan to stay tonight. Then it hits me, I hadn't made a plan for tonight. After already having burned another hour I check my map and see that I am still a good eight miles from the next section through the State Forest, and it is already evening. Then as I am thinking of what I could do I remember an email I received a few days ago from a guy near Petoskey offering assistance when I came through this area. I get online and check it again, find out he lives only a few miles from here right on the road walk section between Petoskey and the State Forest. Now if only I could reach him. I send him an email telling him of my situation and leave my number so he can call me. I hope he checks his mail tonight.

After informing Patti of my plan, I decide to head out, not wanting to burn any more time in case the call never comes and I have to push on in the dark. After taking a picture with the family in front of their house, I say goodbye to everyone and shoulder my pack once again. Kind folks here in Petoskey.

The trail through Petoskey is a combination of sidewalks and a river park trail making for some quick hiking. Not even a mile down the trail from Andy and Patti's home the phone rings. On the other end is John, he received my email and called me immediately. In my email I asked if it would be okay if I pitched my tent in his yard for the night, but he tells me on the phone that he already has a room for me in his house. I tell him where I am and he says it shouldn't take me more than an hour to get there. See you soon John.

On the south end of town the trail crosses the North Central Michigan College campus and the wooded area that it operates around it. At the end of the property, the trail passes through a beautiful meadow with great views in all directions and then ends to take to the roads. Along the first section I encounter a porcupine scurrying across the road to get away from me. By the look of its back it has been in a fight recently and didn't escape without losing many quills and part of his tail. Poor guy.

As I make my way along the roadwalk, I spot a sign by a mailbox with my name on it and a cooler sitting beneath it. I have arrived at my destination, and John and his wife have left me some trail magic. I snap a picture of the sign and within seconds I am greeted by two people. Hence, I meet John and Dove, dedicated NCT members with the Jordan Valley 45 Chapter who have been following my hike pretty closely. They walk me up to their home where they have a fire going and I meet their two kids. For dinner tonight are hotdogs over the fire plus some goodies from the care package these kind folks left for me. I am pleased to find a beer and an Arizona Tea in the cooler (they have been paying attention to my journals).

Also inside is an envelope with my name on it. I open it to find a note and a photo of the Lake Champlain Bridge, what lies ahead at end of the trail in New York. They explained that they got the idea after reading my post about my struggle in the Ottawa National Forest and how my dream that night gave me a surge of inspiration that was enough to keep me going. Now, I had an actual picture of my destination and what I was striving for and I could look at it whenever I felt like giving up if that feeling were ever to come upon me again.

I feel spoiled as I am sitting in a lounge chair in front of the fire with a hot dog and a homemade strawberry smoothie. During dinner, they ask many questions about my hike and I relate the full tale of my journey up to this point, as my posted journals ended about two weeks ago. As darkness descends, John lights off some fireworks as nearby some other folks are having pre-4th of July celebrations themselves. I end up staying up later than I should have, but definitely don't regret it.

Dove says that I can take a shower and leave anything I want washed outside my door. After getting cleaned up I settle into my room, grateful for another night in a soft bed. With a smile on my face I think back on the events of today, three separate events of unbelievably generous trail magic all in the span of one day. A good Independence Day celebration if there ever was one.

Thursday, July 4
Trail Day 095
Miles hiked: 40
Alba, MI

I am served a nice warm breakfast as I prepare to depart this morning. I've enjoyed spending the night here with John and Dove, I do hope I will see them again someday. In a short time I have my gear all packed, freshly cleaned clothes on, and I am ready to depart. We take a few photos together and after a handshake and a hug I am off.

The trail this morning starts on private land before again entering the Mackinaw State Forest. This section is finely groomed and maintained trail. Early on I am faced with the longest gradual uphill climb I have ever encountered, by my estimate stretching almost two miles. I thought I was in decent shape but this climb kicked my butt. They should install a bench halfway up this thing and one at the top, holy smokes!

The trail is interrupted by many short roadwalks, some paved but mostly gravel. I'm not sure why but my feet are not happy today. After turning onto another gravel road I cross a creek running along the edge of someone's yard. No one appears to be home so I get off the road and take a rest on the stream bank. I slip off my shoes and dip my feet in the water for a good soak. I also take this time to filter some water and have a lunch.

After a good fifteen minutes of soaking my feet, I slip my shoes on and begin hiking once more. My feet are much happier now, the cold water did wonders to ease some of the pain. The trail continues down more gravel roads and some sandy two tracks and into the woods again before emerging out onto busy US-131. On the other side of the road the trail looks to not have been maintained in awhile but I head on in to try it out. Maybe a half mile in I lose the trail. The brush has not been cut back so the tread is no longer visible, and I can see no blazes up ahead or on either side.

I spend a good ten minutes looking around for any sign of the trail but am unable to locate it. I don't have time for this, I need to be in Kalkaska by Saturday morning and this small section has not been kept open. With nothing left to do, I backtrack to the road and begin a long roadwalk along the busy highway. There is a federal fish hatchery a few miles down the road where I can hopefully pick up the trail again.

A good distance down the road as I am walking along, I am surprised at how dark it has gotten already. I check my watch and am amazed that it is already late evening. I completely lost track of time focusing on doing as many miles as possible. Within about twenty minutes I need to get out my headlamp as it has grown too dark to walk safely along this road. I hike in the dark for what seems like hours until I notice a little cluster of lights ahead on my right. As I get closer, I realize that I have arrived in a small town, Alba. Having a strong sinking feeling that I have missed a turn I take out my map. Yup, I missed the turn to the fish hatchery in the dark and walked right past it all the way into Alba. This means I overshot my target for the night and missed a section of certified trail that I was looking forward to hiking along the Jordan River.

With nothing else to do, I keep walking to the far side of town and start looking for a place to set up camp. The undeveloped lot behind the gas station is completely empty, a nice flat spot covered in long grass with a few trees to provide cover. This will have to do for tonight.

Friday, July 5
Trail Day 096
Miles hiked: 34
Near Wheeler Lake Road - Pere Marquette State Forest

Despite my incredibly long day yesterday, I am up early this morning. To save time I don't bother to prepare breakfast, but just pack up my gear as quickly as possible and decide to have breakfast on the go from the gas station. As I am paying for my snack, the woman behind the counter asks where I'm headed. I tell her I am hiking the North Country Trail and I am surprised when she says she has heard of it. It turns out she knows the person in charge of maintaining the northern section along the Jordan River, the area that was impassable yesterday. She says she will pass on the maintenance issue and get it resolved and she gives me directions to the quickest way back to the trail.

The trail is only a mile west of town on a gravel road and I reach it in no time. Here I have a choice to make: continue on from here, or go back and try to hike as much of this segment of trail as possible. I decide with the latter, as I feel somewhat guilty for missing the certified trail yesterday despite it being an honest mistake.

I head north on the trail to the nearest trailhead where I drop my pack and carry only my camera. I head back up the trail as quickly as possible to at least see some of the Jordan River before continuing on. I snap many good photos along this stretch before turning around again. By the time my detour is done I have hiked eight miles but have made zero forward progress. It is quite frustrating, but at the time I felt like I needed to do it.

Pack-shouldered again, I head south, finally making some forward progress. The off-road trail is well marked today and I have an easy time staying on course. The trail winds around a few lakes on its journey through the Mackinaw and Pere Marquette State

Forests. It is also hot today, so I take frequent breaks to avoid getting another dose of heat exhaustion like I had back in the UP. Toward the end of the off-road portion, I take a break at a state forest campground and restock on water to stay fully hydrated. I spend a half hour sitting on a picnic table at one of the campsites snacking and drinking water.

The campground is pretty crowded as I am at one of the only open sites. I get really annoyed when some guys on dirt bikes come speeding in and out of the campground while exploring some of the motorized trails in the area. Technically, it's not illegal, but you would think some people would have the decency to not make so much noise when a campground full of people is right there trying to relax in peace and quiet... rude!

When the half hour is up, I set out again and begin a long roadwalk out of the state forest. This brings me through the tiny village of Darrough, where I stop at the gas station for another rest on this hot day. Inside, I am pleased to find a small kitchen where they make homemade pizza and serve ice cream. I decide to indulge myself in both and no sooner have I sat down on the curb outside to enjoy my dinner than people start pouring in. This must be a favorite spot for the locals. Many of the people see my pack and ask where I'm headed. When I tell them about my adventure I am pleased to find that about half of them have heard of the trail.

I still have many miles to go, and it will be dark in a little over an hour so as soon. When I finish eating, I shoulder my pack and head out again. I manage to make it to the next section of off-road trail right at the forest's edge just after dark, where I am greeted by a swarm of mosquitoes (the first since leaving the UP). I take off my pack to grab my headlamp and the mosquito netting so I can hike the last mile or so in the dark and find a decent place to camp.

I find a place where the trail comes out into a clearing where a pipeline crosses the forest. A sandy two-track is located immediately adjacent so I make sure to find a spot well away from this in case any vehicles come by in the middle of the night.

I find a small clearing just inside the trees and set up my tent. As I am driving in the stakes, I notice that I have just pitched my tent on the edge of a large patch of poison ivy. At this point I am too tired to care, so I just do my best to minimize exposure and hang my gear in a tree off the ground. We'll see in the next few days if I managed to avoid getting the nasty stuff all over me.

Saturday, July 6
Trail Day 097
Miles hiked: 14
Guernsey Lake Campground – Pere Marquette State Forest

I had another restless night of sleep, much like the night before reaching St. Ignace (probably from being worried about over sleeping and missing the deadline for getting to the post office in Kalkaska before they close). I have managed to make it within five miles of the town, so to miss it now would be a shame.

I awake at 5 a.m. and decide to just get up and go. I hike the five miles into Kalkaska by 7:30 a.m., and make my way toward the post office. They don't open for awhile, so I find a small diner right on main street and head on in for breakfast. I spend some time lingering, enjoying my omelet and a few glasses of soda before heading out. I am at the post office as soon as they open and retrieve my next food drop, enough food and supplies to get me to White Cloud down in the Manistee National Forest. By 9:30 a.m. it is already 90 degrees, and tomorrow is supposed to be the same. Yup, I'm getting into the thick of summer now.

I definitely need some time to rest before continuing on in this heat. I spend a few hours hanging out downtown, stopping for ice cream at the local joint, and then heading to Burger King to use their WiFi to check email.

Early afternoon I decide to finally get moving again. Heading out of town the NCT follows the TC to K trail through the Pere Marquette State Forest for a few miles before splitting off on its own course again. I reach the Guernsey Lake Campground where I decide to head in and set up camp. Today was a short day, but given the heat and the intense miles I've done over the past week, I think it's a good idea to take it easy the rest of the day. I set up my tent and sit down at the picnic table to have one of my hot meals. Afterward, I relax at the table and read many pages from Tolkien.

After awhile, a man from the adjacent campsite comes walking toward me. Hence, I meet Tony. He had seen my pack earlier when he walked by to get some water. He is here with his family and they are just finishing dinner and wanted to offer me the leftovers. I can't say no to that so I head on over to his campsite where I meet his wife Kelly, and his son Max. They hand me a plate full of macaroni, corn, and a chocolate chip cookie. I spend the next several minutes telling them my story so far and where I am headed after this. They seem interested in the trail and I hand Kelly a piece of paper with a link to my website so they can check it out once they get home. *Thanks for the fine dinner folks, it was nice meeting you.*

I head back to my campsite and head to bed early to catch up on rest from the past few days.

Sunday, July 7
Trail Day 098
Miles hiked: 21
Home of Mark and Tamal - Kingsley, MI

Despite heading off to sleep early last night, I still managed to sleep in pretty late this morning. I decide to cook another meal for breakfast before hitting the trail again. As a result I get a late start, but my pack is now that much lighter from consuming another meal, which in this heat makes all the difference. Heading out I pass by my friendly neighbors, and Tony wishes me luck as I pass.

Leaving the campground the trail passes through the Sand Lakes Quiet Area for several miles. I pass several isolated campsites loaded with people out for the weekend. The trail in this area is a variety of widely-groomed trails and some sandy two tracks.

After a few hours, my phone rings and I am talking to Mark from Kingsley. He had sent me an email awhile back showing interest in hosting me for a night, and has called to set up a meeting place. We make plans to meet at the end of the day near the point where the NCT crosses Hwy 186. Despite the heat, I manage to make good progress and make it through the forest and out to a short roadwalk where Mark plans to pick me up. I get maybe a half mile down the road when a van pulls up. Of course, it is Mark here to pick me up for the day (what excellent timing). He says he will turn the van around and meet me down a half mile where the road forks and I can pick up there in the morning.

In a few minutes, I am loading my gear into his van and we head west a few miles off the NCT into the town of Kingsley where Mark lives. When we arrive, I am introduced to his wife Tamal, and pointed in the direction of the shower where I can finally get cleaned up. Dinner is ready shortly afterward and I get the chance to sit down and meet Mark's family. I am asked many questions and spend a good deal of time telling my story so far, and Mark's kids seem very impressed. Afterward, his kids disperse and I am left conversing with Mark and Tamal at the table. Mark relates his experience four years ago when Nimblewill Nomad stayed at his house on his thru-hike and what an inspiration it was to him. Mark hopes to one day have the opportunity to hike the whole trail. We share several other travel stories as Tamal disappears and comes back with a box of Klondike bars for dessert. I have never had one before so my taste buds are in heaven when I finally bite into mine.

After dessert, I spend the next hour conversing more with Mark and Tamal and then it's time for bed. I head to the basement to my spot on the couch and within a few minutes of shutting off the lights I am off to sleep.

Monday, July 8
Trail Day 099
Miles hiked: 30, +1
Unmarked campsite near 15 Road – Pere Marquette State Forest

I am up early for a quick breakfast before Mark needs to head to work. In no time I have my gear packed and am ready to go. Mark has me back on the trail by 6:30 a.m., and I say goodbye to another new friend. **Thanks Mark for your hospitality and sharing your stories with me. I hope our paths cross again.*

As I set out this morning, the rain sets in and stays around most of the day. I am not hiking for very long when a thunderstorm rolls in. After awhile as I am making my way along a ridge above the Manistee River the lightning gets closer and closer until one strikes less than a half mile away. It is so close that I can feel the ground shake as I see a blinding white flash and hear a horrendous explosion directly over my head. This isn't good, I'm in an area where the forest is thinner and I have these metal trekking poles. I decide I need to get to lower ground as quickly as possible to avoid becoming a lightning rod. Luckily, near this spot the trail descends into a creek bed, and I decide to hunker down here on the edge of the river until the lightning passes. My rain coat has managed to keep me mostly dry to this point, so I decide to get out my rain fly from my tent to rig up a temporary shelter to wait out the storm in.

As I am setting up, I am surprised when two hikers come down the trail toward me. Hence, I meet Dave and Patty out for a morning hike. They are members of the Grand Traverse Hiking Club Chapter and were hoping to meet me at some point as I hiked through this area. Despite being completely soaked, they appear to be having a good time. We talk for a few minutes and then they continue on down the trail into the storm.

I sit under my rain fly and take the opportunity to have a snack and study my maps. After the lightning has subsided for ten minutes, I decide it is probably safe enough to continue on. Before too long, I come to a gate and a gravel road. I have a short roadwalk from here to connect to the next segment of trail. The road is supposed to turn within about a mile and I get concerned when I am hiking for more than twenty minutes with no sign of the road.

I decide to hike on a little further, hoping that the map may just be wrong. Soon I hear a vehicle slowing down behind me. As I turn, and the window comes down, and I recognize Dave and Patty. It turns out I *was* going the wrong way! On the map the gate was facing the wrong direction, so it was a little misleading and I hiked the wrong direction. Luckily, Dave and Patty were here to get me back on track. I hop into their van and they drop me back on the trail at the correct place. They wish me luck as they drive way. *Thank you Dave and Patty for helping me out today. If you hadn't shown up when you did I would have wasted time and many miles trying to find the trail again. It was nice meeting you.*

The thunderstorm has passed but the rain continues off and on for the rest of the day. During a break in the clouds, the sun manages to come out for a short time and I stop where I am along the Manistee River for a break. As I cook one of my meals, a van pulls up on the sandy two-track adjacent to the trail. Down goes the window and I meet Terry. Turns out, he has been following my progress on Facebook, so when he saw a hiker with a big pack sitting on the riverbank he knew it had to be Strider. Before he leaves he snaps a picture so his family will actually believe that he got to meet me. Then, he wishes me luck is gone.

Continuing on, the trail parallels the Manistee River for the rest of the day. Toward the end I am again faced with lots of poison ivy lining the trail on both sides. I am careful not to let any of it touch my ankles if it can be helped. Just before nightfall, I come to a nice little campsite that is not marked on the map. Here on the trail it is marked with the friendly tent symbol and it even has a small bridge across a creek leading right to it. I pitch here for the night and settle in for a nice night of sleep.

Tuesday, July 9
Trail Day 100
Miles hiked: 24
Guesthouse of Loren and Dave – Irons, MI

I decided to sleep in this morning; I'm not hiking until after 8:30 a.m. From my campsite it's maybe a half mile to the next trailhead, there to begin a roadwalk into the town of Mesick. I'm there by 10 a.m., and I stop at Ellen's Corner for breakfast. A few slices of freshly-baked pizza does just fine to satisfy the stomach. As I sit outside enjoying my breakfast, a man comes around the corner with a bag of cherries. "Here's something for the road," he says. Hence, I meet James, a local who saw me sitting outside with my large pack. He had walked across the street to a fruit stand to get freshly-picked cherries. He is familiar with the trail and is amazed that I intend on hiking the whole thing. We talk for a few minutes and then he is on his way to begin the day. *Thanks for the treat James.*

Before leaving, I fill up my water and head into downtown, there I run into a guy outside the grocery store with his dog. Hence, I meet Brian, who was out walking his dog and enjoying the nice day. He asks a few questions and then is on his way. I head to the library to use their WiFi so I can check my email. I also take this time to call Loren, president of the Spirit of the Woods Chapter. She left me a voicemail about a week ago asking me to call when I reached Mesick. She lives not far from here, and wants to host me and try to set up a few interviews with the local news outlets, hoping to raise some awareness for the trail. We make plans for her to pick me up at the end of the day at the crossing of the Coates Hwy in the Manistee National Forest.

Plans made, I shoulder my pack and hike on, reaching the Hodenpyl Dam and the northern boundary of the Manistee National Forest. The hike along Hodenpyl Dam Pond is very pleasant. The view is wonderful, no underbrush to block the view through the trees. It is easy to see 100 yards or more into the forest most of the time. Along this stretch there are a few small campgrounds located right on the lake. At the Northern Exposure Campground, I take a short detour and head up the road a quarter mile to Nate's Country Store. Mark told me stop in here when I passed through to try some of their ice cream, so here I am following his advice.

As I walk in, a man comes out to the counter—Nate himself. "You must be the hiker," he says. He grabs an envelope tacked to his bulletin board with my name on it. It turns out one of the local trail maintainers left six dollars for me to use to get one of the famous ice cream cones. *Thanks very much to the generous donor, it's just what I needed on a hot day like this.* Luckily, there was enough money left over after the ice cream to buy one of the Arizona Teas I've come to enjoy.

I sit at one of Nate's tables to cool off and get rehydrated after downing the delicious ice cream. Soon Brian walks in, here to use Nate's WiFi. "Hello again." After finishing my drink, I decide I could still benefit from some more hydration, so I get up to purchase a Gatorade to bring along for the road. Then as I am ready to check out, three men walk in, all local trail maintainers. They recognize me right away and have many questions about my travels. They are particularly interested in their section (if I had any problems getting turned around or if I thought it needed any additional maintenance). Everything is good from my eyes guys, thanks for all your hard work.

At the counter, I pay for my drink and am ready to leave when Nate tells me to wait a second. He reaches down, pulls out a fifty-dollar bill and hands it to me. Wow! *Thanks Nate for your generous donation. I will use it well.* After thanking Nate and saying goodbye, I head out once again, still many miles to hike before day's end.

Shortly after leaving the campground, the NCT meets a junction with the Manistee River Trail, which basically parallels the NCT on the opposite side of the river. I've heard good things about it. Art, back at the Two Hearted River Campground in the UP, said it was an impressive scenic hike. Currently, both routes are acceptable for a thru hike, but I decide to stick to the blue blazes. I am greeted by more nice trail, again no underbrush to block the view and the soil is fairly sandy making it much softer on the feet.

Early evening I reach the Coates Highway, and after waiting only about seven minutes a van pulls up and stops. Hence, I meet Dave and Loren, here to shuttle me to their place near Irons for the night. On the ride over we make nice conversation about the trail in the local area and they give me a summary of what to expect in the days to come.

We arrive at their lovely home and I am directed to the guest house. I am then shown the way to the shower so I can get cleaned up, and then we all sit down to a nice meal. Afterward, I am inclined to retire early as I am very tired from the longer days and the heat. I make my way up to the guest house and crash as soon as my head hits the pillow.

Wednesday, July 10
Trail Day 101
Miles hiked: 29
Guesthouse of Loren and Dave – Irons, MI

Last night, I decided to spend another night with Loren and Dave after they offered. So we made a plan for me to get picked up at the end of the day near the Freesoil Trailhead. After breakfast, I am back on the trail at Coates Hwy. The hike is very pleasant. It starts off on a nice mowed trail through an open meadow with views of the Manistee River below. Back in the woods, I'm on many switchbacks winding up and around a steep incline; I'm in the Udell Hills. I pass a few bikes on this section today as this is one of the few areas where the trail is open to multiple users.

After a few hours the trail crosses the "High Bridge" and leaves the Manistee River to head south. At the Udell Trailhead I see a man walking toward me. Hence, I meet Dave, a reporter from the *Manistee News Advocate*. He is here to interview me about my trail experience so far and he has even brought a comfy chair for me to sit in. For the good part of a half hour, I am in an interview talking into a camera to be posted on the *Manistee News* website. Afterward, I pose for a few pictures and thank Dave for taking the time to come out here. Immediately afterward, I get a call from Brian of the *Ludington Daily News*, and so I have another interview. I don't mind it in the slightest, I can't think of a better way to raise awareness for the trail than getting an article in the local paper or on TV.

The second interview went a little quicker, so after a good hour of sharing my story I am on the trail again hiking south. Before too long I get a call from Loren. She informs me that a few of the chapter volunteers will be stopping over at the house tonight and one of them will be driving right by where I will need to get picked up. I inform her that I'm a little behind schedule so I will need to stop a few miles early at the crossing of Tyndall Road rather than at Freesoil.

With the new plans in place I hike on for a few more hours, ending the day with a long boardwalk section with a swarm of mosquitoes. I emerge onto the road and there is a car waiting for me. Here to pick me up is Joan, one of ten people that has completed the entire trail, and also an active member of the Spirit of the Woods Chapter. I hop into her car and relate some of my experiences so far.

Back at the house, I hop in the shower first thing and then head in for dinner. I am introduced to chapter members Ed and Nancy, here to meet me and hear some stories. I enjoy a fine evening with these folks. Before everyone leaves Joan hands me a bag with some trail goodies for the road.

Afterward, I sit down for dessert with Loren and Dave and get a call from Bruce at NCTA. Tomorrow there is a dedication ceremony for the town of Lowell. It will become an official trail town and since I am not far away they want me there if possible. We make plans for one of the staff to pick me up tomorrow around noon and bring me down to Lowell for the night. With all the excitement of the past few days I am definitely tired, so I head up to my spot in the guest house and settle in for another night of comfortable sleep.

Thursday, July 11
Trail Day 102
Miles hiked: 16
Home of Beth - White Cloud, MI

Last night during dessert, Loren told me to stop by a little convenience store just off the trail and talk to Anne, the owner. She was interested in meeting me and I'll be passing near her store on the hike today. I load my stuff into the van first thing and Dave drives me to Tyndall Road where I will continue my journey south through the Manistee Forest. *Thank you Loren and Dave for hosting me in your guesthouse.*

The hike today is absolutely gorgeous; one of the nicest sections in the Lower Peninsula so far. The forest is thicker here with many oaks and pines growing together, but still very little brush. I enjoy places like this as the tall red pines constantly remind me that I am still in the north woods.

Before too long, I reach a two-and-half-mile section of roadwalk and watch for where the trail turns back into the woods. I locate it and then continue on down the road for another quarter mile to stop in at Anne's store. I find the place, located right off the shore of a lake, and head on in. There is a woman at the counter (who I'm guessing must be Anne). I introduce myself. "You're the hiker!" she says.

She directs me over to the counter where she has a glass case full of many different flavors of ice cream. She asks, which flavor I want, and I respond with Mackinaw Island Fudge. I had this flavor back at Nate's Country store and it has become a favorite of mine. I bring my large cone up to the register and Anne tells me "It's on the house." *Wow, thanks Anne.*

The day has turned very hot, so before leaving I decide to grab a cold Gatorade for the road. In the fridge, I see that Anne has a fine selection of beer as well, including almost all varieties of the Keewenaw Beer from the UP. I decide to grab one, the blonde ale, to enjoy before leaving. I pay for my drinks and say goodbye to Anne; thanking her for her kindness.

About two hours after leaving Anne's store, I come to the crossing of Centerline Road, where I was planning to get picked up today to head to Lowell. I find a note on the ground tied to a small stump. It's from Dave, NCTA HQ. It says he went up to the next road in case I hadn't gotten this far yet, and that I should wait here for him to come back. I'm not waiting more than ten minutes when a car pulls up. Hence, I meet Dave from NCTA, here to bring me down to Lowell to partake in the festivities of the day. We load my gear into his vehicle and begin the journey south, a good two-hour drive.

On the way to Lowell, we talk about many things regarding the trail; maintenance and markings, favorite sections and future plans among other things. From hiking the trail these past many months I have seen the trail from a thru-hiker's perspective and have come up with many ideas that I think could attract more users in the future. I share many of these with Dave and plan to share them with Bruce as well.

We arrive in Lowell mid-afternoon with plenty of time to prepare before the celebrations start. Dave drops me off at Bruce's house where they have already allowed for me to get cleaned up. When I arrive, I meet Bruce's wife, Linda. She invites me in and shows me the way to the shower were I can get cleaned up. Afterward, I head back out into the kitchen where Linda pours me a large glass of juice on this hot summer day. She asks many questions about my hike so far and is glad that I was able to make it down here for the dedication ceremony.

She then tells me how to get from here to the NCT headquarters—only a few blocks away—and I make my way there. I find the place easily enough, located right on main street near the Flat River. I head on in and I am recognized as soon as I enter. Most of the staff are there. The first one I meet is Tarin. I have spoken with her many times, mostly before my hike began to coordinate supplies like maps, apparel, and the GPS unit they have been kind enough to allow me to use. Next, I meet Jill, Beth, Laura, Andrea and Bruce.

After brief introductions, I head back with Bruce into his office. First thing he does is pull up a video from the *Manistee News Advocate* of my interview from a few days ago. It turned out better than I thought. We spend the next several minutes talking trail, and I mention to him many of the ideas I have to attract more users and improve the trail in general.

Afterward, we head outside for a quick walk down the street. On the outside of the NCT headquarters building a new attraction has just arrived. Some of the local art students spent much of the school year painting a mural of the NCT on three large panels that are now attached to the outside of the building. It's a very clever way to raise awareness of the trail. It will play a part in the dedication ceremony happening shortly.

Before long people start gathering on the street. A podium is set up outside the building and a few people with cameras arrive. I am brought aside for a quick interview for the local paper. Also here to capture the whole ceremony, is Brandon. He is an ultra marathon runner and frequently does his workouts on the trail nearby. He has even done the ultra up on the Superior Hiking Trail that happens every fall. He hands me his card and tells me to give him a call when I officially come through the area, about a week from now.

The ceremony begins and lots of people are gathered on the street. The mayor of Lowell and Bruce, are at the podium. All the NCTA staff and the National Park Service representatives are present. The mayor gives an opening speech to welcome the NCT and the NCTA to Lowell. Bruce then gives a brief presentation about the trail, followed by Mark, superintendent with the National Park Service. Mark talks a little about the trail's designation back in 1980, and the partnership with the NCTA.

The presentation concludes with an official ribbon-cutting, and Bruce calls me up to do the honors. With a scissors in my hand (after Bruce gives an introduction about my adventure), I cut the ribbon and Lowell is made a trail town of the NCT! To finish off the ceremony, the coordinator of the mural project comes up and introduces all of the artists who contributed to the great piece of art. Afterward, I stick around for many pictures.

Next, I get a chance to meet a few of the local trail members with the West Michigan Chapter. First I meet Beth from White Cloud, who has agreed to put me up at her place tonight. Also, there is Chuck, who gives me a short rundown of what I can expect the next few days as I enter his chapter's area. Soon the party moves inside and there is a table of food in the back. Here I meet a few others, including Matt, the GIS Coordinator for the NCTA, and Jeff with the National Park Service. I thank Matt for the new maps he has provided me. They have worked very well so far and are more up-to-date than the current retail maps.

I can't linger too long as I need to be mindful of Beth's schedule, so after meeting everyone I head to Bruce's house to retrieve my gear and load it into Beth's van. We head back to her place in White Cloud and she gives me the tour of her nice home. Her house is right on the back side of a small lake, complete with a dock. My feet were bothering me a little bit today, so I decide to hang my feet over the edge in the water for awhile. Beth comes out and hands me a beer and we sit for awhile and talk about the trail. As soon as it gets dark it is time for bed. I have another long day tomorrow.

Friday, July 12
Trail Day 103
Miles hiked: 25.5
Near 96th St. - Manistee National Forest

Beth prepared a nice homemade breakfast, then it was off to the post office to retrieve my next food drop. I call this one my "halfway" box, as I am now very near the halfway point of the trail as it exists right now. En route to the trail we make a quick stop at the local bakery for some fresh donuts (by Beth's recommendation). Looks like we're having second breakfast today.

Before long, I am back at the trail where it crosses Centerline Road. Beth waits patiently as I unload the contents of the box into my pack. This one seems heavier than usual and I soon find out why. My family has sent a few extra items in celebration of crossing the halfway point, including letters from all my family members, some candy, and a tiny bottle of wine. *Thanks, Mom.*

Pack-shouldered and ready to hit the trail again, I say goodbye to Beth, thanking her for being a good trail angel. She snaps a few photos of me and I turn and continue my long journey south through the Manistee National Forest. After about six miles, I reach the Timber Creek Campground where I stop to have lunch and stock up on water.

A few hours later near Bowman Lake I stop for a rest and check my email again. I remember receiving an email many weeks ago from someone in this area...and sure enough here it is. I call the number and talk to John, who has a cabin nearby. He is happy to help me out any way he can, and says he'll meet me where the trail reaches Bowman Lake. I'm only a short distance away as I made the call, so I am surprised when I arrive to find that he is already there waiting. It turns out his cabin is literally across the street from the trail. We head over there where he has a nice patio overlooking the river below.

The day has grown quite hot and humid so it feels really nice to sit down in the shade. Before I can say anything, John brings out a beer and a plate with some smoked salmon for a snack. Now this is some trail magic! I take smoked salmon whenever I can get it. We spend awhile talking and I find out that John has traveled all over the place. He's been to Mexico and South America many times to a point where it's almost become an annual occurrence. He comes back up to Michigan for the summers to pass the time away up here in the woods.

After awhile, we head to the nearby town of Baldwin for a burger at the local pub. John then drops me off at the trail again and I have a few hours yet until it gets dark. *Thanks for your help John, and for sharing your stories.*

I finish the day hiking a fantastic boardwalk through the Sterling Marsh. I am instantly reminded of the Brule Bog back in Wisconsin, as this boardwalk is of a similar length. It, however, is chopped up into about six segments rather than being one continuous structure. Immediately adjacent in many spots, a private landowner has put up fences and flagging to keep hikers away.

Despite a few delays, I make it just past the sterling marsh before it gets dark, and I pitch my tent on a low hill above the trail.

Saturday, July 13
Trail Day 104
Miles hiked: 25
NCTA Schoolhouse - White Cloud, MI

Today is more hiking through the beautiful Manistee National Forest. I am up early and hike for several hours before taking a spur trail into Highbank Lake National Forest Campground to fill up on water and use the facilities. Despite filling up my water yesterday, the humidity is very high today and I need to drink more to stay properly hydrated. The rest of the day is uneventful as I make my way through the forest past many lakes.

Early evening I come to a white-blazed spur trail that should lead me to the NCTA Schoolhouse. I take the spur trail, intent on checking out the former headquarters for the trail. On my map it looks as if the spur is no more than a mile long, so after a half hour of hiking I get concerned when I haven't crossed any roads yet. Soon I come to a sign that indicates the schoolhouse is still a mile and half from here to the north, and a campground to the south.

Totally confused, I dig through my maps and find the new way-point-added maps issued to me from Matt at HQ and realize my mistake. The trail I am on is an entirely new trail that doesn't even show on the older map. I took a spur trail that took me three miles out of the way in a semi-circle around the schoolhouse. Oh well, at least it was a nice hike.

After another half hour, I finally arrive and find a few people camping outside in the back yard. They are volunteers from the

Western Michigan Chapter, out for a weekend of trail maintenance. Here, I meet Paul and Jim, both friends of "Windigo Doug".
They invite me over to the picnic table to share in some appetizers
before dinner, so I sit down and enjoy snacking on some veggies
and a nice cold beer.

Soon a few other volunteers arrive and we spend some time exchanging stories. I tell the story of my hike so far, and they inform
me of local happenings on the trail. This year they are working on
a loop trail that will connect the main NCT to the town of White
Cloud, making it eligible to be a trail town in the future. They're
hoping to have it done this year.

As we are talking, Paul gets a call on his phone; it's Beth and she
is on her way. Paul hands me the phone and I'm on the line with
Beth. She asks if there's anything I want from town before she
heads to the schoolhouse. I've been craving Subway for the past
few days, so I tell her my favorite sandwich, the spicy Italian (pep-
peroni, salami, Pepperjack cheese, with some lettuce, spinach,
black olives and mayonnaise). Delicious!

In no time, Beth arrives and hands me my dinner. *Thanks Beth!*
Another call on Paul's phone...it's Windigo Doug himself. He was
originally planning to come out and work this weekend, but his
plans changed. Instead, we make plans for him to pick me up near
Lowell in a few days and host me for a night.

Afterward, we all head over to the fire for s'more trail talk before
one-by-one dropping off for bed. I shouldn't stay up too late, I
have a long day tomorrow and they're saying it's going to be a hot
one. I head into the schoolhouse with my gear, plop a mattress
down on the floor, and head off to sleep.

Sunday, July 14
Trail Day 105
Miles hiked: 29
Home of Michael and Jane - Newaygo, MI

As I woke up this morning, I took a few minutes to look around the inside of the schoolhouse. The seven-state map of the whole trail is still up on the far wall, and a table is set up with all the brochures. From what I gathered online during my research for this hike, this schoolhouse at one time served as the headquarters for the NCTA. The HQ has since moved to Lowell, but they still maintain this schoolhouse and it's available for hikers to rent for a night or two if they wish. It also serves as a good staging area for the Western Michigan Chapter's trail work weekends such as the one this weekend. Yes, surely a nice asset to the trail.

I'm out pretty early on a roadwalk to hook back up with the trail a few miles from here. After three miles, I approach the first road crossing and I spot a cooler sitting on the side of the trail. My name is written on top. As I open it I find a note inside along with many trail goodies: water, Gatorade, fruit, and cookies. They were left here by Tracy. *Thank you Tracy for your generous care package.*

This road crossing is M-20, and the supposed half-way point for the trail as it exists right now. I snap a photo of the trailhead sign and continue on. A little way down the trail, as I approach the White River, I stop suddenly in my tracks. A slight movement on the edge of the trail caught my eye. I focus my vision and realize I have just come face-to-face with a large blue racer, one of the fastest snakes on this continent.

I'm not a fan of snakes, and this is the largest one I have seen in the wild so far, easily four feet long. It's laying halfway across the trail, so I nudge it with the trekking pole hoping it will scurry off.

Instead, it responds by raising its head in a defensive position. I move a little to the left looking for the best way around and it inches closer to me, head still raised. Finally, I back off a few feet, take a wide turn to give it plenty of room, and get back on the trail. As I do so, it darts in the opposite direction and I lose sight of it in less than a second. I guess the rumors I've heard about racers being aggressive are true.

Shortly afterwards, I can hear the sound of a mower coming down the trail. Sure enough, here comes a small crew of trail volunteers lead my Jim, at the head operating the mower. He smiles and gives a wave as we pass each other. In less than an hour I feel it, the heat has definitely settled in. I take frequent breaks to stay properly hydrated. At one point, I hike a short spur trail down to the roadside park off Hwy 37.

Here I take some time to have lunch, and as I am preparing a meal a car pulls in and honks. It's Jim. The trail crew has broken for lunch and he has driven down here to enjoy the shade of some of the many picnic tables. And so I get to enjoy another conversation with Jim before he heads back to work on the trail, and I decide to eventually start hiking again. *Thanks for the company, Jim.*

The rest of the day includes hiking through Coolbough Natural Area, followed by a short stretch with a unique feature I never thought I would see anywhere near the North Woods. On this short segment, I emerge from the trees into a wide meadow and am surprised at what I see. All around me, growing in large clumps and individually, are thousands of prickly pear cacti! This is very unexpected, but a nice touch of diversity along this great trail.

Shortly afterward, I emerge from the trees once more at the end of a certified section at Croton Dam. This is the end of the Manistee National Forest, and the end of the contiguous north woods. For the next 1,000 miles or so, I will be hiking through more open countryside, through agricultural, suburban, and some urbanized areas through the rest of the Lower Peninsula and Ohio. I won't get back into the north woods again until after I cross into Pennsylvania.

With the heat today I am definitely exhausted, and once at the dam, I take another break. I received an email a few days back from a couple in Newaygo who were interested in helping me out if I need it. I think now might be a good time to accept their offer. I make a call and soon I am talking to Michael from Newaygo. He says he can pick me up any time. We make plans for him to pick me up somewhere along the roadwalk section south of here, so after hanging up I get going.

I manage to make it a few miles to a restaurant parking lot, Hit-the-Road Joes. As soon as the place is in view, a truck pulls in and slows down. I walk over to the parking lot and meet Michael. We throw my gear into his truck and he drives me to his home in Newaygo where I meet his wife, Jane. They offer me their shower and some delicious soup for dinner.

Afterward, I head into the living room and just lie down on the floor exhausted. They ask me many questions about my hike and tell me stories of many of the trips they have taken on the trail in Michigan. They have hiked most of the trail within the forest, and some of the smaller sections further south. They tell me of the time they were hiking through the Manistee a few miles north of the dam and Michael unknowingly stepped over a rattlesnake, not even noticing it was there...Freaky.

After awhile, it's getting late and they hand me a few souvenirs for the road before we all head off to sleep. Michael will drop me off at Hit-the-Road Joes first thing in the morning.

Monday, July 15
Trail Day 106
Miles hiked: 26
Home of "Windigo" Doug - Grand Rapids, MI

Michael had to be on the road early, so I'm back at Hit-the-Road Joes at 7 a.m. Within a few minutes they open, so I head on in for breakfast as I haven't eaten yet. After downing my patty melt and a few glasses of water, I hit the road.

Today is mostly a roadwalk except for a chunk of certified trail through Rogue River State Game Area. By 8 a.m. I can already feel the heat. Today may be my first triple-digit day for temperature on this hike. I take frequent breaks whenever I can, usually in people's front yards beneath a tree for shade.

As I stop for a break in the early afternoon it's definitely in the 100s. I take a few minutes to check my small notepad. Back at the schoolhouse in White Cloud Paul gave me the number of a woman who lives near the entrance to the game area, and is always happy to help hikers. With this extreme heat I decide it would be beneficial to get inside for awhile, especially with the hottest part of the day still approaching.

Soon I am on the phone with Barb. I tell her my situation. "You're only a few miles from my house," she says. Unfortunately, she also tells me she is out of town at the moment and doesn't expect to be back until the end of the day. I am amazed when she offers me to stop by the house anyway, let myself in, and use the shower, sink, anything I need. *Thanks for the offer Barb, but I would feel a little awkward if no one is there, I hope I get a chance to meet you in the future.*

Continuing on, I finally make my way to the entrance of Rogue River State Game Area, seemingly the only forested place in this entire area. As hot as it is, the heavy tree cover doesn't do much to relieve the heat. It is nice to get a break from the baking of the pavement. Somewhere in this forest there is a visitor center where I can hopefully rest for awhile, but I am unable to find it at the road crossing where it is supposed to be. Just as I enter the woods again I get a text message on my phone. It's from Barb, she is on her way back and wants to know my location. I let her know I'm almost through Rogue River and will be at the Red Pine trailhead soon. She responds that she will be there in fifteen minutes.

I arrive at the trailhead and am waiting less than ten minutes when a car pulls in. Hence, I officially meet Barb. After a brief introduction we load into her car and head back to her house—but not before stopping at a convenience store so she can grab a few things. Before getting out she asks what is my favorite drink. I respond that I drink pretty much anything, but I've been craving chocolate milk. She heads in and in a few minutes comes out with a half-gallon of chocolate milk in one hand. "For you," she says. *Wow, Thanks Barb.*

We arrive at her house, literally right next to the north entrance of Rogue River SGA. I leave my gear by the door and sit down at the kitchen bar. Barb pours me a large glass of chocolate milk first thing, and then we start a long conversation while she walks back and forth across the kitchen making preparations. She is ready to cook dinner as her husband will be home soon and she invites me to stay. I gladly accept, happy to be out of the heat for awhile.

Soon her husband Glenn comes home and we have introductions. Barb and Glenn have done a lot of traveling together over the years, and they both ride Harleys. I am also not the first hiker they have hosted. Many hikers have eaten or stayed here over the years, including Nimblewill Nomad back in 2009. Glenn and Barb share the story of when they hosted Nimblewill on his thru-hike over dinner. He wandered in looking for the trail and a temporary respite from the skeeters. Barb ended up fixing him a steak dinner with potatoes, and she tells me how he came to call her "T-Bone Barb". She has a copy of his book nearby that recounts that night from Nomad's point of view (the same book I have on my own shelf back home and have read many times). I hope to one day turn my own experience into a book as well, to keep a history of all the great happenings on the NCT and make it available for future hikers to use a resource.

After the delicious meal prepared by Barb, it's time for me to hit the trail again. We take a few pictures on their front porch before heading out. They take a few minutes to show me access points for the trail a few miles down the road, as there are a few tricky ones that are hidden from sight. Then, it's back to the Red Pine trailhead where I say goodbye to these dear new friends. *Thanks for your kind hospitality Glenn and Barb, it was a great pleasure meeting you.*

There are a few patchy segments of off-road trail on the southern end of Rogue River. The first entrance was a little hard to find, but thanks to Glenn and Barb I know right where it was. I pass a few more cacti fields along a road section. Apparently, the soil is so sandy and dry here that these cacti are able to grow and survive even in the winter months. I've now traveled through a transition zone into a new environment and from here on out I will be in rattlesnake territory until I get clear through Pennsylvania. They are not particularly numerous this far north, but I will need to stay more alert and watch my step on off-road segments.

Back on the road now there are no more cacti, being completely contained within a small area. I cross busy M-46 and enter Long Lake Park on the paved road. Crossing the park takes only a few minutes and soon I am in some residential areas making my way east along farm country roads. Along Indian Lakes Road, I am looking for a small cornfield on one side with an active sprinkler.

I am getting picked up today at this location and before long I identify the house and head on up the driveway. I see three people sitting in the front yard enjoying a few drinks. One of them stands up and comes to meet me. Hence, I officially meet "Windigo Doug" in person! Back at the schoolhouse, when he was on the phone with Paul, we made arrangements for him to pick me up today and bring me to his home in Grand Rapids for the night. It turns out, he has friends who live on this road, and that's where I am now. (Good thing too, there is nowhere to camp between Croton Dam and Lowell.)

After we shake hands, he brings me over to where the chairs are gathered and introduces me to his friend Randy, and his wife Laura. They offer me a chair and a nice cold beer, which I gladly accept. We spend the better part of an hour talking. A quick thunderstorm rolls in and after it passes it is time to move on. We say goodbye to Randy and Laura, load my gear into Doug's van, and we head for Grand Rapids.

Once there, I get cleaned up as Doug starts to prepare dinner. In his kitchen are framed pictures of the various hikes he has done on the NCT. He is on a quest to hike the entire trail, hiking about 300 miles at a time. I recognize most of the places on his wall. Later Paul comes over (as he lives just across the street) and we enjoy more trail talk together. All filled up and tired from the longer days in the heat, I retire to bed.

Tuesday, July 16
Trail Day 107
Miles hiked: 26
Main Street Inn - Lowell, MI

Doug has me loaded into the van pretty early as we head back to Randy and Laura's house. He pulls into their driveway and helps unload my gear. After a firm handshake, I turn and begin hiking. *Thanks for your help Doug, it was great to finally meet you!*

I have a short roadwalk to reach a crossing of the paved White Pine Trail that will bring me into the town of Rockford. It is an enjoyable hike along this old railgrade, but even this early in the morning I need to rest a few times from the heat. Rockford is a wonderful trail town if there ever was one. There's plenty of fine restaurants, ice cream shops, beautiful green space, and much more. I've already consumed a lot of water—despite only hiking for two hours—so I take the opportunity to stock up on some Gatorade and spend time in the shade. Just as I am ready to hit the road again, a nice little ice cream shop on the corner opens up, so I head on in for a cone. With some extra calories stored up, now I hit the road again.

I head out of Rockford on busy ten-mile road. It is extremely hot today and I feel like I'm taking a break every twenty minutes. Today's hike is almost exclusively on paved roads, and I'm often pulling off into people's yards to enjoy a small speck of shade beneath a tree to rest. At one point, toward the end of the day, a woman comes out of her house, gets in her vehicle, and pulls out as I am sitting at the end of her driveway beneath a large tree. She spots me on the way out and stops. "Are you okay? Need anything?" I respond "No I'm fine ma'am, just taking a rest in the shade, thanks for the offer though." I sure have met some kind folks on this trail, total strangers concerned for the well-being of others, very refreshing.

By the end of the day, I make it to a gravel road just north of Fallasburg County Park where Andrea from HQ will be picking me up shortly. I'm not waiting more than five minutes when she arrives, ready to haul me and my gear into Lowell. Tonight I will stay at the newly opened-motel in town that has a room set aside for me. On top of that, she also took the time to pick up my resupply box at the post office in town. **Thanks Andrea!* She drops me off at the motel and tells me to head to the Flat River Grill down the street in thirty minutes for dinner.

Not wasting any time, I head on in and check into my room. This new motel is very nice, freshly-furnished rooms and a nice balcony at the back right on the river. I enjoy a nice cool shower first, and after changing into my fresh clothes I head down the street for dinner. Here Andrea is waiting for me, and soon after I arrive a few others join us. Jill and her husband, Darl, are here as well as their daughter, and Andrea's boyfriend Ted. We have an enjoyable time talking trail over some delicious food. **Thanks All, for the delicious meal and for the company!*

Afterward, I head back to my room for some much needed rest. I found out that it reached a scorching 103 degrees today and I got quite sunburned...no wonder I feel so worn out!

Wednesday, July 17
Trail Day 108
Miles hiked: 25
Lowell, MI

Last night, after I had already fallen asleep, I received a text message from Andrea. Since leaving the Manistee National Forest there has been a lot of roadwalking, and with these hot temperatures it is definitely not the most pleasant place to be. On her way back from the restaurant last night she stopped by the motel to give me an NCTA ball cap to help with the heat. But, the doors had already been locked. She left me a note saying she left a cap behind the flower pot outside on the street, so last night I went out and retrieved it. **Thanks again Andrea, this will definitely be a valuable item in the coming weeks.*

I have quite a busy morning ahead of me. I kept my word and gave Brandon a call last night. He is available today and wants to hike some with me. We made plans for him to pick me up here for breakfast and then shuttle me to Fallasburg Park, where he will park his car and then come join me.

Within a few minutes of getting ready, Brandon shows up and we head to a diner down the street for a nice healthy omelet breakfast before hitting the trail. Brandon drops me off at the spot were Andrea picked me up yesterday. He shuttles his car back to the trailhead at Fallasburg Park and he will hike back this direction to meet up with me. It's about a two-and-a-half mile roadwalk along a gravel road to reach the trail in Fallasburg Park. Along this stretch Brandon meets back up with me and hikes about ten miles, all the way back to Lowell.

Fallasburg Park is a pretty stretch of trail right along the Flat River, complete with an old historic covered bridge, the first of this hike. I make sure to snap a picture with the bridge before continuing on. Along our joined hiked today we pass through Lowell State Game Area. We talk about the trail itself and our running careers. Brandon is an ultra marathon runner and has done the Superior Ultra up on the Superior Hiking Trail in Minnesota. He relates his experience from the many races he has done over the years as we hike along. Before we know it we are back in Lowell where I again stop in at headquarters. I say goodbye to Brandon at this point, thanking him for his company. After a firm handshake, he is off to retrieve his car.

While here at HQ, I have a few quick errands to run—a trip to the post office to mail a package home and a quick meeting with Bruce before heading over to the rotary club meeting for lunch. Afterward, I have a meeting at Flat River Grill with Howard Myerson, a journalist writing an article for the *Grand Rapids Press*. He's here to get a detailed interview about my experience for the paper. While we are sitting in our booth enjoying some more delicious food, Dave from NCTA, and Jeff from NPS, happen to walk by. We have a brief conversation before we all need to get back to our tasks. The interview lasts for over an hour and then it's time for me to hit the trail again. I thank Howard for his time and interest in the trail and then I head out the door.

I hike the short section in town through the Kent County fairgrounds and then it's a roadwalk the rest of the day. After several hours, I pass a new section of trail built this year on some property owned by Trout Unlimited. Unfortunately, it's a dead-end segment, so there will be no hiking it on this trek. After this, I pass by the Maher Audubon Preserve on a narrow, fairly scenic gravel road, and reach the next segment of trail. This is a narrow two-track at the entrance to Middleville State Game Area...and my target destination for today. I'm not waiting too long when a trail angel arrives and I'm back in Lowell. After downing a pint of Ben & Jerry's ice cream, it's time for bed. I have another potentially long day tomorrow in the heat.

Thursday, July 18
Trail Day 109
Miles hiked: 15.5
North of Yankee Springs Recreation Area

I decided to sleep in an extra hour this morning; feeling no need to get out extremely early. Then it's back to the narrow two-track at the game area to begin today's hike. This morning, I decided to wear my blaze orange bandana over my hat while I hiked, as this section was on the south side of a shooting range. Just in case anyone is out there with a gun I am much easier to spot!

Within a couple hours, I am approaching the town of Middleville, and as I am making my way toward downtown the phone rings.

On the other end is Jean, of the Chief Noonday Chapter. I met her at the Lowell trail town dedication last week and she told me to stop in when I came through. Amazing timing. Within a few minutes I make it to her office and she gives me the tour of Michigan's first official NCT trail town. For lunch we stop in at the local bakery where she shares my story with the servers and most of the locals. Fine folks here in Middleville. After lunch, Jean walks me down to where the trail leaves town following the paved Paul Henry Trail. She snaps a picture at the trailhead and away I go. *Thanks for your hospitality, Jean.*

Along the bike trail the mosquitoes are back! In fact, they are the worst I've encountered so far since leaving the UP. I pick up my pace to try and outrun the little buggers with little success. Finally, as I emerge at the other end into a wide open clearing that serves as a trailhead, I take a break in the shade at a picnic table. Today is another scorching hot day and I can feel weariness coming on, so I decide to take a little nap in the shade.

An hour later, I wake up. After drinking many full gulps of water I am on the road again. The trouble with these roadwalks is, unless you're in a wooded area or a heavily-developed area with access to a gas station or other public facility, there are very limited places where you can safely do your business. Luckily, just down the road is a church. I stop in, and sure enough the door is open. Once inside, the kind lady at the table shows me the way. When I come out there is a bucket of ice sitting on the table with two full bottles of water. Wow, this is some timely trail magic. *Thanks folks.*

Only a few miles to go now I make it to the next off road segment of trail just north of Yankee Springs. Then, I call it a day. I'm kind of bummed about taking a shorter day, but under the circumstances I think I need it. These last few days have been in the 100s along mostly paved roadwalk sections, and I haven't taken a full day off since leaving Marquette over a full month ago. It'll be nice to rest for a few extra hours to get my strength back.

Friday, July 19
Trail Day 110
Miles hiked: 25
Hickory Corners, MI

The hike today begins through Yankee Springs Recreation Area. This is a gorgeous stretch of trail, perhaps a small island of the north woods has established itself here. Many pretty lakes and tall trees are passed along the trail route. There are also many trail junctions to contend with but for the most part they are well-marked and color-coded, different colored carsonite posts indicate which trail you are on. I navigate through this area without incident.

After a six mile stretch through Yankee Springs, I'm in Barry State Game Area for a little while before emerging out onto a gravel road. At this access point there is a note posted: "Trail ahead not maintained, turn west here to Norris Road and follow down to designated roadwalk." It looks like this segment has been recently abandoned, so I follow the detour.

This brings me through a little area known as Circle Pine Center. I was curious about this place on the map and I quickly discover what it is, a summer camp for kids. It looks like they have been busy recently. I saw a brand new picnic pavilion complete with a running drinking fountain. Across the street were a set of small houses and cabins, one likely belonging to the care takers of this property.

Off in the woods I think I see what appear to be trails zigzagging around in various directions. I stop at the picnic shelter for a quick rest and to refill my water at the drinking fountain. Within a few minutes a large group strolls up, most of them appear to be kids between the ages of 10 and 12. They must be getting back from a hike.

One of the group leaders spots me and comes over. Hence, I meet Josh, around my age. He seems a bit curious as to why I'm lingering here. I tell him my story, where I came from, and where I'm headed. He seems surprised to see a long-distance hiker out here and wishes me luck as he gets back to his group.

As I continue on down the road, I get maybe a quarter mile away and I hear my name being called. I turn around and I see Josh jogging toward me. He says the group is just getting ready for lunch. "The caretakers know you're here and said you can stay for lunch if you want, we have plenty of food." I thank Josh for the offer but explain that I need to continue on if I am to make the mileage I want to get to tonight.

After this encounter the rest of the day is entirely a roadwalk. Before long I reach the little berg of Prairieville. It shows on the map as a single icon, a restaurant. I find the little diner situated at an intersection of many roads and I head on in. Questions start coming instantly. This appears to be a family-run business. They can tell I have traveled far, and are still surprised when I explain where I came from. They bring me a glass of water and ask what I might want to eat. I inquire about any fruit they may have, they respond that unfortunately the closest thing they have is Jello in small quantities.

My eyes light up, "Would it be possible just to get a big bowl of Jello?" "Sure," they reply. Within a few minutes a bowl is placed in front of me filled to the brim with Jello. Afterward, I decide to get a burger as well and select the olive burger...it sounds intriguing.

As I am waiting for my food, some locals come in for dinner; all mighty fine folks interested in my travels. I take the opportunity to tell my story, and not surprisingly, they haven't heard of the NCT. I point out the blue blaze on the telephone pole across the street and explain that the trail is marked by these for all 4,600 miles of its length, from North Dakota all the way to New York. They had always wondered what the blue marker meant, and when they found out they were very excited. "Well, I learned something today!" says the waitress.

While enjoying my delicious olive burger, I find out from the locals that some bad weather is coming tonight. They are saying hail for sure, possible tornadoes. Darn, looks like I should get going to try and get to the next sheltered spot before it hits. One of the locals says he is heading to Battle Creek and offers me a lift. I thank him for his offer but explain that I really can't take rides to skip any trail unless it is an emergency, which this probably isn't. I tell them I can make it to the next town before the storm hits.

So back on the road now, I pass a beautiful piece of property on my right called the Lux Arbor Preserve, owned by Michigan State University. I imagine it must be a similar concept to the Ekre Grassland Preserve back in ND, kind of a summer research station for students in environmental or outdoor programs. It would be cool if the trail could pass through this property, just from the road it looks amazing.

I end the day at the little berg of Hickory Corners. Not much here, a diner, a church, a gas station, and a handful of houses. I head over to the diner and take a seat in the bench on their front patio. I can see the storm building to the north, it's definitely going to be a bad one. As I am sitting out front composing some of my journal entries, I wait to see what happens with the weather. A few of the locals passing by stop to talk. A few of them stay to chat once I explain what I'm doing. They seem interested in the trail.

At one point, a woman comes walking down the street and asks where I'm headed. I tell her I'll be in Battle Creek tomorrow, but I'm here now to wait out this impending storm. She says she happens to know the fire chief in town, she will go ask if he will let me in to the fire station for the night. After I agree to that idea she disappears and never returns.

About twenty minutes later, as I am sitting outside the diner talking on my phone, two young cops show up and walk right up to me. As I hang up the phone they load me with questions and ask to run my ID. I spend several minutes explaining what I am doing, where I'm headed, why I'm here, and the fact that there is an impending severe thunderstorm literally a few miles away. Apparently, I was labeled as a suspicion person by a few of the locals (I suspect that woman) and these young cops clearly took advantage of the opportunity to find some trouble.

After running my ID, they came up with a bogus story that someone from Detroit with my name had a criminal record and they thought it may have been me. After explaining that I'm a Minnesota native only passing through to get out of this storm, they said I couldn't stay here in town, and asked me to move along. I don't argue with them and simply shoulder my pack and head out...not in the mood for unnecessary trouble. This is ridiculous. Cops are supposed to protect us and help us, not force us out into a thunderstorm on foot with no cause.

I'm sorry boys, but you leave me no choice. I wait until they're out of sight, then I hang a left turn to walk in a semi-circle around the outer edge of town. I circle back to the church, and unfortunately it's locked. However, I find a semi-secluded spot along a hedgerow behind the storage shed between the church and the cemetery where I decide to pitch for the night. It's the only spot that has any reasonable cover from wind, debris, or possible falling power lines. If this storm is as bad as they are saying, the church may be my only chance for survival. Hence, tonight it looks like I'll be stealth camping...hoping like hell I don't get swallowed up in the storm.

Saturday, July 20
Trail Day 111
Miles hiked: 29
Ott Biological Preserve – Battle Creek, MI

I was woken up several times last night by pelting rain against the fly of my tent, coupled with pools of water forming inside on the floor. I had decided last night to leave everything in my pack accept for the tent itself. In case I needed to make a quick getaway, everything would be in one place. I'm glad I did that, because if my sleeping bag had been in the tent with me it would have gotten soaked. It was so hot and humid I really didn't need it anyway.

As I officially wake up this morning, I can tell that it rained pretty hard, but there is no sign of hail damage. The storm swung east pretty early on so the worst of it just missed us. I reckon many of the towns east of here got pelted pretty hard though. It's first light now so I don't waste any time stuffing my tent into my pack and hitting the road early.

Before long, I have made it to the next segment of trail at Kellogg's Farms. Much of it is in the woods near the edge of the property, around some field edges and some open meadows. At the southern end is a biological forestry station, with a visitor center and another one of those historic covered bridges. This one has the NCT logo attached right to the front of it and is now only open to foot traffic. What a neat place. The trail heads south from here along the edge of a field, though I am a confused at first as there are no markings once I leave the woods. The edge of the field has not been mowed so I'm not positive I'm going the right way, but I follow it down the edge of the trees and come through a gate to a trailhead. I guess it was the right way after all.

I'm now in the town of Augusta, where a short roadwalk connects to another segment through Fort Custer National Cemetery just east of here. While in town though, I spot a restaurant across the street from the trail and head on in. The name of the establishment, The Barking Frog. I enjoy another fine olive burger before continuing on.

Just outside of Augusta, a car pulls over to the side of the road. Down goes the window and guy asks, "Are you Strider?" Totally caught me off guard. It turns out this guy has been following my progress on my website and on the NCTA's Facebook page. He wishes me luck and then continues on his way.

From here I pick up a wet segment through Fort Custer National Cemetery and then follow the paved Linear Park bikeway through the city of Battle Creek. Riding in a car through Grand Rapids was one thing, being in a big city now on foot is a great culture shock after being in the woods for three months. There are people everywhere, music playing in people's cars as they drive by, lights, noise, distractions. I hike through this section as quickly as possible, and by evening I'm clear through the other side and hiking a wooded section through Ott Biological Preserve.

I emerge from the woods on the far side of Battle Creek after about fourteen miles of urban hiking it is evening. There is one motel nearby and I am disappointed when I find out that there are no rooms available. Looking for a place where I can pitch for the night, I hike to the next section through Kimball Pines County Park. When I arrive, I am utterly confused by what I see. If there were any pines here in the past, there are none here now. All that remains is a very narrow path through nothing but brush and lots of wooden debris. There is a gravel parking lot a short ways in where I could pitch but the remnants of recent campfires with alcohol containers scattered about makes me think twice. This has clearly become a party spot for the local kids. I decide to head back to the road, there is a McDonald's right on the trail where I can duck in and use their WiFi and maybe find a place nearby where I could camp.

Just as I emerge back onto the crowded street, a guy walks out of a gas station and flags me down. He is familiar with the trail, saw my pack, and came to the conclusion that I must be out for a lengthy trek on it. When I tell him I am attempting to hike the whole thing he is greatly impressed. I learn from him that Kimball Pines was destroyed by a tornado back in 2011, and the county hasn't started the full rehabilitation yet. Currently, all that exists are the bathrooms and a roughly cut trail through the middle of the debris.

I tell him my issue of not having a place to stay since the motel is closed, and he recommends I pitch in the Ott Preserve. "It's pretty quiet, no one will bother you in there." Thanks for the tip Sir, I will take your advice. So, with that I head back into the Ott Preserve, bushwhack a good distance off the trail and pitch for the night.

Sunday, July 21
Trail Day 112
Miles hiked: 26
Days Inn - Albion, MI

I'm up at first light and hiking out of town. After passing Bridge Park the rest of the day is mostly a roadwalk. Within a couple hours, I reach the outskirts of Marshall. As I am turning a corner, a car pulls up to the side of the road and I meet Jim. He knows about the trail and is curious where I've come from. He is amazed when I tell him I have walked here from North Dakota and am heading all the way to New York. He snaps a picture of me before wishing me luck and continues on his way.

In Marshall, there is a small section of trail, a riverwalk maybe a half mile long. It winds through some small woodlots and ends at a decent sized dam. I stop here for a lunch break, many families are out enjoying the bright summer day. After this, the rest of the day is a long roadwalk into Albion. This is the only town within walking distance that has a motel. There is no public land in this area, so naturally my options for lodging are limited.

When I arrive, I find Albion to be in a state of disrepair. Many of the buildings on the outskirts are abandoned, windows are broken or boarded up. There is debris lining the sidewalks, weeds growing up through the cracks. The center of town is better, but still not a very pleasant place to hike. As I pass through I get that feeling of dread that I'm being watched.

I head over to the Days Inn for a room, clear on the other side of town across the interstate. The woman at the desk seems very annoyed. She almost reluctantly gives me a key, and when I get to my room I find that it hasn't even been cleaned. There is still trash in the garbage cans, the beds are not made, nothing has been cleaned. Disgusted, I head back downstairs to the desk and explain the situation. The woman hands me another room key and when I get to this room, it's the same thing.

Finally, the third time does the trick. The woman at the desk (getting extremely impatient) hands me another key. This room is finally clean! This is the worst experience I've ever had in a motel. I hope the lack of lodging isn't the reason the trail route does the weird jog. To me, it would make more sense to bypass this town and head straight from Marshall to Homer. This was an unfortunate experience for me and I hope this area is more hospitable for future long distance hikers.

Monday, July 22
Trail Day 113
Miles hiked: 28
America's best value inn - Jonesville, MI

I'm happy to leave this motel this morning! I hope there aren't any more incidents like this on this trek. Today's hike is entirely a roadwalk, except for a small section in the village of Homer where there is a short pedestrian walkway crossing a river. I stop here in town for a break and a refill of my water and then move on down the road.

The day is uneventful as I pass through the town of Litchfield and beyond, to end the day at Jonesville where I check into a motel a short distance off the trail. I check my email and there is a message from Dave in Hillsdale. He was interested in hosting me for a night when I came through town. He also wants to interview me for a show he does on his Youtube channel. I send him a response, saying I will be passing through Hillsdale tomorrow and would be glad for any assistance he could provide. So, at some point tomorrow I will be meeting with Dave in Hillsdale.

Today ends with a little bit of trail magic as I head to the vending machine with just enough change for a single soda...but it gives me two! How about that? Afterward, I catch up on a few journal entries and then head off to sleep.

Tuesday, July 23
Trail Day 114
Miles hiked: 26.5
Student rental house - Hillsdale, MI

From Jonesville the NCT follows an unmarked bike trail running adjacent to busy M-99 for a ways into Hillsdale. Where the bike path ends I lose the trail as it has not been marked through town. I have a very hard time locating where the trail is supposed to go, and eventually end up at the school. At this point I give Dave a call asking for directions. He says he's nearby and will pick me up for lunch. That sounds good. It's another hot day today and it'll be nice to get out of the sun for awhile.

Within a few minutes Dave shows up and we head to a nice pizza joint for lunch. He asks me about my experience so far; particularly along the Chief Noonday and Chief Baw Beese chapter's segments where I've been for the past several days. This segment was all good until I got to Hillsdale, no blazes or markings of any kind through town that I could see.

After lunch we head over to the city park where Dave sets up his video camera for an interview. He has a show on Youtube where he posts occasionally about enjoying the outdoors. He has several videos from various NCT hikes he has gone on and now he wants to add to it by interviewing me. We spend about an hour filming in the park, talking about the trail itself, various hazards and planning logistics, gear and other things. After it's all done, Dave shows me where to go through town and says he will pick me up again at the end of the day.

After finding my way through town, the trail is clearly marked again on the far side where it returns to more traditional tread along the Baw Beese Trail. I pass by lovely Baw Beese Lake and through the little berg of Osseo before heading south through Lost Nation State Game Area. This is the last off-road segment in Michigan so the rest of the day is a roadwalk straight south along farm country gravel roads.

Late evening I give Dave a call and tell him I am ready to get picked up. He will be out in a half hour, so I manage to get in about two more miles before he picks me up at Camden road, just a few miles short of the Ohio border.

Back in Hillsdale, he brings me into an empty house. It turns out, Dave is involved with a local church and they own a house that is rented out to college students during the school year. Being summer, there are no tenants currently living in it, so Dave has set it up for me to use for the night. *Thanks Dave, I appreciate it.

After taking a nice shower, downing my leftover pizza and half a bottle of Gatorade, I'm pretty tired so I settle in for a nice night of sleep in a quiet house.

Northland College, south of Petoskey

OHIO

July 24 - September 3, 2013

Wednesday, July 24
Trail Day 115
Miles hiked: 29
Rotary Park - Wauseon, OH

I'm up early this morning, in fact it's still dark. Dave has breakfast to go, and he drops me off back at Camden Road at first light. *Thanks for all your help Dave, it was nice meeting you.*

It's about 3.5 miles to the Ohio state line at Territorial Road. When I arrive, I snap a picture of the sign and continue on. In a few hours I reach the town of Aldvorten where I have my next food drop. I'm here a little early, the post office isn't open yet so I have to wait about a half hour until I can retrieve my package. When I go inside the woman at the counter knows who I am instantly. She and others were wondering if I was every going to show up to retrieve this package.

Afterward, the roadwalk continues into West Unity where I pick up the Wabash-Cannonball Trail. It's a multiple use trail, at this point beginning as a two-track. I encounter two woman on horses a little distance down the trail. I find out that horses do not like packs, in fact they are afraid of them. The two women have to dismount and let the horses sniff my pack so they would know that it was harmless. I suppose to a horse, a human with a giant pack doesn't look like a human anymore, but rather some strange animal.

The quality of the Wabash Cannonball Trail is hit or miss; some of the open sections have been kept decently cleared, other places are overgrown with branches. Right before entering Wauseon the trail turns to uncomfortable ballast and then becomes paved a few miles through town. This is as far as I will go today. There are only a few pieces of public land. I hang around the pond at the Rotary Park, wait until dark and pitch my tent in the woods.

Thursday, July 25
Trail Day 116
Miles hiked: 32
Young Cemetery - Liberty Center, OH

Before leaving town this morning I head over to the grocery store first thing, hoping for some fresh fruit for breakfast. I find a nice batch of fresh strawberries and raspberries and spend a few minutes out in the front of the store enjoying them. As I am sitting there on the sidewalk, a woman walks over and hands me an ice cold bottle of water. "Here, I got this for you." She must have seen me while she was walking in and wanted to make sure I didn't overheat. I don't even know her name, I simply know her as "The Woman in Red." *Thank you very much madam. What a nice way to start the morning, with a bit of trail magic.*

Not far out of town the pavement ends and the Wabash-Cannonball Trail turns to ballast once again. Soon the ballast stones become bigger and more difficult to navigate. It is very slow and unpleasant to walk on and at a railroad crossing the trail appears to narrow and then disappear completely. With no sense of direction on where exactly I'm supposed to go, I just continue along the edge of the active railroad tracks and get off at the next road crossing. I take to the roads for awhile to get around this mess. A few miles further down the trail is supposed to again turn to pavement, so I plan get back on at that point. My detour takes me through the town of Delta where I stop for a break under the shade of a gas station awning. The woman out trimming the grass for the city smiles and waves as she passes by on her ATV.

I pass by many orchards along the roadwalk today, and a few miles outside of Delta I get another small dose of trail magic. A pickup truck pulls up next to me as I am passing one of these giant gardens, and down goes the window. "Are you hungry? Would you like a fresh peach?" A woman reaches out her hand with a giant peach and hands it to me. Wow, this is amazing.

Finally, I make it back to the Wabash-Cannonball Trail where it is once again paved and continue heading east. I am soon in Oak Openings Metro Park, located near the outer suburbs of Toledo. This is the closest I will ever get to Lake Erie on this trek, only twenty miles away. Within a few moments, I spot a carsonite post with the NCT logo on it and a foot path heading into the woods. This trail is not on my map, but I decide to follow it anyway and I find that it is well marked and maintained, though it has not been blazed. Oak Openings is a pretty park indeed, lots of giant trees, well-maintained trail, and some very neat picnic shelters made of stone. I stop at one of these to enjoy dinner before continuing on.

On the south end of the park, I emerge onto a road and spot another carsonite post across the street. Again, this section is not on my map but I decide to follow it. This leads me into a chunk of the Maumee State Forest. I'm not sure what this area is meant for, but the trails I am following now are very wide; wide enough for a two-lane road and markings become sparse. Soon I regret my decision to enter this place as following the road would have been much safer (as far as getting lost is concerned). Many of the intersections in this place aren't marked, and I end up having to consult with my gut feeling on many of them, hoping I turn the right way.

In the end, it turns out I made all the right decisions because I emerge onto the next road and figure out exactly where I am. If they build some single-track trail away from these strange wide, open clear cut trails, and build some quality single track, this forest would actually be a good spot for an Adirondack shelter in the future. This area of Ohio has very few campgrounds and even fewer right along the trail. This first stretch of Ohio may be a challenge to find adequate camping spots...we'll just have to wait and see.

After a short roadwalk I am back on the Wabash-Cannonball Trail, heading southwest now toward Neapolis. Just outside of town, the pavement ends once again and the trail becomes a grassy two-track. This section is generally better maintained than the northern section, and along this stretch the mosquitoes come out. I need to put on my bug shirt for the first time in many weeks. Eventually, the trail ends where an abandoned railroad begins and I finish off the day with a short roadwalk into Liberty Center. Back in Jonesville, I took the opportunity to scout ahead online for any spots of public land I could use to pitch a tent in this part of Ohio. I found a cemetery in Liberty Center. I never thought about cemeteries as possible options until I heard about Ed Talone camping out in a few back during his thru-hike in 1994. It's actually a clever idea if you think about it. Many cemeteries have running water and a bathroom, and most people wouldn't think of them as being private land. So, with my campsite identified I run into the gas station to grab some snacks, and once darkness settles in I head to the cemetery and find a spot in the corner between the fence line and a mound of gravel (well away from the headstones). This will be an interesting night.

Friday, July 26
Trail Day 117
Miles hiked: 28
Super 8 Motel - Defiance, OH

I'm up at first light hiking another roadwalk. This leads me to Hwy 424 and the first blazed trail in Ohio, a segment of canal towpath. This section is well maintained and ends on the outskirts of Napoleon where another roadwalk begins. On the way into town, I find that my passage is blocked by road construction. The road leading into town has a bridge crossing over a creek and they just happen to be working on it. I spend a few minutes inspecting the area looking for a way around because otherwise I would have to backtrack and take a detour many miles around. After much contemplating, I find one place where some debris has piled up enough into the creek to allow me to pass without getting wet. I move as quickly as possible to avoid getting in the workers' way, scramble across the creek, and make it safely to the other side.

I make my way to the far side of town and find more blazes; these being of the Buckeye Trail (BT), which I will follow through Ohio for about 700 miles. From town is a long continuous stretch of trail along the Miami/Erie Canal Towpath. It's wide, flat and makes for easy hiking. Today the mosquitoes are out, but nothing like they were up in Michigan. Along the way are many benches installed by Eagle Scouts over the years. The main attraction of the day is the stretch through Independence Dam State Park where this segment of certified trail ends and another roadwalk begins that brings me into the town of Defiance.

My progress is slowed way down along the roadwalk. I'm exhausted and my feet are pounding, begging me to stop. It turns out the BT map was wrong about the mileage on this section, it takes me a full hour longer than the map says it should to reach Defiance where I head across town to check into a motel for the night.

Saturday, July 27
Trail Day 118
Miles hiked: 24.5
Auglaize Chapel Cemetery near BT

I slept in this morning, exhausted from the long day yesterday and from not having a decent rest day since leaving Mackinaw City way up at the north end of the Lower Peninsula. I am overdue for a day off. Today's hike is mostly a roadwalk with a few isolated segments of off-road trail. Leaving Defiance, I pass by a large berm on my right, on the other side is the Defiance Reservoir. The trail keeps to the road, though I suspect in the future it may be moved to the top of the berm. Many people are out along the reservoir walking or running, enjoying the day.

The few off-road segments today are along the former towpath of the Miami Erie Canal. At the north end of the longer segment is a sign marking the place where another canal joined with this one before making its way to Lake Erie near Toledo. At this trailhead there is a car parked and a man comes out to meet me. Hence, I meet Sam, BT supervisor of the Delphos Section. He heard I was coming through and wanted to meet me and give me some pointers on possible camping spots along his section. He also wants to set me up with an interview with the Delphos paper when I pass through tomorrow. *Thanks for coming out to meet me Sam, your advice was helpful.*

Along the off-road segment, I come to a stile crossing that is blocked by a large herd of cattle. I go around the pasture, not wanting to disturb the herd, and take the road back on the trail in the woods on the other side. Here I find the first official campsite for the Buckeye Trail at the remains of Lock 21. I stop here for a break on the bench and have lunch before continuing on.

As I leave the shelter of the woods and come back out to the road, the sky is pitch black to the west and the wind is so strong that my hat is blown right off my head. I couldn't have been at the campsite more than a half hour but a large storm has rolled in. I pick up the pace and follow the blazes south until I reach a road intersection with a gas station, a place called Charloe according to the map. I look back and the storm is now directly north of me, I managed to hike my way out of its path.

Further along the roadwalk, I pass the site of Fort Brown on the Auglaize River and stop here for a moment. Sam mentioned this was a possible place to camp but I feel like I'm here a little early,

I have enough daylight to make it many more miles. I decide to push on to the next segment of towpath trail. When I arrive I am disappointed to find it overgrown. However, there is a cemetery nearby about a half mile off the trail so I make my way there and pitch for the night on the edge of the trees. So glad I decided to go the extra miles.

Sunday, July 28
Trail Day 119
Miles hiked: 34
Old Acadia Park - Spencerville, OH

I am up at the crack of dawn and hike the nine miles into Ottoville where I head into the local subway for breakfast. From here it is a ten-mile roadwalk to Delphos where just outside of town Sam passes me in his truck. He has set up an interview with the local paper and will be waiting at the city park.

When I arrive, I get a chance to sit down at one of the picnic tables and give a brief summary of my journey for the local paper. Afterward, Sam asks me how far I'm planning to go today and I tell him it would be nice to get to Spencerville. He tells me there is a city park there where they don't allow camping, but says he knows the sheriff and will find out if he can get permission for me to stay there. Thanks Sam, that would be great.

On the way out of town, I stop at The Creamery, Delphos' famous ice cream place. I walk up with my big pack on and order a large cone. Of course the pack generates many questions from the ladies inside. When I give them the brief rundown of my hike to this point they are very enthusiastic and very amazed. One of them even asks me for my autograph, while another tells me that she "feels special" that I stopped here. I sit down to enjoy my cone and as soon as I take my first bite I come to the conclusion that this may be the best ice cream I have ever tasted. Nice work ladies. Nearby many locals also see my pack and the usual questions come. None of them have ever heard of the trail even though it follows the street right in front of this fantastic ice cream establishment. I point out the blue blazes on the telephone poles nearby and explain what they mean; just like I did for the kind folks back in Prairieville, MI.

Then, as I am getting ready to leave, my phone rings. Sam is on the other end and says he got permission from the Sheriff's office in Spencerville for me to camp in Old Acadia Park for the night. *Wow, thanks Sam. I really appreciate it!*

I've still got many miles to go, so I follow the BT out of town along the canal towpath and make it to Spencerville before dusk. I pull into the picnic pavilion at Old Acadia Park and cook dinner before setting up my tent beneath a small locust tree and heading off to sleep.

Monday, July 29
Trail Day 120
Miles hiked: 23
Minster, OH

Hiking along the canal towpath has made for some easy hiking the past few days. This environment through western Ohio is not the most scenic, but it does allow for high mileage days and easy access to services. I have passed through at least one town every day since crossing the border from Michigan. From here until I reach Cincinnati I won't need as many food drops, because I can pick up most of what I need right on the trail in the small towns. Today the surface of the towpath changes from grass to dirt, then to crushed limestone. Also along the trail are remnants of the old locks (by the end of the day I will have passed 21 of them). Just outside the town of St. Marys, I come to a culvert underneath Hwy 33. The trail uses this to cross under the highway. These are quite common on some other trails, but this is only the second one for me on this hike, and the first since my first day in Wisconsin as I passed into Pattison State Park.

From here the trail leads into St. Marys, a nice trail town. There is an old canal boat still floating in the canal downtown across from the city park. I take a break for lunch at a local bar to check email and charge my phone a bit before continuing on. A few miles south of town, I find a spur trail leading away from the canal to a newly formed park complete with a new trail shelter built by some Eagle Scouts. I stop in to see the new shelter and to take a quick break before making the final push for the day.

There is another man here and he walks over to talk as soon as I sit down. Hence, I meet "Tall Drink", another hiker. He is not following any particular trail, but making his way from San Diego up to Maine. Instead of a backpack he pushes his gear around in a backcountry stroller. The was the stroller much like the one Bart Smith used when he hiked the trail over a few years on his quest to photograph all eleven National Scenic Trails. Tall Drink is going further than I am, but he is still very impressed when I tell him about the North Country Trail and my attempt to thru-hike it. We spend a few minutes talking trail, and after signing the guest book at the shelter I shake his hand and move on.

I finish the day following the canal towpaths through New Bremen and Minster. I linger for awhile in Minster to have dinner at the McDonald's and use their WiFi to figure out where the hell I am going to camp tonight. As darkness descends, I head out and pitch for the night in the small clump of trees next to the drive-thru.

Tuesday, July 30
Trail Day 121
Miles hiked: 34.5
Roadside Park north of Piqua, OH

I am up at first light and make my way back to the trail along the canal towpath. Most of the day is easy walking. Early on, I pass through Lake Loramie State Park, and then the village of Fort Loramie where I have a food drop waiting. I arrive a little early and have to wait until the post office opens to get my package.

Afterward, I stop to enjoy some treats that were sent in my box and as I am sitting there in the park I get a call from Andrew, executive director of the Buckeye Trail Association. He is hoping for an update on some of the trail conditions I have encountered the past couple days. He also informs me of a few volunteers that know about me and want to help out any way they can. So I take down their contact information. This is great news. Over the past few days I have noticed that my pack is coming apart at many of the seams. After telling Andrew of my situation, he gives me the number of some contacts in Dayton that may be able to help me out with that. He also informs me that a section of the trail through the Wayne National Forest will be going through a rehabilitation, and will likely be closed when I arrive there in a few weeks. He concludes by telling me to stop by the BTA office in Shawnee when I pass through. *Thanks for the help Andrew, I hope I get a chance to meet you during my trek through Ohio.*

The easy walking continues until I reach the village of Newbern. At this point the towpath becomes overgrown in spots, and I become lost when I arrive at the Lockington Dam. There are some blazes missing in critical places and the description on the map is not enough to navigate without them. Before I know it I miss a critical turn and end up walking extra miles. I stop to look at my map and find a way back to the trail. After a short time, I realize that I missed yet another turn and ended up going even further in the wrong direction. I can't believe the same thing happened twice in the same day!

Eventually, I do figure out where to go but it ends up being a five-mile detour to get back to an identifiable spot on the trail. Totally exhausted, and with my feet on fire, I find a roadside park right across the street from where the trail heads into Piqua. Below the picnic shelter along a creek is a nice flat spot out of sight of the road. It is there that I decide to pitch for the night, not able to walk any further.

Wednesday, July 31
Trail Day 122
Miles hiked: 29.5
Super 8 Motel - Vandalia, OH

I had a nice night of sleep in my little spot on the edge of the creek. At first light I'm up and back on the trail across the street. In Piqua I stop in at the gas station for some convenience store breakfast. At this point in town the trail turns from grassy canal towpath to paved bike trail and continues all the way down to Cincinnati. It'll take me a few days to traverse this segment through suburban Ohio.

The bike trail brings me through Troy and Tipp City with a surprising amount of historic sites. There's an abandoned nuclear plant in Piqua, remnants of old locks and a lock tender's house in Tipp City. I reach a short off-road segment of trail through Taylorsville Metro Park. This is where the NCT leaves the bike trail and heads into the woods and through the remains of an old abandoned village. Somewhere toward the end of this stretch, I miss the turn to Vandalia where I plan to spend the night at the Super 8. The road crossing was not marked and I walked right past it. By the time I figure it out, I need to backtrack four miles on dangerous Hwy 40 to cross the river to Vandalia...no shoulders and high-speed traffic! With much frustration, I make it safely to Vandalia and check in at the motel. I enjoy a nice shower and hot meal before catching up on a few journal entries and heading off to sleep.

Thursday, August 1
Trail Day 123
Miles hiked: 17
Comfort Suites - Dayton, OH

The thing I enjoy most about spending the night in motels is the continental breakfast. I get a chance to pig out on sausage, eggs, and waffles; something different from my dehydrated meals and trail snacks. The first thing I do this morning is head on down for another breakfast, and then hit the road.

I have quite a few miles on the road before hooking back up with the trail a little ways south of here. I decide to take an alternate route from the one I took yesterday because of the heavy road traffic and the busy shoulderless highway and a bridge crossing. Between me and the trail there is a steep hillside and an active railroad, so I find the next road crossing on my map and head for it.

Shortly after crossing I-70 along the shoulder of the road, I suddenly feel a sharp pain in the bottom of my foot. I limp across the road to the sidewalk on the next street corner, drop my pack, and take off my boot. My sock is covered in blood and I see a piece of glass embedded inside. I am horrified when I pull the thing out and it's almost an inch long! Immediately, I take off my sock and as I do so blood starts oozing out of the puncture wound. I reach into my pack and grab my first-aid kit and proceed to clean and bandage the wound as best I can right there. This is the first time I've had to use the medical supplies (besides the blister kit), and at this moment I am very grateful I have it. I clean the wound as best I can with water and disinfectant, and then bandage it up with gauze and duct tape.

Once back on my feet again the first few steps are painful. But, like a batch of fresh blisters, once your feet get into a rhythm the pain isn't so bad. On the paved trail today I pass through several metro parks into the very heart of Dayton, Ohio. At one of them I stop in at a picnic table for a break and make a phone call. On the other end is Brent, works for Five Rivers Metro Parks. He is the contact Andrew gave me regarding getting my pack looked at. Brent has been expecting me and is glad to hear that I made it to Dayton. I tell him my pack situation and he says he and his coworker will meet me in Eastwood Metro Park.

With plans in place, I continue on through Dayton, even arriving at the entrance to downtown right as the large fountain goes off. I snap many pictures and stop for a few minutes to admire the water show. From this point the trail turns away from downtown and heads east along the river, and soon I am in Eastwood Metro Park.

Within a few moments I see two people walking toward me down the trail, Brent and his coworker Angie. We walk together for awhile toward the trailhead where their vehicle is parked. I planned on taking a short day today and getting a motel in town as there happened to be one right off the trail about a mile ahead. Brent says he'll hike there with me, and Angie will take my pack and bring the car up to the motel. She snaps a photo of me in front of the NCT/Buckeye Trail sign, and then Brent and I head down the trail. It takes us all of about fifteen minutes to hike to the end of this section right on the river, coming out right behind a Comfort Suites Motel. Well, this is convenient.

We head on inside to the lobby and Angie is there with the pack. Brent knows some people at GoLite as he used to work in the backpack business. He makes a call. Through some negotiation he manages to get my pack to the top of a long waiting list for maintenance. On top of that, he has about five packs of his own that he no longer uses and says I'm welcome to use any one of them until mine gets repaired and sent back to me. Wow, this is just incredible.

We make plans to meet here again tomorrow morning. Brent and Angie need to head back to work and I head upstairs to my room. After a nice shower I take a good look at my foot. The wound appears to have closed and there are no signs of infection. I'll keep an eye on it over the next week and watch for any color changes. In hind sight, it probably would have been smart to go to the hospital right away for a tetanus shot, but so far it looks okay.

Next, I order some dinner to be delivered to the room, then I spend the good part of an hour making some travel arrangements. You may notice that I have not taken a zero-mile day since Marquette. So far I have taken one day roughly every 500 miles, so I am well overdue for one as I've come more than 1,000 miles since my last one.

Part of the reason I have not, is that a few days from now I plan on taking a brief break from the trail. My good friends Tony and Ashley are getting married next weekend, and I have decided to fly back to Minnesota for their special day. I couldn't commit until now because I had no idea where I would be. But now it is only a week away and I will be within range of Cincinnati. I had planned ahead and posted a request on the Buckeye Trail group page about volunteers for a possible shuttle, and I got a few responses.

In my motel room I am on the phone with Byron, trail supervisor of the Old Man's Cave Section. He volunteered to pick me up and drive me to the airport. He knows a fellow hiker on the outskirts of Cincinnati he can leave me at, and they can take me to the airport the following morning. With plans in place, I purchase my ticket online and then spend the rest of the night relaxing. Short days like this are nice when you've gone over 1,000 miles with no rest.

Friday, August 2
Trail Day 124
Miles hiked: 24
Oldtown Reserve north of Xenia, OH – BT

Another continental breakfast to kick off my morning, and then Brent and Angie are back in the lobby with a few packs. I find a Gregory that fits pretty well, but it's quite a bit smaller, so I actually have to ditch some of my gear. I hand my pack off to Brent and he will send it in to GoLite headquarters to get repaired. *Thanks for all your help Brent and Angie. You've done this hiker a great service and made Dayton a nice memory.*

It's another hot day here in southern Ohio, and the entire hike is along roads and paved trails. I pass through the town of Fairborn to the east of Dayton, and then take a temporary turn away from the blue blazes. When Nimblewill Nomad came through in 2009, the NCT continued all the way to Springfield. But, since then that section has been abandoned. Luckily for me, it allows me to cut off a good chunk of mileage and avoid going in the opposite direction.

I get back on the trail a little ways north of Yellow Springs, a very fine trail town if there ever was one. There are lots of little Mom 'N Pop places to eat ,but unfortunately the place is mobbed with people and long lines. I end up having dinner at a place called the Corner Cone.

I don't linger in town long as I still have a few miles to go and it is already late evening. As I'm hiking south out of town where the trail parallels the road, I hear someone call out in load voice, "Strider!!!!!!!" I turn to see a jeep pass by, slam on the breaks, do a U-turn, then pull up on the side of the road. Out the door and running down the hill to meet me is Dave, on his way home from work. He has been following my progress on Facebook for awhile and instantly recognized me when I was walking by.

Apparently, meeting me is the highlight of his day. He snaps a picture and wishes me luck as he jumps back in his jeep and moves along. I continue on until I come to Oldtown Preserve to the north of Xenia just before dark. I pull off into the trees and pitch for the night.

Saturday, August 3
Trail Day 125
Miles hiked: 29
Morgan's Riverside Campground – Little Miami Scenic Trail (BT)

I'm up at first light this morning and stop in the grocery store in Xenia for some breakfast. After downing my fruit and muffins, I continue on down the trail. Here in town the trail comes to a confusing junction at a place called Xenia Station. The trail can go one of many ways, but none of them are explicitly marked as the BT or the NCT.

I study my map closely, trying to figure out which way is the correct one before ultimately deciding on a direction. Luckily for me I chose wisely, and make my way to the next trail junction on the edge of Caesar Creek State Park. At this point the Buckeye Trail heads off the paved trail and through the park and the NCT continues south along the bike trail.

I pass through the towns of Spring Valley and Waynesville and eventually toward Fort Ancient Memorial where I begin to look for a place to camp. Within a few miles, I spot a campground across the river and luckily there is a road bridge up ahead that I can use to get to it. I check my map and decide that this must be Morgan's Riverside Campground. I head on in and get a tent site right on the river for tonight.

After setting up camp, I head back over to the concession stand and order a rib sandwich for dinner. As I am enjoying my food at the picnic table nearby, the woman at the stand asks me many questions. She saw my pack when I checked in and has many questions about my travels. Hence, I meet Lauren, co-owner of the campground. With the Little Miami Scenic Trail and the BT/NCT right across from the campground they get plenty of hikers and bikers in here every summer. I am surprised that she has never heard of the NCT. I tell her that it follows the Buckeye Trail through most of Ohio, but that it starts way back in North Dakota and ends in New York. Many questions follow and I give the usual story of my trek so far.

After I finish eating it is well past nightfall, so I say goodbye to Lauren and head back to my campsite. Just as I am about to enter my tent I see movement at the edge of the bushes. I shine my light in the direction and find a raccoon scurrying through my campsite. I chase it off, and finally head into my tent and drift off to sleep.

Sunday, August 4
Trail Day 126
Miles hiked: 25.5
Terrell Park Shelter – Milford, OH

I awoke early, determined to have a quick breakfast and hit the trail right away. I open my odor-proof food sack and find my daily ration pack missing. I always keep the food that I will need for the day in the side pocket of my pack and I always put it with the rest of my food in the stuff sack at night. Then, I suddenly realize what happened. Last night I completely forgot to put my food for the next day in the stuff sack, so I left it in the side pocket of my pack. That's why the raccoon was in my camp last night! Those little buggers came and stole my food for today in the middle of the night. Realizing it was just a dumb mistake, I don't think too much about it and simply transfer some food into a Ziploc bag for the day. I will just need to replace my daily food sack at the next opportunity.

The Little Miami bike Trail is packed with bikers today. I would be willing to bet that at least 1,000 people pass me by the end of the day. In Loveland, I stop for lunch at Paxton's Restaurant for a great burger. The lovely hostess Carissa, makes sure I'm well hydrated on this hot August day and makes friendly conversation. After awhile, a couple sitting at the table behind me come over and ask me a few questions. They overheard my conversation with Carissa and are curious about my journey over the NCT.

Hence, I meet Barb and Tom. They know many people that have hiked the AT over the years so they are very intrigued that a sister trail comes right through Ohio. I really enjoy sharing the trail with people as I hike along. It's nice seeing such positive reactions when they find out this amazing resource passes right through their backyards and they didn't even know about it. It's a great feeling to know that many folks will now get out for at least a day and go for a walk in the woods and enjoy this national treasure.

After gorging myself with the fantastic meal I hit the trail again. Many more bikes pass by, though the numbers are thinning now that evening is coming on. At some point a woman sees me with my big pack on and asks me a few questions. Hence, I meet Heather, a Buckeye Trail member and volunteer. She figured I was most likely doing a thru-hike of the BT, but is blown away when I tell her No, in fact I am thru-hiking the NCT. She wishes me luck on the rest of my trek and continues on down the trail. Not a mile further down I have a similar encounter with Betty, a local just out for an evening walk. (People sure are curious when you walk through a populated area with a giant pack on.)

By the end of the evening, I reach the town of Milford, my destination for today. Milford has the designation of being a crossroads for many thousands of miles of trails and the only official trail town for the BT at this time. From here the Little Miami Trail continues south about twelve more miles, to a park in downtown Cincinnati. The NCT turns east and crosses the river through Milford and along the southern tier; sometimes seemingly only a stone's throw away from the Kentucky border.

Milford is often called "Trail Town USA", as supposedly over 20,000 miles of trails converge here. The Buckeye Trail, North Country Trail, American Discovery Trail, Sea-To-Sea Route, Little Miami Trail, and Underground Railroad Cycling route are the more popular ones locally among a few others. To take advantage of this unique designation, the city has built an Adirondack Shelter right in town at the small city park where I set up camp for the night. It's amazing to think that I have hiked almost 3,000 miles on this trail and this is only the third shelter I've stayed in.

Monday, August 5
Trail Day 127
Miles hiked: 23
East Fork Lake State Park - BT

I had a comfortable night of sleep in the shelter last night. It was surprisingly quiet, despite being right in the middle of a town with a busy highway nearby. For breakfast I head downtown to the local diner. There are a few locals inside, otherwise the entire town is still asleep. The outfitter right on the Main Street is still closed when I leave the diner. I was told by many BTA folks that I should stop in when I get to Milford, but it looks like I won't get the chance.

I follow the blue blazes along the sidewalks to the edge of Milford where I come to a newly constructed off-road segment. I follow it as it zigzags around what appears to be an abandoned farmstead along a nice mowed path. It comes to end of the segment as it dumps back out onto the road near the school. From here it is a roadwalk all the way to East Fork Lake State Park where I plan to spend the night.

The roadwalk along Round-Bottom Road is very dangerous. There is no shoulder and I have to stop every thirty seconds and pull off into the ditch. Many places are filled with poison ivy to give the autos a clear space to pass. In many places there is no ditch at all, just a guardrail. And on the other side, a steep drop of more than fifty feet down into a gully.

During a lull in the traffic, a car pulls up next to me and a woman asks. "Are you hiking the Buckeye Trail?" I respond that I am hiking part of the Buckeye Trail on my way to thru-hike the NCT. Hence, I meet Laura, who hiked the AT a few years ago and is familiar with the NCT. She offers me a ride as she tells me this road is incredibly dangerous. I respond that I would like to but I really can't as I need to hike every section of trail to the best of my ability. She understands completely and tells me to stop in at the Cincinnati Nature Center up the road a ways where she works if I need a break. Thanks Laura, I will do that.

Not even ten minutes after Laura drives away, the traffic flow increases again and I almost get hit by a car...twice missing me by mere inches! One idiot actually swerves closer to me and turns away at the last second. I don't know what the BTA was thinking when they routed the trail onto this road, but I need to get off it as quickly as possible. Man, if I would have known this road was this dangerous I might have taken Laura up on her offer for a ride.

Finally, I see the sign for the Nature Center, and anxious to get off this road, I cross and head on up the hill to the nature center for a rest. Unfortunately, this road isn't much better, but the amount of traffic is much smaller. Soon I arrive at the gate and the woman at the toll booth tells me to head on in. As I make it to the parking lot, Laura is there and walks with me into the visitor center.

At the desk, I am greeted by Lester and soon another employee, Paula, walks over with a camera to take my picture. I take off my gear and rest for a bit while I make conversation with the employees at this fine establishment. Laura mentions that she once tried to get in touch with the BTA about possibly bringing the trail through the nature center to avoid most of the dangerous roadwalk. They already have a system of hiking trails and even have some abandoned bunkhouses that could possibly be restored to allow hikers a place to stay. If nothing else, it may be possible to build a shelter at the same site or even just a place to camp.

I am glad to hear that she is interested in making this place accessible to hikers and I will definitely pass on the information to the BTA once I get to their office in Shawnee. Soon a man walks over and Laura introduces us. Hence, I meet Bill, the executive director of the Nature Center. Paula takes a few photos of the three of us together for their newsletter and then I spend a few more minutes relating the story of my hike to everyone present.

After an hour at the center, I need to hit the road again, so I fill up all my water bottles and even receive some trail magic from the staff. Lester hands me five dollars to help with my hike, Paula offers me some left-over brownies from a meeting this morning, and Laura hands me a Hershey bar from the vending machine. Kind folks here indeed.

Laura can't be gone for too long but she does offer to drive me back down to Round-Bottom Road, which I gladly accept to avoid backtracking on the narrow road. I find out on the short drive that she hiked the AT with her husband a few years ago and that she too has a trail name, "Sundance." As I unload my gear from her car she wishes me luck and turns back around to work. *Thanks for all your help Laura, I appreciate it.*

I follow the roadwalk into Batavia where there is supposed to be a grocery store. I originally had a food drop here, but since I will only be on the trail for three more days before taking a break, it didn't really make sense to send an entire box. I decided to just buy three days' worth of food here in Batavia. Unfortunately, I find out that I was given bad information and that the main part of town, where I am now, does not have a grocery store...only a post office! Batavian residents happen to live several miles south of here in a residential area where all the stores are located. So, I need to take a detour several miles out of the way to reach the grocery store in Amelia.

It's a scenic walk to get there, and then the hike through Amelia is the sidewalk adjacent to a busy highway. There is a Walmart here, so I head on in and pick out enough food to last three days. I end up lingering in town a little too long and don't make it to

East Fork Lake State Park until nearly dark. I don't have enough time to make it to the backcountry campsite, so about a mile and half into the park I pull off the trail and pitch for the night in the trees nearby.

Tuesday, August 6
Trail Day 128
Miles hiked: 25
Home of John and Theresa - Williamsburg, OH

The trail through East Fork Lake State Park starts off decent past the first campsite and the first trailhead. The rest of the day is hit or miss depending on the section. Much of the trail within the park is open to multiple use, and is in really bad shape from some recent horse traffic in wet conditions. The going becomes painfully slow over deeply-rutted trail and some poorly marked intersections.

I take a wrong turn several times by the end of the day. Along some intersections today, I see the first markings for the American Discovery Trail that coincides with the BT for about 300 miles through southern Ohio, from Milford clear through the Wayne National Forest. At one point the trail leaves the woods and wanders straight through a farmer's cornfield. I feel very out of place, thinking for sure I have taken another wrong turn. However, as I am bushwhacking through the corn, I soon come to a small clearing in the middle of the field with a few small rocks. One of them has a blaze painted right on it.

By sheer dumb luck, it appears I have managed to stay on the trail in an area with no markings—save this one lonely blaze. Eventually, I do manage to find the trail again where it enters the woods, by using only my instinct and gut feeling as a guide. To add to the confusion, in a lot of places the trail is crossed by large cobwebs. I have to stop several times to clear the sticky stuff off my gear and trekking poles. By the end of the day, as I emerge onto the road from the woods, I feel like I have just passed through the forest of Mirkwood and the webs of the giant spiders from Tolkien's great work.

Back on the road, I come to an intersection and realize I have taken yet another wrong turn. I had intended to take the alternative route into Williamsburg for some dinner, but instead ended up taking the shorter route that completely bypasses the town. With much frustration I backtrack over a mile to Williamsburg where I stop for dinner at Grandmas Pizza. Afterward, I head up to the gas station to refill my water once again, as today was another hot day and I have consumed most of my supply.

On the way out of town I decide to linger at the bar for awhile and charge my devices. While there I study my map to look for a possible place to pitch tonight. After my first beer, a man at the table across from me asks where I'm headed. Hence, I meet John and his wife, Theresa. They are familiar with the Buckeye Trail, as it is currently routed on the road right in front of their house down the street. I find out that they have a son and daughter who did the AT a few years ago. They are very enthusiastic when I tell them my story and that the BT is just a small part of my journey to Vermont from North Dakota.

John offers to buy me another beer, an offer I can't refuse. Theresa asks me where I'm planning on staying tonight. I tell her that I'm not sure, but the only spot that looks feasible is the city park across the river. She responds by telling me I am welcome to spend the night at their home. I accept her offer and thank them both tremendously.

It's pretty late when they are ready to head out so I load my gear into the car and get a ride to their place. I bring my gear inside and set it by the door. John and Theresa say I'm welcome to use the shower and they will set up a mattress for me in one of the spare rooms. I don't hesitate one second. After a shower, I settle down onto a soft mattress on the floor. It feels nice to be clean again.

Wednesday, August 7
Trail Day 129
Miles hiked: 27
City Park Gazebo - Russellville, OH

I slept in a little later than I would have liked, but I needed a little extra sleep after staying up late last night. Theresa is up right behind me and cooks me some eggs and bacon for breakfast. Afterward, I take a few minutes to change back into my dirty hiking clothes and I find some trail magic in the top of my pack (a package of licorice, and some granola bars). *Thank you John and Theresa, it was a pleasure meeting you.*

Another humid day as I continue on my way through southern Ohio. The entire day is a roadwalk except for a short segment near a historic covered bridge. By the end of the day, I make it to Russellville where I stop in at the local bar for dinner. The server asks me many questions about my hike and asks where I'm planning on staying. I respond that I have no idea. She suggests that I could sleep in the gazebo at the park next door and no one would bother me. She even takes the extra step to notify the sheriff that I will be staying there just so they know.

She says it won't be a problem, and I can feel free to set up there once I leave. She also says she will be here early and invites me to come back for breakfast, on the house. Wow this is incredible, I will definitely be back tomorrow!

251

I leave the bar and head to the gazebo in the city park next door. I unroll my sleeping pad right on the floor and prop my gear against the wall and settle in for a night of sleep in my gazebo shelter.

Thursday, August 8
Trail Day 130
Miles hiked: 17.5
Home of Bruce and Denise "Ladybug" - Cincinnati, OH

I had a bit of a restless sleep last night; lots of semis driving through town all night long. I still managed to get up early and head back to the bar for breakfast—on the house as promised. Leaving Russellville, the hike is once again entirely a roadwalk to Bentonville where I end my hike for the day. I had arranged for Byron to pick me up here and bring me to Cincinnati to board a plane first thing in the morning. (The plane would get me back to Minnesota for my friends' wedding.)

There is nothing here but a vending machine outside an apartment, right where the two roads come together. Luckily, the apartment has free WiFi, so I grab a soda from the vending machine and enjoy some time browsing videos on Youtube after answering some emails while I wait for Byron to arrive.

Around 3 p.m. Byron pulls up in his car and we meet face to face. I load my gear into his car and we head to Cincinnati where we will have dinner with a local hiker who will bring me to the airport in the morning. We spend time talking trail on the way there. Byron gives me a heads up on what to expect on the upcoming sections of the BT leading up to his section through Hocking Hills. It sounds like some sections between here and there are in rough shape.

We pass through Milford where I was only a few days ago, and shortly before dinner time we arrive to the outskirts of Cincinnati where I will be spending the night. At the door we are greeted by Denise, aka "Ladybug". She's a 2011 BT thru-hiker and Byron's friend. She gives a quick tour of her home before her husband Bruce arrives with dinner. Ladybug has also thru-hiked the AT and PCT as well as part of the CDT before an injury forced her off the trail.

The room I am standing in now is filled with everything for the hiker; maps on the walls, books on the shelf; all related to hiking America's great trails. Shortly afterward, Bruce arrives with dinner and Ladybug introduces us. The menu tonight is take-out from Skyline, a Cincinnati tradition. I get a double order of the delicious stuff pasta and fries drizzled with melted cheese, a hiker's dream.

After dinner, Byron has to head back home, but says he will definitely see me again as I hike through the Hocking Hills region. *Looking forward to it Byron, thanks so much for your help.* Afterwards it's time for me to get cleaned up and enjoy a nice evening with a fellow hiker. On top of the beer I had with dinner, Ladybug was prepared for my arrival and has many sodas in the fridge just for me.

We spend a good while at the table talking trail, about my NCT thru-hike attempt so far, and about her own experiences on the AT and PCT. I thank Ladybug tremendously for allowing me to stay here tonight, and for letting me stash my gear here while I'm away for three days. I turn in for bed early as I will have to get up quite early for a morning flight to Minneapolis.

Friday, August 9
Trail day XXX
Miles hiked: 00
Strider's Family Home – Minnetrista, MN

I'm up at 5 a.m., and Bruce has me at the airport by 5:30 a.m. where I have about an hour to catch up on journals. My short trip this morning actually allowed me to cross into another state on this journey. The Cincinnati International Airport is actually a few miles across the river in northern Kentucky, another state I have never been to. So I get to cross another one off my list.

The flight from here to Minneapolis is pretty short, and when I arrive Roxanne is there to pick me up. She is happy to see me and we talk about my travels and recent developments here in Minnesota. When we arrive at the old family farm I actually feel out of place. This is my first time in my house since I left for Lake Sakakawea way back in March, over four months ago. Everything somehow seems small and close together, even the trees outside seem like they're encroaching on the house. It's a very strange feeling and one I did not necessarily expect.

There are lots of goodies waiting for me as I look through the cupboards and the fridge—fresh fruit, candy, pie, you name it. I don't think my family quite realized I was only going to be here for a day and a half, but I'll try to consume as much of it as I can while I'm here.

Right around noon, Karlee pulls into the driveway and stays for a long visit. We enjoy a nice chat in the yard waiting for lunch to be served. We spend a good deal of time talking about my recent experiences in southern Michigan and Ohio, and about her recent trip overseas to Croatia. After lunch, the conversations continue until about 4:30 p.m. when more people start showing up. First my dad comes home from work, followed shortly by Matt and

Trevor, all excited to see me.

Around dinner time a few friends, relatives, and neighbors come over for a campfire cookout while I tell of my travels since leaving four months ago. Many questions and much laughter follows as I recount the highlights (and lowlights) of the hike and how much further I still have to go. Based on the maps, I estimated that when Byron picked me up in Bentonville I was right around the 3,000 mile mark, which means I'm 2/3 of the way thru.

After dinner, a few people head back to their own homes gearing up for a busy weekend. Around 6 p.m., Karlee says goodbye once again and I'm reminded of the day she left back on the SHT at the Fox Farm Road trailhead, where this long journey I'm on had its roots over three years ago. The same sad emotions come to the surface as I say goodbye, and after a long hug she is gone.

Back at the fire there are a few of us left; my family and a few friends from high school. Our good friend, Josh came up all the way from Iowa just to touch base with me and hang out with us for a bit. Some of us end up talking late into the night and my planned day of rest turned out to not be a day of rest at all. I don't get to bed until after 2 a.m. Despite my derailed plans for recovery, I have a feeling this will be a night I will remember long into my years.

Sunday, August 11
Trail Day XXX
Miles hiked: 00
Home of Bruce and Denise "Ladybug" – Cincinnati, OH

I'm back in Ohio after a nice weekend in Minnesota. It was a gorgeous wedding I attended on Saturday, and I was grateful to be able to see my two best friends start their lives together. Most of my closest friends from college were there as well, so it was a nice change of pace from the day-to-day grind of the trail. There was a lot to catch up on after being absent for four months. *Dear friends, I'm glad I was able to be there for your special day.*

I spent the night with friends and left for home the next morning, just in time to take care of some last-minute planning for the remainder of the hike. I enjoyed listening to music on my Zune in the car on the way home, it never sounded so good after being basically absent for four months. Also the feeling of driving a car 70 mph on the freeway for the first time in four months was definitely a strange experience.

I got to spend a few more hours with my family before catching my flight back to Cincinnati. Bruce was there at the airport right at 7:00 to pick me up, and we headed back to his place for another home-cooked meal. After looking over some maps with Ladybug and packing my gear to prepare for the trail tomorrow, I head off to sleep.

Monday, August 12
Trail Day 131
Miles hiked: 25
Pavilion at House of God Church & Cemetery near Shawnee State Forest

I didn't get near enough sleep last night. I down an entire box of cereal before loading my gear into Bruce's car and heading for Bentonville. Despite downing most of a soda after breakfast, I am still incredibly tired and end up sleeping most of the way there. Before I know it we arrive at the intersection with the vending machine—the only landmark in town. I shoulder my pack, Bruce snaps a picture of me and shakes my hand, as he wishes me luck.

Then, I turn and begin the roadwalk toward the Shawnee State Forest.

The entire day is a roadwalk through hilly country. Before long it is clear that I have entered Appalachia and the foothills of the famous mountain range. There are lots of angry dogs to fend off today as I pass farmhouse after farmhouse. These trekking poles are great for efficiency and balance while hiking, but in times like this they also double as a weapon. I get by unscathed by the dogs and continue along the narrow winding roads. I end the day at a church with a picnic shelter nearby where I decide to spend the night. Across the street is the entrance to the Shawnee State Forest, where tomorrow morning I will enter and make my way to the next off-road segment of trail.

Today has been a strange day. I thought I would be more excited to be back on the trail, but today is somehow different. After spending three days back home with the best people I've ever known, and to come back here to southern Ohio where so far the trail, it has been less than ideal with little redeeming value made for an ugly transition. For the first time I'm not looking forward to the next section of trail. Instead, I'm looking back on the places I've been so far; places like the Manistee National Forest, Pictured Rocks National Lakeshore, and Porcupine Mountain Wilderness State Park.

I'm picturing my first day on the trail at Lake Sakakawea State Park and the snowy transition I had to make to finally reach the Superior Hiking Trail. It was there that I set my eyes on Lake Superior once again, the setting of so many fond memories. I remember what it felt like to see a friend come up to the cabin to visit me, how it felt to see them leave, and that I've missed them every day since then. Today, that feeling was deeply amplified and I just feel empty inside.

Tuesday, August 13
Trail Day 132
Miles hiked: 28, +5
BTA property off Mt. Unger Road

Despite getting to bed early last night, I slept in this morning later than I should have. I down a quick breakfast and head across the street to the Shawnee State Forest. After a short roadwalk, I reach the access point for the off-road trail and find it to be over grown. There is a bypass route intended for horses that would take me around this section directly to a campsite, and would save me half a day of hiking. But, I head on in and give the trail a try. There are lots of blowdowns to contend with on this section and I'm on the lookout for snakes. The first few miles are not in the best shape, but after awhile the trail becomes better maintained.

After the first road crossing the trail changes drastically. Bull dozers have been in here recently and have widened the trail to about eight feet. There are also no switchbacks on this section; the bulldozers simply drove right up the mountains and back down again. I say mountains here because that's exactly what they are. This region of Ohio includes the foothills of the Appalachian Mountains and are known locally as the "Little Smokies." The name fits, as many of the over-looks provide a great sweeping view but in the distance the view becomes hazy.

At the base of the first climb, I am surprised to see a water spigot in the middle of the woods. There is no campground nearby or anything, it's just here by itself. After the first climb I can tell this will be a tough section. The trail heads straight up the bulldozer track and straight down the other side. This goes on for many miles until I reach the edge of Shawnee State Park, where I stop at a picnic table to take a break and cook dinner. There are a few people enjoying the park today, most of them walking or fishing.

As I pass through, I look straight ahead at the mountain in front of me and after reaching the entrance head on in, and up. After a few miles I come to a confusing intersection along on old road. I take out my map and figure out where I am. I decide that I need to turn left here. A few miles further it has become apparent that I made the wrong turn. With no blazes or markings on the trail whatsoever, I had mistakenly misplaced my position on my map and walked in the completely wrong direction.

After almost two hours, I am standing at a point I have already passed once, near the road crossing. Well this is just great! It's going to be dark in a few hours and I now have to re-hike a very challenging section and hope that I don't get lost *again*. I wish I would have taken the bypass route. If I had known how poorly marked this section was I may have done that to save myself this frustration and heart break.

I decide to head back down to the parking lot and refill my water before attempting to continue on. Frustrated, I take one last look at my map and prepare to head out. Just then, a fisherman walks by on the way to his car to head home for the day. He asks where I'm hiking, and I explain my situation. I told him how I was supposed to make it to a campsite, but now I have no idea where I'll be because I wasted two hours walking in the wrong direction. He tells me to show him on the map. After he realizes where I'm headed, he tells me to get my gear, he'll drop me off at the other end of the road. Wow, this is great!

Assuming the road is clear, I can get dropped off very close to the point where I initially took the wrong turn and continue on from there. This will save me lots of backtracking. It takes us awhile to get there by car, all the roads are very windy and narrow. We make conversation as we go, I tell him why I'm out here and my ultimate goal of reaching Vermont. As I explain where I've been through Ohio so far, he makes a few comments. He asks if I have a snake bite kit, to which I respond "No."

"Ohio is really bad for that. You need to watch your step," he said. That's very curious because I've been watching where I step constantly, particularly since leaving Milford, and have seen no evidence of snakes anywhere up to this point. He also makes sure I know that this part of Ohio does have black bears, which a lot of people don't realize. I didn't know for sure, but I have been hanging my food just in case. It turns out that my driver, Tyler, is a fisherman and hunter. He is very knowledgeable about Ohio wildlife and thus, knows so much about the snake bite issue and the bear population.

Before too long we start seeing blazes along a narrow gravel road so I know we're on the right track. Eventually, we reach a junction with an old road that has to be where the trail comes out. Tyler drops me off here and wishes me luck as he drives away.

I am now very close to where I got lost in the first place and I have many miles to go to reach a legal camping spot on a piece of BTA property on Mt. Unger Road. I manage to make it there just after darkness descends, and I have to set up my tent with my headlamp on. No time to hang my food tonight, so I find a low branch in a cluster of trees and hang it so it is at least off the ground away from my tent. Today was a very long and frustrating day...I'm glad it's over.

Wednesday, August 14
Trail Day 133
Miles hiked: 23
Woodlot behind high school - Peebles, OH

The hike today is mostly a roadwalk and quite an eventful one. Right off the bat this morning I have a short walk down a narrow gravel road from the BTA property to the small berg of Wamsley. On the way there I pass a home with many animal cages. As soon as I come into view, I know instantly that they are all filled with dogs. I count at least twenty-five; each of them barking loudly and darting back and forth as I pass by. To make matters worse, I soon discover that not all of them are chained up.

Before I know it, the five largest ones are out in the road to intercept me. They come at me in two groups, one group of three and one pair. The pair jumps out in front of me trying to cut me off as I turn to face the group of three. I manage to slip through a small gap between them and the edge of the road using my trekking poles as extensions of my arms. I turn to face them all as one group as they try to circle me, now growling and showing their teeth.

I respond in the only logical way; I mirror their behavior, not showing any fear. I show my own teeth and make loud growling noises. This face-off continues for a good five minutes as I slowly hike backwards down the road, not to take my eyes off the aggressive attackers. Finally, after having metal poles swat at their faces for long enough, they give up and walk back to their home. Whew! Of all the wildlife encounters I've had so far, this was probably the most dangerous.

From Wamsley it is a long roadwalk on country roads (still with no shoulder) all the way to Davis Memorial. This turns out to be a very cool place. It's a state unit owned by the Ohio Historical Society that contains a network of natural dolomite formations with groves of cedars, and surrounded by groves of native bamboo. It's a pool of incredible diversity. I never even knew bamboo occurred naturally outside the tropics. I take a break at the stone shelter at the far end of the park to get rehydrated and have some lunch before continuing.

After a short walk along the gravel road the trail heads back into the woods on another bulldozed trail. The climb is very steep and I need to take a break halfway up. At the top the trail flattens out and follows the ridge line for a way before dipping back down into the next valley. At this point, the blazes stop and I get turned around again. I walk back and forth a few times to try and find any evidence of the trail. It would be easy just to follow the skid trail, the only problem is at this point there is more than one of them.

There has been a recent logging operation up here on the ridge and many paths converge in the clearing. I finally make a decision to follow my gut and take the straightest path down into the valley. The damage from the logging operation has not been cleaned up yet, as even on this skid trail I need to walk over, under, and around large blowdowns (or cut-downs). At the far end, I come to an opening in the trees and it brings me right to a back yard of a house. There is a woman nearby hanging laundry on a clothes line.

She looks over at me and I speak to her, "Am I still on the Buckeye Trail?" She responds, "Yup, you're in the right place." I thank her and continue walking across her yard until I pop around the house and spot a carsonite post right at the road edge. I head toward it and spot the Buckeye Trail logo right at the top. It looks like my gut was right, and I navigated the mess up on the ridge accurately...thank goodness!

From here, the rest of the day is a roadwalk into Peebles where I've got a food drop waiting. I arrive too late and will need to wait until tomorrow. With nothing left to do, I head down to the McDonald's for dinner and use their WiFi to find a place to camp. As darkness descends, I hike a mile and half to the wooded lot next to the high school and pitch for the night.

Thursday, August 15
Trail Day 134
Miles hiked: 25
Butler Springs Christian Camp

I'm up at first light and head to the post office to wait for my package. I cook myself breakfast in the parking lot while I wait and read a few pages of *Tolkien*. Once the post office finally opens, I waste no time in getting my package and hitting the road.

It is very hot today as I hit the pavement and head for Serpent Mound. On the way, I pass many houses and I spot a guy sitting in a lawn chair in his front yard. He sees me approaching and heads into his house. As I pass his driveway he comes back out with an ice cold bottle of water in his hand and hands it to me. "Here, you might need this today." I thank him for his kindness, hiking in this hot weather isn't the most fun.

Before too long I reach the entrance to Serpent Mound State Historic Site. The name speaks for itself, the main feature of this park is an ancient Native American earth work, a giant mound in the shape of a snake. The mound is certainly massive, I estimate it's about a half mile hike around it. Right in the park there is a fire tower where one can climb to the top and see the entire thing. I head up and get some great photos from the top.

After checking out the mound, I linger for awhile as I eat lunch, and then I leave the park on a newly-constructed piece of trail. Right next door is a property owned by the BTA where it is possible to camp. From what I hear, the plans are to build an Adirondack shelter here in the near future.

More trail magic as I hit the road again heading toward Sinking Springs. A guy mowing his lawn stops as I pass and hands me a cold bottle of water. I need to stop several times today and take a break from the heat, including a stop in Sinking Springs at the convenience store where I enjoy a cold drink and a slice of pizza. I finish the day by hiking through the off-road section of trail through Fort Hill State Memorial. More spectacular dolomite formations remind of the Davis Memorial I hiked through yesterday.

At the main parking lot I stop for a break and check my map. Fort Hill ends just up the trail a short distance, and the map shows a campsite located outside the boundary. I decide this would be a good place to stay tonight. Less than a mile from the parking lot the trail climbs a ridge, and I notice a spur trail going off to the right and I can see a structure down below. At a closer look it is revealed to be a ropes course. The ropes course I climbed at Wolf Ridge back home when I was a kid is much larger than the one I'm standing in front of now, but It triggers a memory. This must be the place on the map indicated by the campsite icon.

I continue down the trail and come out into a large clearing and see a full setup of recreation activities. This is clearly some sort of summer camp meant for kids. There are cabins across the clearing from where I am now, tennis courts, and bikes available for rent. I see a house so I head over and knock on the door. The owners of the resort are home and I explain that I am thru-hiking the trail and am wondering if I could camp here tonight. They point out a broad area between the road, and the shower house where it is pretty quite, and I can feel free to set up anywhere I want. I ask about the fee and they tell me not to worry about it, I can camp for the night free of charge. I thank them and find a spot on the lawn to pitch for the night.

I take a shower and cook my dinner under the nice shelter complete with patio furniture. It's nice to cook dinner on an actual table. I have enough quarters for a soda from the vending machine and enjoy a nice hot meal. I finish the night by reading a few pages of *Tolkien*, and finally settle into my tent for a night of sleep.

Friday, August 16
Trail Day 135
Miles hiked: 19.5
Pike Lake State Park

I'm up and back on the trail at first light. After crossing OH-41 the trail conditions are not as good, and I need to pay attention to stay on track. The hike today is very choppy; short sections of trail followed by short roadwalks. At one point early on the trail is not clearly marked, and I miss a turn along a roadwalk and end up taking a longer detour before I realize it.

Along the detour I pass by Cave Lake Family Campground where I stop in for a break on another very hot day. As I am sitting on the front porch of the camp office enjoying an ice cold Gatorade, I notice that my ankles appear very dirty and have a bunch of dark and red spots. I noticed this in the shower last night and was puzzled by it. I thought that any dirt would have come off and perhaps the red spots were tiny scabs from something. Suddenly, as I focus my eyes, I feel like one of the specks is moving. I pull it off to examine it. As I strain my eyes I can barely make out what appears to be tiny legs poking out from the sides. I have actually just pulled off a tick so tiny I thought it was a speck of dirt and didn't notice it until it started moving.

I don't recognize the tick as one I have seen before. It doesn't appear to be an ordinary wood tick, or a deer tick; it is far smaller than either of them. I start scratching to remove some of the dirt from my ankles, and within a few seconds I am horrified as the reality of my situation sinks in. There isn't dirt on my ankles at all, only tiny ticks, hundreds of them! No wonder they didn't come off in the shower, they're already bitten in, every single one of them. I start picking them off as best I could, but many of them are simply too small to grab with my finger nails.

Then I get an idea. I reach into my pack for some duct tape. With no other tool to use I rip off a large strip of tape, taped it to my ankle as tightly as possible, and then ripped it off in one swift motion. To my surprise it actually works! The tape is strong enough to remove many of the ticks. I spend the better part of an hour doing this before finally deciding to move on; determined that I have removed most of them. If there are any left they are impossible to see at the moment.

I hit the road again, following busy OH-124 (with no shoulder) for many miles to the small town of Latham. There is a gas station here where I head in and stock up on Gatorade. I have no idea how long those ticks where embedded into my skin, but there's a good chance they were there long enough to infect me with any disease they may have had. I need to stay well hydrated until I get to more populated areas in case any sickness comes over me. My cell phone has no signal here but there is a pay phone outside the gas station. You don't see many pay phones around anymore, but here is one in the middle of Appalachian Ohio. I take this opportunity to call home and inform Roxanne of my situation. I tell her not to panic, but to research every tick species in the Appalachian Mountain Region and send whatever she finds in my next food drop.

I get back on the trail north of Latham, but soon find myself in a maze of poorly-marked trail. To make matters worse, horses have been out here recently after a rain and the trail is just a mud hole. I can't tell which trail is the BT and which isn't, so I use my best judgment again and eventually find my way to the road that will bring a hiker into Pike Lake State Park. I soon pass a carsonite post marked with the BT sticker, so I didn't come out at the right spot, but at least I know I'm back on track now.

I reach the park campground and stop for a few minutes at the dam and study my map. If I hike a few more miles I can reach the Pike State Forest and pitch there for the night, instead of paying for a site within the state park. Just as I am about the leave, a woman flags me down. Hence, I meet Cheryl "Questseeker", currently thru-hiking the BT. She asked if I am the guy that's thru-hiking the NCT. When I respond that in fact I am, she is very excited. She brings me back to the campground where she introduces me to Dan and Ruth of New York, who were currently section hiking the whole NCT. They are shuttling Cheryl around on her thru-hike while they hike other sections on their quest to hike the whole trail. After a few stories, they offer to host me at their campsite tonight so I don't have to pay for my own. I accept their offer and set up my tent behind their van. We spend a good hour at the picnic table swapping stories and then at nightfall it's time to turn in.

Saturday, August 17
Trail Day 136
Miles hiked: 25.5
Home of Mike and Connie – Richmond Dale, OH

I'm up at a decent hour this morning and enjoy a nice breakfast with the kind folks that invited me to share their camp last night. Ruth and Dan tell me many stories of their own adventures over the NCT so far. They have done pretty much all of New York, and most of Ohio now. They are well on their way to achieving their goal. After breakfast it's time to leave, so I say goodbye to my new friends and head past the dam and up the trail.

The trail heading out of the park is in nice shape, but after about a mile or so it quickly deteriorates and becomes overgrown. It proves to be a very frustrating day overall. I find another hundred ticks around my ankles by the end of the day, and need to stop and remove with the ol' duct tape. Once I'm out of the Pike State Forest, I have a long roadwalk to a short segment of trail on private land. I can tell this segment is going to be rough going as it hasn't been cleared this year. But to get around it would be an impossibly long road-walk, so in I go.

This segment is the worst maintained trail I have encountered so far on this journey. It's short, but I spend the entire time fighting my way through rose bushes taller than myself, and waist-high poison ivy winding up many of the trees. By the end ,my arms and legs are severely scratched up from all the multi-flora rose bushes, an invasive species. At the end of the segment I have to scramble over a pile of debris at the edge of someone's field and follow a fenced corridor down to the highway. The only problem is at the very end of the corridor is a fence crossing with no stile, and right in front of it is a dog house with two large dogs chained up right on the trail.

As I approach, they see me and start barking up a storm. I'm not getting close to these guys, so I take a wide detour around the perimeter of the fence through the yard of the nearest house and follow their driveway down to the road. A short roadwalk brings me into the Scioto Trail State Forest, where I follow the bridle trail a short distance and then finish the day at a five-way road junction.

Yesterday, as I passed through Sinking Springs, I had a message from Bruce at NCTA HQ. A couple along the Scioto Trail section heard about me and offered to help out anyway they could. While I was in town I gave them a call and they agreed to pick me up at this road junction tonight and host me at their home. I am not waiting very long when a van appears and pulls over to the side of the road. Hence, I meet Mike and Connie, my hosts for the night. We load my gear into their van and head back to their home in Richmond Dale.

When we arrive, they show me around and direct me to the guest room in the basement where I will be staying. After a nice shower and the removal of a few more ticks, I head back upstairs for dinner. Mike and Connie have hosted many hikers over the years, most of them travelling westbound on the American Discovery Trail. They also hosted Andrew Skurka for Thanksgiving during his C2C hike back in 2004. Here, yet again, I am following the tracks of a previous thru-hiker.

We share many stories during the delicious meal and the question of my next food drop comes up. My next drop is in Londonderry, which I should reach tomorrow. The problem is, tomorrow is Sunday, so the post office will be closed. Luckily, Connie knows everyone at the post office and says she'll make some calls for me. After dinner Connie comes out with good news. She tells me she will run over to the post office first thing in the morning, someone will be there with my package.

This is truly amazing. Despite the harsh nature of the trail in Ohio I've had some of the best trail magic here...and when it is needed the most! *Thanks Connie.*

Sunday, August 18
Trail Day 137
Miles hiked: 25
Home of Joe – Blue Lick Road (BT)

Since I can't get my package until a little later this morning, there is no harm in sleeping in. Before leaving for the post office, Connie made a nice breakfast and I down it pretty quickly. When she returns with the package, it takes only a short time to rearrange my gear and then we load into the van again. Mike and Connie shuttle me back to the five-way intersection where they picked me up yesterday. So now, once again I say goodbye to some dear new friends, wonderful people along this NCT. "If you need anything in the next few days just give us a call." *Thanks Mike and Connie!*

The trail today starts off well maintained and very nice. There's very little underbrush to contend with. The decently maintained trail comes out to a road above the Scioto River and I've a short roadwalk across to reach the next segment at the base of Hang Gliders Hill. Getting to the top is no problem, but once I'm there I'm disappointed to once-again find a lack of maintenance. There are no markings up here, no blazes, and no visible tread.

I follow the only discernable path as I fight my way through eight-foot tall rose bushes. More bloody arms and legs as I slowly fight my way through. Soon the trail becomes lost in a thicket of these multi-flora monsters, and I am forced to turn back. I backtrack the way I came to the base of the hill and begin a long roadwalk around this section, eventually coming through Richmond Dale and Londonderry where I stop for a break.

This huge detour has wasted several hours of forward progress and it's almost dark now. I sit outside the gas station in Londonderry consuming a Gatorade, trying to figure out what I'm going to do tonight. I can't stay here, so I have no choice but to push on in the dark until I reach the state forest boundary outside of town. I reluctantly shoulder my pack and go. While passing by the local donut shop, a guy sees me and waves me over. His name his Monk, lives right on the BT just up the road. He offers me a place to camp in his yard.

He gives me directions on how to walk there, and before darkness falls I find my way down Blue Lick Road where I should be. The houses are numbered a little weirdly, so it's hard to tell which one is which. I single out the one I think must be Monk's and knock on the door. It turns out it is not the correct house, but I happened to knock on door of Joe, his son. Joe's wife answers the door and when I explain how I came to be here she invites me in. Joe comes out to meet me and says I can pitch in the yard outside.

It turns out I am not the first hiker who has stayed here; they've had many hikers pitch in their yard over the years. Joe's friend Scott is visiting this evening, so after I set up my tent he invites me inside for a few beers and I relax as I watch Joe and Scott battle it out on Wii Golf. They ask many questions about my hike as they play and seem very entertained by the adventures I've had. After enjoying a few drinks and some company, I thank Joe again for his hospitality and head out to my tent for some much-needed rest after this difficult day.

Monday, August 19
Trail Day 138
Miles hiked: 26
Hocking Hills State Park

Yesterday, as I was relaxing in Joe's house, he mentioned that he had recently been up the trail behind his property and into Tar Hollow State Forest and it was not in very good shape. He recommended not wasting my time with it and instead hike around until I reach the beginning of the Old Man's Cave segment. Not wanting to have a repeat of yesterday, I take his advice and hike up OH-327 on the edge of Tar Hollow and pick up the trail again where the Old Man's Cave Section begins.

The segment starts off on a bridge and a privately held road that has allowed access for hikers. At the top of the ridge, the unmaintained road intersects with an ATV trail and the BT follows this for a good distance before heading back to the road just north of Eagle Mills. The rest of the day is mostly a roadwalk and pretty uneventful, with the exception of a strange piece of trail art (a tree with every branch capped with an empty can of PBR). With all the places I've eaten at, all the bars I've stopped into, and now this. The PBR definitely appears to be the beer of the trail. Hiker trash beer.

On the far side of Pretty Run, as I am hiking across a lawn through a grove of black walnut trees, a car pulls up next to me. Hence, I meet Jamie, Byron's brother. He had heard I would be passing through here today and wanted to let me know that his place is available to stay at tomorrow. We make plans for him to pick me up at the end of the Old Man's Cave section. He hands me a piece of paper with his contact information on it and wishes me luck before driving off.

Soon the road walk descends into a valley and suddenly I feel like I'm in the north woods again. I have reached Hocking Hills State Park and I can tell this will be a special place. All around there are large hemlock trees, even a few cedars here and there. I haven't seen any conifers in this large of a cluster since leaving the Manistee National Forest. I appear to be in a small canyon, there are sheer sandstone cliffs and towers on either side of me.

Before long, I reach the trailhead for Ash Cave and stop here to have dinner. A few folks passing by on their way out stop to chat, wondering where I am headed. They all seem amazed when I tell them I walked here from North Dakota and still have two full states to go to reach my journey's end. One young couple offers me a fresh peach from their cooler before they load up their vehicle and drive away.

The park in Hocking Hills is gorgeous. The temperature is cooler in this canyon and there are caves and waterfalls all around. I take many pictures at Ash Cave before continuing on. The trail heads up a fine system of staircases and walkways to the top of the next ridge. As I reach the next parking lot, the sun is beginning to set rapidly and I find that a newly constructed barricade is across the BT here. A sign says that the trail is closed and to follow different trails around to Cedar Falls. I've had bad luck in Ohio so far when it comes to detours, so I decide to stick to the trail regardless of what the sign says. I hop the barricade and head on in a few hundred yards and find a spot off the trail to pitch for the night. I pick a cool flat spot right on the edge of a ravine with a sheer drop on two sides and after hanging my food nearby I am off to sleep.

Tuesday, August 20
Trail Day 139
Miles hiked: 27
Home of Jamie - near Logan, OH

Nobody bothered me last night in my spot on the rim of the ravine. I'm up at first light and hike the trail to Cedar Falls. I quickly see why this segment was closed. A bridge got washed out so now one must pick their way through a mess of boulders in a stream bed. The stream is now bone dry so it's very easy to pick my way through and I arrive at the other barricade with no problem and rejoin the open trail at Cedar Falls.

The trail through the park is well marked and I have no doubt this will be the highlight of Ohio, especially considering the condition of the other trail in southern Ohio. Before long I'm at Old Man's Cave with swarms of people running around, despite being a Tuesday. I stop here for awhile to have a snack and take some good photos. As I am sitting here at the edge of the small lake, a couple comes up and asks me some questions about my hike. Others nearby listen in as I tell my story. Hence, I meet Don and Pam. They live near Lisbon where there is some certified NCT and I will be hiking through there in a few weeks. Don hands me his contact info and offers to help out any way he can. Thanks so much Don.

On my way out of the park I stop at the visitor center concessions for an ice cream cone. It is hot again today, and from the park I've got a short roadwalk to the next section of trail through the Hocking State Forest. This section is just as gorgeous as the park itself. There are plenty of cool sandstone formations, cliffs, gorges and that north-woodsy feel. Some of the cliffs here are tall enough that there are some rock climbers out today. Unfortunately, there is also some horse damage on this section but otherwise it's a very well maintained and gorgeous trail.

The rest of the day is mostly a roadwalk with a few short off-road sections in between. There is a cool trail register of the ammo box variety that is painted blue and marked with the symbols of all three trails I am currently on: NCT, BT, ADT. I am a little behind schedule because of the heat today, and the last segment of trail across private land proves to be a challenge because it has not been mowed this year. I need watch my step and navigate around debris.

I finally make it to the church at the end of the Old Man's Cave Section where Byron and Jamie are waiting. We quickly load my gear into the vehicle and head to Jamie's house for the night. Byron orders a few pizzas for dinner, and after I'm done with a much-needed shower, I head to the kitchen where we wait for dinner to arrive.

Jamie recently got back from a hike of the AT, so we spend some time swapping stories. Byron is curious to hear about my adventures since he saw me last week. The weather is supposed to be brutal. The past few days were just the beginning of a massive heat wave that is supposed to linger over the area for at least a week. After hearing the bad news the pizza arrives and we spend the rest of the night relaxing.

Wednesday, August 21
Trail Day 140
Miles hiked: 21.5
BTA Office - Shawnee, OH

Yesterday, sometime before dinner, Byron put a call in to the BTA office to let them know that I will be passing through today. He told me they are ready to have me, and I can even spend the night if I want. This morning I am dropped off at the church where Byron and Jamie picked me up. We snap a few photos before we shake hands and I thank them for hosting me last night. I shoulder my pack and head down the road.

The day is mostly a roadwalk, paved roads until I reach the boundary of the Wayne National Forest, and then mostly gravel once I enter. The day starts off hot but before I make it to the first section of off-road trail the temperature drops rapidly and the sky turns dark. Within a few minutes a big thunderstorm rolls in as I hike along a wide gravel road. Up ahead is a pretty big exposed hill and lightning is flashing overhead. I decide it's time to take cover.

I bail off the road and head into the forest, a good fifteen-foot drop from the road bed. I struggle to find a clear spot to put my pack down away from the thorn bushes. I find one, sit on my pack, and wait for the lightning to pass. I'm in this spot for more than thirty minutes before the lightning gets far enough away that I can continue on. With my rain coat on I head back to the road in the pouring rain and hike on.

This road section isn't blazed very well and I miss a turn. I figure it out at the next junction and make my way back to the trail. At one point along this unintended detour, I pass by a trailer house a good distance off the road. I am startled when an angry dog, barking at the top of its lungs, comes charging out at me clear into the road. I have a few rocks in my pocket, and not wanting it to get close enough for me to use my trekking poles, I lob one and land it right in front of him. No sooner did this occur than an angry voice comes booming out from the trailer. The owner had seen the encounter and warned me not to throw another rock at his dog or it will, "get me in big trouble in these parts." Excuse me dude, but your dog acted aggressively while I was on a public road, I'm not just going to let him bite me!

Not daring to turn my back on the savage animal that's now staring me down, I continue walking down the road until it loses interest, and then I turn and pick up the pace. I'm not entirely sure over the sound of the rain, but I think I hear a door slam as soon as I turn my back. I have this strange feeling I'm being followed. I make a turn at the fork in the road, cross Salt Run on a bridge, and pick up the trail again there.

Just as I make the corner, some headlights come into view behind me. Not wanting to find out if it is the pissed-off dog owner, I make a dash for the trees and lunge myself a good distance into the brush and lie flat and still. The truck passes by and doesn't stop, if it was him he didn't see me. My mind is probably just going into survival mode, but for the first time on this trek part of me wishes I had a firearm or something to defend myself against potential encounters like this.

I slowly get up off the ground as the sound of the engine disappears and I continue on, with the nagging feeling I'm still being watched. I quickly dash across the road to the other side and pick up the trail once again. At the next road crossing I dash across again just as a bolt of lightning comes out of nowhere and hits the ridge right above me. The rain quickens again and right on the edge of a creek I stop once again and hunker down with my pack until the lightning passes. After forty-five minutes or so, the thunder and lightning pass on and I am finally able to keep going.

I start off trudging through three inches of water. I've got a few more miles to cover here in this part of the Wayne and once I hit busy OH-93, I bail off and follow the road into Shawnee where the BTA office is located. I find the place and knock on the door. It is after hours and no one appears to be around. I backtrack a little and make my way to the gas station and grab something to drink. As I am sitting outside, my phone rings. On the other end is Richard, GIS Coordinator for the BTA. He is wondering where I am, and I tell him that I just arrived in town and am waiting at the gas station. He will be here in a few minutes to pick me up.

Sure enough, in a few minutes a car pulls up and I meet Richard in person. We load my gear into his car and he shuttles me to the BTA office where I will be staying tonight; the top floor is actually an apartment where he currently lives. After I grab a shower, we head back down the gas station for some freshly-made subs and soda, and bring them back to the office for some trail talk. He is curious to hear my thoughts about the trail conditions so far and gets out his maps. I spend the next ten minutes pointing out all the areas where I had difficulty navigating because of poor blazing, unmaintained trail, or confusing intersections.

I also take the opportunity to inform him about my visit with the folks at the Cincinnati Nature Center and how Laura was interested in talking with the BTA to see if they could route the trail across the property. Richard's face lights up with excitement, it turns out he has been hoping that opportunity would come up for many years now. I guess someone just needed to be in the right place at the right time to make it happen.

I purchased most of my maps for this hike almost two years ago and many of the ones I have for the BT are the older additions. Richard takes a few minutes to print me off a new set of the areas I haven't been to yet, that are more up-to-date. After talking over the changes I head upstairs to the guest room and drift off to sleep.

Thursday, August 22
Trail Day 141
Miles hiked: 20
Home of Andrew and Claudia - Glouster, OH

Just as I am getting ready to leave this morning, Andrew comes into work. We spend awhile talking trail; he is interested in my feedback on the BT. He cringes as I relate my story of the tick infestation and how I am watching very closely for signs of sickness. He also informs me that the trail in the Marietta unit of the Wayne is not yet open. That, combined with the likelihood of me getting sick from a sudden tick illness along that stretch, I decide it would be safer to bypass the long roadwalk through Marietta, and instead take the alternate BT route through the AEP Recreation Lands.

If the thirty-five miles of trail in the Wayne is not open, then there is no point in walking 150 miles further on remote forest roads just to walk past it. Instead, I can instead hike almost forty miles of alternate existing trail that is in good shape with a shorter roadwalk and still end up at the same place. The past few days I've felt a little off, if I do get sick it's going to be sometime in the next four or five days. Being in the remote corner of the Wayne would be the worst possible place to be when it happens.

Andrew asks what my plans are for tonight and I tell him I can probably make it to Burr Oak State Park. He gives me his cell number and says I can stay at his house tonight if I can't make it there. Before leaving, we snap a picture in front of the historic building downtown and then Richard drives me back to the trail. After the first few miles, the rest of the day is mostly a roadwalk except for a small segment of trail through a horseback resort and a wildlife area. In a small unit of the Wayne outside Burr Oak State Park, I follow the last chunk of off-road trail to a stile crossing to find that a large tree has fallen on it and there is no way to get over or around it. Additionally, the fence is too high to climb over, so I have no choice but to turn around here and roadwalk around.

As I backtrack to where I left the road, I notice dark clouds overhead. I give Andrew a call; looks like I won't quite make it to the park after all. He says he'll pick me up near Tom Jenkins Dam in about an hour. To get around the impassable stile crossing I need to walk along busy OH-13, again with no shoulder. It starts to rain again a half hour into my trek to the dam, and just as I approach the entrance Andrew pulls into the driveway. What good timing!

We load my gear in the back and head for his house in Glouster. When I arrive, I am introduced to his wife, Claudia. My first order of business is to take a shower and then catch up on some emails before Claudia has dinner ready. Afterward, Andrew gets a call from Herb, one of the volunteers with the BTA. My pack has been repaired and Brent from Five Rivers Metroparks in Dayton has sent it to him to be delivered to me.

We make arrangements for Herb to meet me in Stockport day after tomorrow at the old hotel in town to make the exchange. I'll be getting my own pack back and handing off Brent's pack to Herb to be returned to him later. After handing up the phone and talking trail for a little while, Andrew sets up the fold-out couch in his living room and I drift off to sleep.

Friday, August 23
Trail Day 142
Miles hiked: 30
Home of Ken and Karen - Chesterhill, OH

This weekend is the BTA Annual meeting at the century barn in Deersville, so Andrew and Claudia will be dropping me off en route. After a nice breakfast, they shuttle me back to Jenkins Dam. I thank them for their hospitality, and after shaking hands they drive away.

A short walk from the dam I cross into Burr Oak State Park. Very pleasant scenery along the route today, right along the shore of the Burr Oak Reservoir. The trail is well maintained, a nice change of pace for southern Ohio, but it is pretty slippery from the rain. All the moisture from the storms doesn't help the heat situation at all as the humidity makes hiking in this heat unbearable. I need to stop frequently for breaks to stay hydrated.

Despite the nice scenery in this park, it brings back memories of passing through East Fork Lake State Park east of Milford. The reason… the cobwebs are back today and are just as thick (if not thicker) than they were back then. During my frequent breaks, I'm ripping the sticky netting off my body, my clothing, and my gear. At one point while hiking along, I feel something crawling on my neck. I reach back and pull a large clump of webbing off and am shocked when I inspect it. There, clinging to the strand of sticky web, is the unmistakable black widow! I always thought they were a southern species, but as I edit this, I have discovered there is a northern subspecies, and southern Ohio is along the edge of its range. I avoid getting bitten and watch myself more carefully after the discovery.

After leaving Burr Oak, the rest of the day is a roadwalk and I stop for a break at a place Richard told me about, a tall hill near a water tower with a pavilion. The heat wave is definitely back in full swing and I have a few text messages on my phone from Andrew regarding local trail angels who would be happy to help out. I also have a voicemail from Ken in Chesterhill. Apparently, he and Andrew talked last night and Ken wanted to offer to help out anyway he could. I give him a call back and he doesn't answer, but he did include his address in the message he left.

In a few hours I complete the roadwalk to Chesterhill, and easily locate Ken's home based on the information he left me in his message. I knock on the door and a woman answers. It's Ken's wife, Karen. She happily lets me in. She knew I may possibly be stopping by, and the first thing she does is sit me down at the kitchen table and bring a pitcher of ice water.

We talk for a few minutes before Ken comes in from his work on the guest house next door. It's a work in progress, not finished yet, so I will be sleeping in a guest room upstairs tonight. So I meet Ken in person, and we spend a good amount of time talking about my adventure and future plans for the trail. Ken tells me he hopes to host a section of trail and a campsite on his property in the near future for hikers to use.

Karen says she will have dinner ready soon, so the next thing I do is take a shower so I'm not completely disgusting during the meal. Once I'm finished, I'm treated to more ice water and a delicious dinner. The evening is concluded after much storytelling with good company. Afterward, I head upstairs to the guest room for a comfortable night of sleep.

Saturday, August 24
Trail Day 143
Miles hiked: 21
North of Onion Run Road - AEP Recreation Lands, BT

I sleep in a little this morning and then Ken shuttles me into Stockport to retrieve my next package. On the way back to his place we make a detour to a historic site. It is a little distance off the trail where the Indian Wars began. Ohio sure does have lots of history despite the poor trail conditions in some spots.

Back at Ken's house, Karen serves some extra food for breakfast, and after thanking them both tremendously for a lovely stay at their home I hit the road.

As I leave Chesterhill, I pass by the point where the ADT leaves the BT behind and heads southeast to West Virginia. It's another blazing hot day on the roadwalk to Stockport. Along the way I get a call from Herb; my pack was delivered to his house this morning. We make plans to meet in Stockport in a few hours. At a fork in the road from Chesterhill—literally in the middle of the intersection—is a well with a freshwater spring. The rest of the roadwalk into Stockport is uneventful, except for a feeling of doubt caused from an uncomfortable dream I had last night, and I am distracted most of the day.

I roll on into Stockport and stop at the gas station for some Gatorade and a rest in the shade. No sooner have I finished than I get a call from Herb. He has just reached town and is wondering where I am, to which I respond, I have also just arrived in town. Another case of perfect timing. I head on down to the old Inn on the river and meet up with Herb. He's a dedicated member involved with both the BT and the ADT.

My pack looks almost brand new! I spend a few minutes switching gear from Brent's Gregory, into my GoLite, while Herb gives me a few pointers on the section of trail I will be hiking the next two days (between here and Belle Valley). He says there is a nice camping spot a few miles up the trail where they plan to install a shelter next year. My goal for today is to make it to that spot. I thank Herb for taking the time to bring my pack to me and he wishes me luck on the rest of my hike.

I decide to linger for awhile in the shade in front of the old Inn before continuing. The rest of the day is almost entirely a roadwalk to the beginning of the next off-road segment on the edge of the AEP Recreation Lands. At this junction of the wilderness loop, known locally as the "stupid loop", it continues along remote gravel roads on a forty-mile segment of off-road trail in the Wayne on a strange 150-mile detour to Belle Valley. Up ahead on my route I have forty miles of off-road trail through recently reclaimed AEP lands to reach Belle Valley day after tomorrow. I will never understand why the NCT takes the long detour to Marietta over some historically poorly-maintained trail a stone's throw from West Virginia when this chunk of existing good quality trail is here.

I head on in and up the finely-maintained trail to the first ridge. I lingered too long in Stockport so I won't make it to the camping spot Herb spoke of. I find a nice flat spot up on the ridge just off the trail and pitch for the night.

Sunday, August 25
Trail Day 144
Miles hiked: 20
Bicentennial Campground – BT

I'm on the trail fairly early this morning but it remains a slow day. The heat has really intensified and it's showing no signs of letting go anytime soon. Parts of the trail through some of the open areas are overgrown with weeds up to my waist, but the sections through the woods are nice. There is a small cave early on the hike this morning and there are some nice views of some nearby lakes. I pass a trail register along an open stretch and figure that this must be the site of the future shelter. I stop here for a quick break under a shade tree before continuing on.

The afternoon sees the trail following some mowed service roads through previously strip mined land. It hasn't been mowed in awhile so the grass is up past my ankles, and unfortunately some

ATV's have been out here and created some muddy rutted areas. Along this stretch, my time scanning the ground for snakes finally pans out, but what I find isn't what I expected.

Across the trail, maybe eight feet in front of me, is a huge black snake. It is so large in fact, that the seven-foot corridor I am hiking through now can't contain its entire body. I freeze, as the horror of what I've stumbled upon sinks in. I've mentioned before that I'm not a fan of snakes. When I was younger, I had a near-phobia of the buggers. We all have that one thing we have an irrational fear of, and where I stand now that fear takes hold again.

I stamp my feet, hoping the vibrations will scare it off, but there's no movement. I edge a little closer continuing to stamp my feet but nothing happens. I stand motionless for what seems like forever, trying to control the fear and think rationally about how to navigate around this. The brush is too thick on either side to make an easy time getting around so I am left with little choice. I close my eyes and take a deep breath as I leap and hit the ground running, literally!

Not daring to open my eyes (knowing the fear will take hold again if I see the massive beast moving and thrashing around), I run the length of half a football field before opening my eyes. The trail here is wide and straight, so there are no worries of running into a tree. Miraculously, I didn't step on the beast or stumble on a rutted ATV track, and made it to the base of a gentle uphill climb. I follow this to a gated-entry off a paved access road leading to the nearby campground and stop here for a break.

My water is almost gone from the heat of the day so I head on down the road to the campground and fill up. This heat wave has really worn on me and I can tell my strength is starting to diminish. I decide to take a nap here in the campground on the picnic table at one of the empty sites. Nearly two hours go by before I wake up and decide to cook myself a hot meal once I realize I'm hungry. After a good meal and rehydration, I hike a few more mils and finish the day at the Bicentennial Campground, where I get a spot and pitch for the night.

Monday, August 26
Trail Day 145
Miles hiked: 25
Property of Jerry - Buffalo Hills Resort

It's only a few miles to the end of the trail through the recreation lands, and then a short roadwalk to the small town of Belle Valley. I have another food drop waiting for me there. When I arrive, I am disappointed to find that the post office doesn't open until 1 p.m., so I now have several hours to kill. I decide to consume some of my extra food and catch up on journals to pass the time. There is a gas station across the way and today is another blazing hot day so I purchase more Gatorade to stay well hydrated.

At 1 p.m. the post office finally opens and I can get hiking again. The day is mostly a roadwalk except for a small section through Wolf Run State Park. There is a nice section over an earthen dam and then a few more cobwebs to contend with in the woods at the end of the section. Along the roadwalk is another historical site. It is one of the many crash-sites of the USS Shenandoah, an American zeppelin that was ripped apart by severe thunderstorms and rained down on the countryside below. The trail passes right by one of the sites of the wreckage and I snap a photo of the sign marking the spot.

Later on, I pass through an Amish community on the way to Buffalo Hills Resort. I've passed through a few of these on my trek since leaving the North Woods. I passed a fellow along a roadwalk in Michigan riding his horse and buggy that was even familiar with the trail. He asked me flat out if I was hiking the NCT and wished me luck, just amazing.

Arriving at Buffalo Hills, I head on into the office to possibly see about pitching my tent somewhere on the grounds away from everyone else. My map says the resort is private and permission of the owners is needed. Unfortunately, the woman at the counter won't let me stay because the owners are off-site. So I have no choice but to push on.

I follow the BT through the huge campground where there are many campers and small cabins are occupied. I find the gate where the BT leaves the resort and heads into the woods, but it is currently blocked by a large tree that has fallen right behind the gate. I look for a way around but there doesn't appear to be one. I wander around looking for a place to leave the resort to get out onto the highway on the opposite side, but there doesn't appear to be an easy way out.

As I am wandering, I pass an occupied site with a pavilion, and a camper and the occupant flag me down as I approach. Hence, I meet Jerry, the tenant of this lot. After a brief conversation he offers his lot for the night. I can set up my tent anywhere. He was quite frustrated when he heard the woman at the counter wouldn't let me camp here. Well this certainly worked out and was extremely helpful, Thanks Jerry.

Before I can get my tent set up completely, Jerry has to leave for awhile to meet with some friends. He tells me to make myself at home and enjoy his pavilion. There is a wall on the north side with a fireplace and some patio furniture around to sit on. I relax in one of his chairs as I enjoy some dinner and read some pages from *Tolkien*.

After awhile, Jerry returns and offers me a beer. I gladly accept and he gets a fire started as we start chatting. He is familiar with the BT and the ADT, but the NCT is a mystery to him. He is excited that I am here, and when he learns there may be more like me in the future he tells me he would be willing to open his lot up for hikers to camp in and even set up a register box. *I will definitely pass on your request to BTA headquarters Jerry.*

Many drinks and many hours later, it is far past time for me to get to sleep. I thank Jerry for his generous hospitality and head into my tent for a night of sleep.

Tuesday, August 27
Trail Day 146
Miles hiked: 22
Salt Fork State Park

Staying up late last night means I'm sleeping in this morning. After a quick breakfast I say goodbye to Jerry and thank him for letting me stay on his lot. I then hit the road. The entire day is a roadwalk, and my goal is to make it to Old Washington.

The massive heat wave that began a few days ago continues, and I heard there was a motel in town so I'm going to try and stay out of the heat as much as possible. I arrive to find that there is no motel, only a truck stop. I ask one of the locals about nearby lodging and they tell me there isn't anything for at least eleven miles down I-70.

Exhausted, and with nowhere to camp in town, I have no choice but to push on another seven miles to Salt Fork State Park. When I arrive, I find that the trail at the back of the group campground is impassable, and I encounter the worst Mosquitoes since leaving the UP. With nothing left to do, I pitch my tent here and struggle to get a good sleep. I was thoroughly exhausted and overheated. I can't tell if this is the heat or the possible impending tick infection (or maybe a combination of the two), but I definitely feel off and am dazed and disoriented. I am getting really tired of Ohio.

Wednesday, August 28
Trail Day 147
Miles hiked: 27
Piedmont Lake Inn

I awoke this morning after a very restless sleep. Even in the dead of night it was still an unbearable 90 degrees. On top of that, around 1 a.m. I saw lights as a vehicle pulled up at the front gate of the campground. I thought it may have been rangers from the park until I heard a loud gunshot. Then, I watched as the lights turned and passed away as the vehicle peeled out of the driveway. Some hooligans had pulled up and fired a round at the entrance sign. I wondered if they had even seen me as they pulled up. I was camped behind the sign a good distance away on the edge of the tree line. Luckily, their shot did not hit me and I got through the rest of the night with more restless sleep.

Since the trail leading out of the campground through the park is impassable, I will need to roadwalk around this segment. Last night while looking at my maps, I discovered that there is a B&B further down the trail that I may be able to reach to get out of this heat for a night. That is my goal for today.

The hike starts out on mostly gravel country roads and field service roads. One of these travels through an impressive stone gateway, two giant stones propped facing each other forming a sort of half arch. Shortly after passing through this arch, I leave the designated roadwalk and head for paved US-22. I hope this will allow me to save time by walking on pavement instead of gravel, and lower the risk of getting lost on the often unmarked back roads. Like most of the roads in Ohio however, there is no shoulder, and it is heavily travelled by large trucks. I have to hop off the road repeatedly to avoid being hit.

This road turns out to be a workout as it descends into, and then out of a large valley—the upward climb out being longer and steeper. Along this roadwalk a pickup truck slows down and pulls up along-side me. Hence, I meet Mike, who was out doing his rounds for DirecTV. He asks me where I'm headed and indicated that he passed me along the road yesterday. He wishes me well and continues down the road.

Not an hour later, I see a truck stopped on the side of the road in a pull-off and recognize the driver as Mike. He calls over to me. I cross the road and wander over to his truck where he hands me a bottle of water and a banana to get me through the rest of the day. *Thanks for the contribution Mike.*

I finish the day with a short off-road section along the shore of Piedmont Lake before finally making it to the Piedmont Lake Inn, the B&B I discovered on the map last night. A sign on the door lists a number to call to request a room as it is after lobby hours. Just as I am about to make the call, a truck pulls into the parking lot and man gets out. It happens to be Tom, the manager of the Inn. I tell him my situation and ask if he has any vacancy. He regrettably informs me that he doesn't have any rooms available. He is currently renovating the place and the few rooms he does have available are currently being rented by some of the oil workers in the area.

I then proceed to ask him if I can pitch my tent behind his place and he responds by telling me, "No, but you can stay in the lobby tonight." I gladly take up his offer and he lets me in and shows me around. He said I can use the shower and laundry machine if

I want. He then tells me the nearby places I can get some dinner. The one that's just down the road is not very good, but he tells me of a great pizza place a few miles away in the next town. He offers to drive me there. I gladly accept his offer and soon we are in the town of Freeport, where I order a large pizza with everything on it. He then brings me back to the Inn. I thank Tom tremendously for everything he has done for me today—allowing the use of his air-conditioned lobby, driving me to get dinner, and for letting me sleep on the couch in the lobby...free of charge! *Thanks again Tom!*

After Tom heads out for the night, I enjoy watching some TV while consuming my delicious pizza. Folks following my hike were worried about how I was faring in this incredible heat wave, so afterwards, I give Bruce at NCTA a call and let him know that after twelve days of being in the constant heat, I finally made it inside and got some relief. After touching base with a few people back home, I watch a little more TV as I rehydrate, and then settle down on the couch and drift off to sleep.

Thursday, August 29
Trail Day 148
Miles hiked: 25
Home of Mary - Dover, OH

I woke up surprisingly early this morning and enjoyed the left over pizza for breakfast. I glance over my maps looking at the mileage for today. I received a call last night from a trail angel named Cathy, who heard about my struggle with the heat. She wanted to extend an invitation to help out. She agreed to pick me up at the end of the day near Tappan Lake Dam. After packing up and hydrating some more, I take a few moments to leave Tom a nice note in his guest registry for allowing me to stay the night. Pack shouldered, I take one last glance around the room to make sure I didn't forget anything, and then turn as the door locks behind me.

It is already hot this morning as this monstrous heat wave continues. A half mile down the road I stop at the convenience store to get more Gatorade before turning onto back roads on another roadwalk. Eventually I hit another paved road (OH-799), and follow it to some off-road trail providing nice views of Glendening Lake. Many fisherman are camped right on the road bridge enjoying the day. I stop for a break near a Boy Scout camp entrance before continuing on.

More roadwalk brings me to a fork in the road where I take a detour into the small town of Deersville. I had heard they had some pretty spectacular homemade ice cream here at the general store so I head there to try some. Easily some of the best ice cream I have ever had, so I stick around to have seconds and enjoy some more time in their AC. Also nearby is the BTA barn where the BTA holds their annual meetings. Unfortunately, I'm not quite sure where it is, and decide I can't waste any time trying to find it. So, I hike back out of town and continue on the road walk toward Tappan Lake where more certified trail awaits.

When I arrive, I am disappointed to find that most of it is overgrown; lots of multi-flora rose around to scratch me up pretty good. There are also several blowdowns, many of which are too large to get over or under, and so I must go around and through the impenetrable brush. Only a few miles left to go, and I arrive at a boat landing to find the trail leading out of here is suddenly in good shape. After this nice change of pace, I make good time to Tappan Lake Dam where a van is pulled up, and I meet Cathy.

We exchange greetings, load my gear into her van, and head for her home in Dover. When we arrive, I am introduced to Mary, Cathy's mother, and am able to do laundry and enjoy a nice cooked meal. From being exposed to this heat for almost two weeks non-stop, minus the cooler stormy day in the middle, I am utterly exhausted and have no trouble falling asleep.

Friday, August 30
Trail Day 149
Miles hiked: 22
Home of Mary - Dover, OH

I awoke well rested this morning and was treated to another home-cooked meal for breakfast. It was decided last night that I will spend another night here, and so Mary has decided to loan me a day pack to use so I don't need to carry all my gear with me. I happily accept as it makes all the difference in this heat.

After packing what I need for the day, she shuttles me back to Tappan Lake Dam and I continue on from there. An uphill climb on some last certified trail for the day, brings me to the road where I will remain the rest of the day. Not having my heavy pack on makes all the difference as I can tell I am not getting fatigued as fast, even in this heat.

I make decent time into Bowerston, and after passing through town I decide to diverge from the designated route and take more direct paved roads. This brings me through the town of Sherrodsville, where I stop to rest at the city park picnic shelter. Feeling the effects of the heat once again I decide to lie down and take a rest. I wake up nearly two hours later and continue on at a much faster pace now to ensure I make it to the rendezvous on time.

Mary intercepts me at the end of the Bowerston section of the BT (the three-way intersection off Hwy 212), and I call it a day. For dinner we head to Bob Evans, and then it's back to Mary's home for another night out of the heat.

Saturday, August 31
Trail Day 150
Miles hiked: 26
Home of Sam - Magnolia, OH

I am excited to get going this morning because today I leave the Buckeye Trail behind and head east on true NCT. After a quick breakfast, I finish packing my gear and am out the door. Mary drops me off at the intersection where I left off yesterday, telling me not to hesitate to call if I run into trouble. *Thanks Mary, it was a pleasure staying with you and your family.*

Today is mostly a roadwalk, except for a short segment just south of the village of Zoar where the BT and NCT diverge. I have only eleven miles to go to reach that spot, so I expect to be there around noon. Right after being dropped off, a guy pulls up in a van and asks if I'm hiking the BT. I let him know that this is actually my last day on the BT as I head east to New York. He wishes me well as he drives off.

A short distance further down the road I pass a house with a woman sitting on her front porch. As I approach she comes out to the road to meet me. Hence, I meet Barb who is here to offer me some fruit and a cold bottle of water. It turns out that the guy that pulled up in the van was her husband. He called ahead to let her know I would be hiking by. This is turning out to be a nice day so far.

After saying farewell to Barb, I continue on the roadwalk. After almost an hour, I find it very strange that I haven't turned north yet. The road I am on continues to veer southwest. After crossing an intersection I check my map. Yup, I missed a turn that wasn't marked over two miles ago. Great, even the last day on the BT can't seem to be a normal day.

After figuring out how to get back to the trail, I continue on, mostly uphill. At an intersection after seeing a blue blaze on a telephone pole, I know I have made it back to the trail...but only after going five miles in a semi-circle the wrong direction.

At last I reach the last chunk of certified NCT along the Buckeye Trail. It has nice towpath with crushed limestone surface. From here the trail diverges from the BT and crosses an old bridge over the Tuscarawas River into the historic village of Zoar. This town bears somewhat of a resemblance to many of the historic forts I have passed by on this trek; providing a look into the past of America's history.

I stop to rest and rehydrate on more Gatorade at the convenience store at the far end of town. I check my phone and receive a message from Bruce at NCTA. Don and Pam from Lisbon are trying to get in touch with me to offer assistance as I reach their area. As it so happens, I still have their number from when I met them at Hocking Hills a few weeks ago. I give Don a call and tell him that I won't make it much past Magnolia tonight, but I will be in his area tomorrow. We make arrangements for him to pick me up at the end of the day somewhere near Hanoverton tomorrow evening.

I still have a long roadwalk left to make it to Magnolia, so I hike on and make it into town a little before dark. I spend the little daylight I have left searching for a possible place to camp. The only suitable place appears to be a cemetery, but unfortunately, the police station is right across the street. With nowhere to go, I decide to head into the bar to relax and get a break from the heat. I'm the only customer here for the moment, so I find a seat right at the bar. Here I meet Cheryl, the cute and friendly bartender.

I order a beer with a glass of water to start off. She sees my pack and asks the usual questions. I give her the entire story of my hike so far—where I'm headed, what I've experienced. She congratulates me on making it this far and then goes back to work getting the place ready for the evening rush.

Before long, people start coming in; many of them noticing the pack and asking me about my hike. I realize I've been in here more than two hours and I'm getting hungry. I order a large order of spicy nachos and another beer, to tide me over for the evening. After I am finished, Cheryl comes over and mixes two drinks right in front of me. "Since you've come so far, I need you to be able to say you had a Wizard in Magnolia." She hands me one of the glasses and then it's bottoms up. "Cheers." I have no idea what a Wizard is (some sort of a large shot), but it was definitely tasty.

She asks me where I plan to stay tonight and I tell her I have no idea. I thought there would be a park or something nearby, but arrived in town to find nothing. She mentions to me that I may be able to crash with her tonight if I have nowhere to go. *Thanks Cheryl, meeting you has been the highlight of my day!*

Soon, I am surrounded by locals. A guy next to me asks about my story. Hence, I meet Sam, who happens to live a few blocks away. After telling him my story and that I still have almost 1,000 miles to go to finish my hike, he invites me to spend the night at his place down the street. At this point it is getting late, I am exhausted. I don't think I can wait until 2 a.m. when Cheryl gets off work, so I take him up on his offer. He says we can leave whenever I am ready. Another guy sitting nearby had overheard our conversation, and he insists on buying me a drink before I leave. *I'm sorry sir I forgot your name, but I thank you for my final drink of the night.*

At 11 p.m. I'm ready to go. With pack shouldered I say goodbye to Cheryl, give her a firm handshake, and am out the door—stumbling slightly from the drinks I've had. Sam has a nice couch for me to sleep on, which beats sleeping on the ground.

Sunday, September 1
Trail Day 151
Miles hiked: 28
Motorhome of Don and Pam – Lock 30 Woodland RV Campground - Lisbon, OH

I woke up surprisingly early this morning, probably anxious to get out of Ohio and into Pennsylvania. After hydrating and filling up my water bottles, I am out the door and ready to start the day. Sam decides to get his workout in for the day and ride his bike ahead of me. He knows a shortcut through an old strip mine that is now reclaimed forested land; it would shave more than a mile off my hike to Waynesville. I follow him in, and in no time we are following remnants of an old rail grade into the town of Waynesville. Sam stops and points me to the correct road to lead me out of town, and with a hand-shake he turns and rides back to Magnolia. *Thanks for your hospitality Sam. It was a pleasure meeting you.*

I haven't eaten yet, so I decide to stop for breakfast at the Waynesville Grill before continuing on. It's still early morning and it is already scorching hot. The rest of today is all a roadwalk. The next town up the road is Malvern, and I stop for a Blizzard at the Dairy Queen. Afterward, I head over to the picnic shelter in the park next door and take a short nap under the picnic shelter to escape the heat.

Finally, at the end of the day a few miles outside of Hanoverton, I give Don a call. I tell him where I am and what roads I will be hiking on. He says he will be around in an hour to pick me up. After one last push to get as many miles in today as possible, and totally exhausted, I see a vehicle slow down and pull up beside me. Don has arrived to pick me up and shuttle me to an RV campground near Lisbon where he and his wife, Pam have set up their motor home for me to use for the next two nights.

When we arrive, we check in at the registration station to let them know that I will be staying here. At the motor home, Pam is inside and has some snacks prepared for me. Don shows me where everything is and how to work all the appliances. This is just an incredible thing Don and Pam have done to help this hiker out. This heat wave has taken everything out of me and I have no energy left to continue. I am going to take tomorrow off from hiking and take a much needed zero day.

Tuesday, September 3
Trail Day 152
Miles hiked: 32
Home of Rick and Sherry - Darlington, PA

Don and Pam picked me up and shuttled me to their house for dinner last night. What a fine cooked meal that was. Pam had even baked a tray of brownies with my name on it, for dessert. They are here again this morning to drop me off again at the trail. Alas, it is time for another sad goodbye. These folks have been so good to me the past few days. I will surely miss them.

The day starts off with a road walk and then a short segment of bike trail leading into Lisbon. Here, I take a detour to the post office to pick up a drop box with more food and the maps for Pennsylvania. My goal for today is to make it the thirty miles to the Pennsylvania state line so I don't waste any time after getting resupplied.

The next segment of the hike is a long roadwalk past the RV campground, to the entrance of Beaver Creek State Park where a six-mile segment of certified trail begins. The trail is in much better condition than most of the trail in Ohio; a good way to finish off the state. The trail follows along Beaver Creek and past some old canal structures before reaching a road on the other end.

Along the road walk I get a call from Don. Yesterday he had gotten the contact information from a guy at the campground, who apparently lives near the trail in Pennsylvania. He was interested in helping me out as I approached his area. His daughter wanted to meet me, so Don wanted to give me his contact information. In a few minutes, he shows up in his car and hands me a piece of paper with a name and number on it, as well as a final care package from Pam. *Thanks again Don for your help.*

Right after this, a guy in a truck slows down and pulls alongside me. He asks if I need any help and says he lives right down the road and to stop in if I need anything. I have only a few more miles to go now before I am out of Ohio and into Pennsylvania. My pace picks up as I am pumped with the excitement. Then, up the hill comes the same guy on an ATV. He pulls it off into the woods and comes out to meet me. Hence, I officially meet Brad Bosley, one of the leaders of the Great Trail - Sandy Beaver Canal Chapter, NCTA.

He has just returned from a trip out of state and knew I would be coming through. He decides to hike the rest of the trail through Ohio with me. Before long, we pass his house where he mentions he wants to, one day, provide a campsite for hikers in his back yard, complete with a shelter. Only a few miles from the state line now we come to the last segment of certified trail in Ohio, an old rail grade through Sheepskin Hollow Nature Preserve. This is not typical rail grade, as the ties have not been removed and many of the spikes are still in place. It still makes for an enjoyable hike.

Before long, we emerge onto a road segment, bringing us past a golf course and finally to the Pennsylvania State Line! When we arrive, there is a welcome party waiting for us. Members from the neighboring Wampum Chapter (Rick and Sher) live nearby in Darlington, and knew I would be arriving today. They had come out to meet me and invite me to stay at their home tonight. We take a few pictures and then load the vehicles as I say goodbye to Brad and head to Darlington with Rick and Sher.

At their home, I am amazed to see a homemade banner attached to their mail box with the sole purpose of welcoming me to Pennsylvania. They snap a picture of me with their daughter Candice. I then meet Candice's husband, Bobby, who has come out to meet me as well. They say they have pizza on the way for dinner so I unpack my gear. Rick shows me where the shower is so I can get cleaned up and join everyone for dinner upstairs.

Also here for dinner is Dennis and his wife, Karen. Dennis has a bunch of maps and information for me regarding the trail in the Wampum chapter area. He also offers to pick me up at the end of the day tomorrow and drive me to Moraine State Park where they have a cabin available for me to rent. I take him up on his offer and we make a plan for tomorrow.

After dinner, everyone heads out for the night, as it is now well past dark. The couch downstairs is very comfortable and I am happy to be inside on the supposed last night of this deadly heat wave.

Hocking Hills State Park

PENNSYLVANIA

September 4 - September 13, 2013

Wednesday, September 4
Trail Day 153
Miles hiked: 25
Davis Hollow Cabin - Moraine State Park

Rick and Sher have fixed me a nice breakfast before heading out this morning; including a care package for the road. It's a short drive to the trailhead at Gameland 285, where I ended my hike last night at the OH/PA state line. Here a crumbling cement obelisk marks the boundary between the two states. Rick takes my picture at the sign. I have a big smile on my face as I put Ohio in my rearview mirror and begin my trek through Pennsylvania, the sixth state of this trek. I'm also now in the triple digits for mileage remaining on this hike, less than 1,000 to go! The hike today will bring me right by Rick and Sher's house, so Rick tells me stop by again as I hike through.

The beautiful trail through the gameland is a nice change of pace. Along the way I pass a spur trail to a newly-built shelter on private property. I stop in to admire the work done by the Wampum Chapter volunteers and consume one of the snacks from Sher's care package. After this, another spur trail leads off to the left to a place known as Indian Rock. Some very nice trail through this section indeed. From here it is a roadwalk to the town of Darlington and beyond.

Soon I come to the Eiler's home where they are getting ready to leave for work, and there are some people with them. Their neighbors had intended to come over last night but they were unable to make it, so they are out here this morning to meet me and wish me luck. Then with one last hug from Sher, and a hand shake from Rick, I continue on down the road.

Within a short distance I'm passing by a home construction site and woman flags me down. Hence I meet Beverly, a local who knows about the trail and asks if I'm hiking the entire thing. I tell her my story so far, and she snaps a photo of me and wishes me luck.

In Darlington I get a call from Dennis. He has my third pair of boots from the post office in Wampum and wants to know where he can find me. I tell him I am in Darlington, and within minutes he is here at the gas station to meet me. We make plans for him to just keep them until I see him again tonight at Moraine State Park (no sense in loading my pack with extra weight).

The road walk continues across two busy four-lane highways (one with no legal crossing) before I reach the next segment of trail through Gameland 148, which leads me into Wampum. I have a few more miles of certified trail before I reach the point where Dennis will pick me up off Snake Run Road. This last section brings me past an old lime kiln and an abandoned house in the middle of the woods known locally as the haunted house.

I finish the day on schedule where Dennis is waiting for me. He loads me into his car and we drive to Moraine State Park, where we have gained admission to a meeting of the Butler County Recreation Club—most of them also members of the Butler County Chapter, NCTA. Here I meet Joyce and Dave. Dave mentions he lives near Clarion and would be happy to help me out when I reach that area. After the introduction by the club, and the group meal, Dennis drives me to the Davis Hollow Cabin where I will be spending the next two nights.

Like the NCTA School house in Michigan, this cabin is operated by the NCTA. Now it is available for campers and hikers to rent. The inside has been beautifully restored and decorated with all kinds of hiking club merchandise. The upstairs is complete with two rooms full of bunk beds...and I have the entire place to myself.

Before settling in, Dennis lets me know he will be here around 7:30 a.m. tomorrow to pick me up. Soon after, Joyce stops by to give me some contact information for the remaining chapters in Pennsylvania. She also informs me that tomorrow we will be having dinner here at the cabin with the park manager and some others. With that, she wishes me good night and I settle in for a cozy night of sleep in the Davis Hollow Cabin.

Thursday, September 5
Trail Day 154
Miles hiked: 25
Davis Hollow Cabin - Moraine State Park

Last night before I went to sleep, I spent some time unpacking my gear, sorting my drop box, and studying my maps. From where I ended my hike yesterday to this cabin, is twenty-five miles, a good full day. So I will be spending another night here. I decided to leave the gear I won't need so I can travel light. Dennis is at the driveway early with some breakfast from McDonald's. After we eat, he hauls me back to the trail and says goodbye. I may not see him again on this journey. *Thank Dennis for all your hard work and for helping me out the past few days.*

After hiking a short section of trail on private land, the route becomes a roadwalk to the border of McConnell's Mill State Park. At the trailhead there are a few picnic tables, so I stop to have a snack before heading in. The trail through the park is gorgeous, following the river most of the way through the Slippery Rock Gorge. There are lots of hemlock trees along the rocky ridge, so I am surely in the north woods again. The hike is only about seven miles through the park, but it is slow going because of the difficulty of this tread. Large boulders the size of basketballs and larger are all over the place. I have to be careful that I don't take a bad step and sprain my ankle.

Before long, the trail emerges onto a road, uses a covered bridge over the river, and then brings me right to the old mill. Here I stop to take a video enjoy the view. From here it is a short roadwalk to Moraine State Park through mostly residential areas. Once inside the park I am pleasantly surprised at the quality of the tread. It has been widened out and some of it covered in wood chips to keep the weeds from coming up. On top of that, it is well blazed and easy to follow.

The gorgeous trail follows along the shore of Lake Arthur for a few miles before turning more inland. I reach the spur trail that will take me to the Davis Hollow Cabin, and I hike it on down and find a few cars in the lot out front. Joyce is here with a reporter from Pittsburgh to interview Jake, the park manager, and me.

After meeting everyone, we head inside and I am surprised by what lies before me. They had gone to Slippery Rock earlier and brought back a full meal and a pitcher of beer courtesy of North Country Brewery, where the annual meeting was held this year. We spend the next hour or two enjoying the fantastic meal and talking about the trail, my journey thus far, and my long-term goals. They are pleased to find out that my main goals are to raise awareness of the trail and increase usage and interest so it can be better cared for and protected.

After the interview, time for more good-byes. **Thanks Joyce for helping me out the past few days. And thanks to you Jake, for allowing me to stay in your beautiful cabin free of charge.*

Friday, September 6
Trail Day 155
Miles hiked: 22
Tamarack Campsite – Gameland 95

Joyce left me some breakfast in the fridge last night, so I linger in the cabin to enjoy it before packing up and heading out. The cabin is pretty much in the middle of the park so I have many miles to cover on finely-groomed trail. Once outside the park, the trail connects immediately to trails within the Jennings Nature Center... a fine hike indeed.

This section ends at the Old Stone House, a historic landmark of the area. After this, it's a roadwalk of several miles to reach Gameland 95. The trail here passes by Glade Dam Lake and then heads into dense woods where there is one campsite. I pitch here for the night on one of the tent pads and call it a day. There must be a school nearby, as I can hear the roar of a crowd cheering in the distance as I drift off to sleep.

Saturday, September 7
Trail Day 156
Miles hiked: 24.5
Super 8 Motel - Clarion, PA

I had a nice breakfast on my stove this morning, then I was out and going as quickly as could be. Today's hike is mostly a road-walk, except a small section through Gameland 95. This section is really nice; lots of cool rock outcroppings and some creek beds. Once I reach the town of Parker I have to make a decision. First, another heat wave has just settled in today so I have needed to stop more often. Also, between here and Clarion there is no official place to camp, so I need to decide if I should stay here in town or try and find a way to get through some of this area.

I decide to call Dave, who I met at the meeting of the Butler County Recreation Club. I tell him my situation and he agrees to pick me up at the end of the day in Callensburg, where he will shuttle me to a motel in Clarion. I plan to stay there the next two nights, and slack pack tomorrow.

After getting off the phone with Dave, I stock up on Gatorade before leaving town. The trail leaving town follows a pedestrian walkway along a big blue highway bridge over the Allegheny River. On the other side I pass the Allegheny River Trail, a bike path that makes a big loop towards Clarion. This is a suggested route for the NCT, but has not been made official and I doubt much of it ever will. The maps given to me by the NCTA do not include it, so I take the straighter route and official roadwalk through Callensburg.

Along the road walk I have to fight off many more dogs with my trekking poles. One dog is so adamant on getting to me, that he even crosses the busy highway with cars going full speed. The owners scream as he is almost hit multiple times. Eventually, he backs off and I can continue on my way worry-free.

I reach Callensburg where Dave awaits at the local convenience store. We load up his car and he shuttles me into Clarion where I get a room at the Super 8. We make plans for tomorrow and then he heads home. I enjoy a nice air-conditioned room for the night.

Sunday, September 8
Trail Day 157
Miles hiked: 18.5
Super 8 Motel - Clarion, PA

It was so nice waking up in an air-conditioned room on a soft bed this morning. After a nice continental breakfast, Dave is here at 8 a.m. to shuttle me back to Callensburg. The day begins on a roadwalk through some small Amish communities before turning off onto back roads through more gamelands. This is one of the nicest roadwalks I have had this trek, providing some great views.

After the gamelands, the roadwalk continues through some residential areas, across I-80, and finally meets the certified trail through some private property. Soon the trail reaches PA-322 only a few miles west of Clarion. On the other side of the road, the trail enters Gameland 72 with lots of rocky and open areas.

I was warned by Dave to watch the trail closely as this area has the largest population of venomous snakes in the county. I heed his advice as I have heard from many AT thru-hikers that it was in Pennsylvania where they saw the most snakes, and the most rocks. I'm not as concerned with this, as I made it through the entire state of Ohio without seeing a single rattlesnake or copperhead. The fact of having the most rocks did end up being true however, so I watch the trail in front of me closely.

I hike the few miles through the Gameland and am close to the trailhead off Breniman Road when Dave appears around a corner, hiking toward me. We hike the short distance back to his car together and he shuttles me back to the motel. It is now mid-afternoon, but the heat has intensified. I decided to take a shorter day and recuperate as I will be on my own now at least until reaching New York. Dave drops me off at the motel and I enjoy some Applebee's car-side to go for dinner, before catching up on some journal entries and preparing for the next few days on the North Country Trail.

Monday, September 9
Trail Day 158
Miles hiked: 20
Cook Forest State Park

I was more tired than I originally thought. Getting up this morning was the slightest bit difficult. After the continental breakfast, I pack my gear then make a quick trip across the street to get some supplies at Walmart. The odor-proof bag I keep my toiletries in has ripped open, so I need to replace it as best I can.

Back at the motel, I check out, shoulder my back, and walk the two miles or so into town to retrieve my package at the post office. There is no sidewalk for the first mile and the highway is very busy with traffic (not the safest place to be). When I arrive, Dave is waiting for me and he has brought a reporter from the *Clarion News*. So after retrieving my package, we have a quick interview out front on the sidewalk. Then, I repack the box with my old shoes (as they are now worn out), and I hope to make it the rest of this trek with the pair I now have on, my third pair.

After one last stop at the gas station to grab some Gatorade to get me through the hot weather, Dave drops me off at the edge of Gameland 72 where I finished yesterday. Thus, comes another goodbye that has become so common this trek. **Thanks Dave for all you have done to help out this tired hiker.*

The hike today begins on private, well-maintained trail. However, the tread in this area provides a challenge as all the blowdowns have been cut very narrow to keep out horse traffic. They are so narrow in fact, that my fully-loaded pack cannot fit through without shaving the sides off my sleeping pad. After a few miles of this, the trail opens up into a former strip mine. Little drizzle sets in, followed by lightning. I keep a close eye on the sky as I am now more exposed and an easier target. All around me there are piles of trash, mostly metal and other recyclable materials. Apparently, this place has become a trash dump for the locals.

After a few minutes the rain stops and I hike the short roadwalk to bring me to Gameland 283. This section has been well maintained, well-marked, and has many ups and downs. From here the trail enters Cook Forest State Park where I hope to reach a shelter for the night. Through the park the NCT follows the Baker Trail, the blazes painted half yellow and half blue. As soon as I cross the boundary the rain comes again in a steady downpour. This makes the going really slow because a lot of the trail is solid rock and everything is slippery.

The trail through the park is gorgeous, mostly following along the banks of the Clarion River. Trees that I have never seen before grow here in large numbers, the rhododendrons. As the trail turns away from the river I have a steep uphill climb to reach Cook Forest Fire Tower. About halfway up the slope, I have to scramble among the rocks to keep my footing as the trail is slippery from the rain. Suddenly, I feel a sharp pain on my wrist and I bring it up to toward my face to examine it. Is this it? Have I made it all this way to be bitten in the end by an unseen Copperhead?

As I look at the burning hand, I see instantly a single puncture wound with puffy red edges. Then I turn as I hear a buzzing noise to my left, and see a very large Yellow Jacket flying away. I've never had a sting hurt this much! My hand still on fire, I hike the rest of the way up the slope to the fire tower, and there stop to take a break.

My entire arm around the immediate area of the sting has swelled up. I've been stung many times before but I have never had a reaction this intense. I wonder if this is a different variety of hornet than we have in Minnesota. Whatever the case may be, I keep a close eye on it and listen to my body to make sure there are no severe complications. An allergic reaction can happen at any time to anybody and I am not taking any chances.

I drink plenty of water to keep my body fully functional. After a few more miles it is getting dark, and I am forced to pull off into the trees and pitch for the night, unable to make it to the shelter.

Tuesday, September 10
Trail Day 159
Miles hiked: 25
Campsite east of Kelletville - Allegheny National Forest

I woke up surprisingly early this morning. It is so early in fact, that it is still dark when I emerge from my tent. The first thing I do is retrieve my food bag that I hid among some logs last night, as my bear anchor got stuck in a tree I was trying to hang my food. That's the third time that has happened this trek. I think they are simply too light to be of any real use. I need to find something heavier to hang my food with.

After packing up my gear, I head straight for the visitor center, but arrive to find not a visitor center at all, just an old cabin, a few shelters, and a picnic area. I decide to stop and cook breakfast here at the picnic area before heading out today. As I am finishing up, some tourists arrive and they are just as confused as I was when I emerged from the woods to this place. They ask me if I know where the visitor center is, and I reply that I too thought it was supposed to be right here.

Finally getting moving, I am still on the Baker Trail that takes me out of Cook Forest State Park onto some section lines following gas pipelines. I follow these for a few miles before reaching the southern boundary of the Allegheny National Forest. The hike through the Allegheny starts out nicely, but after awhile the trail starts to deteriorate. Multi-flora rose is present in many spots, the trail has not been mowed in probably two months. Eventually, the trail travels through some more open areas and the weeds are over waist-high. It is September now and many wild flowers are growing in profusion and the waist-high foliage presents a hazard; swarms of yellow-jackets. The stretch of trail I am on now is full of them, buzzing everywhere from plant to plant gathering what pollen they can. I have no idea how I am going to get through this without being stung.

With nothing else to do, I raise my trekking poles and run! I run until I am clear to the other side of the meadow and back in the wooded hill sides. I managed to get stung only six times, but it still hurts like hell. I am a little worried now as I have again swelled up, each sting more swollen than the one preceding it. I take a few minutes to rest on top of a large flat rock to rehydrate before continuing on.

The trail here winds through a few rock cities before finally coming out onto a forest road, that in a few miles will lead me into the little berg of Kelletville. There are many campsites along the river here, so I set up camp for the night.

Wednesday, September 11
Trail Day 160
Miles hiked: 17
Minister Creek Area - Allegheny National Forest

I woke up this morning totally exhausted...not surprisingly. Another heat wave has come through and the past two days have been unseasonably hot. I pack up camp as quickly as I can and hike the short distance down the road to the Kelletville public campground, where I stop to have breakfast and camel up on water.

I check my phone and don't have a cell signal, but luckily there is a pay phone at the back of the campground. I make a call to Keith, president of the Allegheny National Forest chapter. I tell him my situation—about the extreme heat and how tired I have been—and he says he wants to take me out for breakfast tomorrow. We make plans to meet at the next road crossing tomorrow morning, which is a full day's hike away.

I waste no time in getting moving again, but after hiking only a short distance I can tell this is going to be a rough day. After an hour I am already exhausted, the steep terrain not making the hike any easier. Early afternoon I decide I simply can't go on. I need to stop and rest. I find a spot near Minster Creek to pitch my tent and struggle to get as much rest as possible. Heat exhaustion is definitely taking its toll on me again.

Thursday, September 12
Trail Day 161
Miles hiked: 34
Red Bridge Campground - Allegheny National Forest

With much difficulty, I actually managed to get some sleep and stay asleep for much of the night. I hope this heat wave vanishes soon, or I will probably need to take another zero to recover my strength.

Quitting early yesterday means I need to get up early to make it to Henrys Mills where Keith is supposed to meet me. It's over ten miles away, so I am up at 4:30 a.m. hiking with headlamp on, watching every step, trying not to trip and fall on my face. This early in the morning it is already unbearably hot, and makes me wonder what is coming later in the day.

I manage to make it to the trailhead in Henrys Mills without incident and just relax until Keith arrives. He is there in only a short time, and he shuttles me into Sheffield to have breakfast at the bowling alley in town. We have a nice chat as we wait for our order. Keith talks about his time working on the NCT, the recent developments in his chapter, and in Pennsylvania in general.

He tells me that the trail ahead has been rerouted because of recent oil drilling in the area. He gives an example where cooperation between the trail and other organizations is crucial. When contacted about the issue of impacting the trail, the oil company responded by actually helping reroute it and get it on the ground, amazing! He also informs me that the heat wave is supposed to break this evening and that it will cool off quite dramatically over the next few days. Now there is some good news!

After breakfast, Keith gives me a few things to take along with me, including an NCT bandana, which I have gotten into the habit of collecting. (I have quite a few now.) I also leave with some advice from his wife, who is a nurse. She said that I should always be carrying an epipen with me on long hikes.

Keith drops me off back at Henrys Mills and we snap a picture at the trailhead. Then, with a firm handshake and words of encouragement from Keith, I am pack shouldered and heading uphill on the trail. Shortly after getting dropped off, the rain starts and continues off and on most of the day. This doesn't impede my progress much as it actually lowered the temperature, making the hike much more enjoyable than yesterday.

Keith had told me about a good place to have dinner in the little berg of Blissville, just off the trail. I head there and make it just before dark. The place is fairly empty and I am served right away. Fine folks here at Bob's Trading Post. I waste no time in ordering a large homemade pizza for myself before settling down at the bar for a nice glass of cold soda. Soon I get asked the usual questions by a woman behind the counter. Hence, I meet Pauline, co-owner.

I tell her my story so far and about where I am headed. From this point it is thirty miles to the New York State Line, and I intend to do my best to make it there tomorrow. She has hiked most the trail in this area and says the last section along the Allegheny Reservoir is pretty rough; lots of ups and downs. "You have a shot, but it will be tough." Challenge accepted.

Soon my pizza arrives and I waste no time in digging in. If this isn't the best pizza I have ever had I don't know what is. During the course of my meal, I talk more with Pauline and her daughters who run the kitchen. They are very impressed with my hike and enjoy hearing my stories, specifically the ones about the many animal encounters I have had.

At this point, I am the only customer left in the place and it is a half hour from closing time. Another man walks in and it turns out to be Jeff, Pauline's husband and co-owner. Pauline asks me what my shirt size is, and after I tell her she returns with a Bob's Trading Post T-shirt, promoting the Allegheny National Forest on the back. "A souvenir to remember us by." As if that wasn't a kind enough gesture, as I am ready to pay for my meal, Pauline says "It's been covered."

She then goes on to ask me if I want a ride to the campground. She tells me it's two miles away over a bridge, has no shoulder, and it's dark outside. With no more persuasion needed, I accept her offer. These have to be some of the nicest folks I've ever met. *Thank you so much Pauline, and kind folks at Bob's Trading Post.*

Full and ready for a good night's sleep, I load my gear in Jeff's truck and he drops me off at the Red Bridge Campground. I make camp and get in a nice hot shower to end this amazing day.

Friday, September 13
Trail Day 162
Miles hiked: 30
Allegany State Park - FLT, NY

Keith was right about the temperature cooling down. It is cold when I get up this morning. I need to put on a layer of fleece to keep warm. I slept in a little later than I wanted to, as I have thirty miles to go to reach New York. However, I don't let that discourage me, and I enjoy my leftover pizza for breakfast. With a good breakfast like that I should have enough energy to get me through the entire day.

The hike today brings me through a gorgeous section of the Allegheny National Forest. Pauline wasn't kidding about the terrain. There are many ups and downs and steep inclines. About halfway through the day, the trail reaches the Allegheny Reservoir and follows along the east bank clear up to Willow Creek Road. This section of trail is gorgeous. It reminds me a little of the Manistee National Forest back in Michigan as there is very little underbrush to obscure the view. Thin soft grass grows between all the trees. This section will probably be my favorite for Pennsylvania.

Along the trail today I spot a man, woman, and two dogs hiking toward me. As they approach they stop. "I know who that is," the man says. His name is Ian, he's been following my progress online and thought I would be past here by now. I explain my reasons for falling behind, but also that I am gaining lots of ground back and still hope to get through New York before the snow flies. He wishes me luck and we part ways.

Early evening now, I reach Willow Creek Road where the NCT leaves the Allegheny Reservoir. From here it is only a mile and a half to the New York State Line. So close to my goal for the day I push on the final distance without stopping. It's nearly all uphill, and reach a large wooden sign that reads: **Allegany State Park, New York**

I've made it! Despite all the odds, all the mishaps and the bad experiences, I have made it to the seventh and final state of my journey. From here, the NCT will follow the white-blazed Finger Lakes Trail for about 420 miles before again diverging and heading more northeast toward the Adirondacks. I pitch my tent a few yards from the sign and call it a day...happy to have finally reached the Empire State.

McConnell's Mill and the Slippery Rock Gorge

NEW YORK

September 13 - October 13, 2013

Saturday, September 14
Trail Day 163
Miles hiked: 30
Dudley Motel - Salamanca, NY

It got very cold last night and it's still cold this morning. I have to put on my fleece to stay warm. I don't waste any time in getting up and out this morning and I begin my trek through New York in Allegany State Park. Soon the sun comes out and it turns into a very nice day. I'm low on water again, so I head to the developed campground nearby to camel up and enjoy a nice breakfast.

Lots of people are out camping this weekend, almost every site is full. Also, along the trail today I pass several Adirondack shelters, the most I have seen in such a close proximity. Despite being on the final leg of this journey, I have only seen a handful of shelters along the NCT, most of which were in Pennsylvania. The Finger Lakes Trail is supposed to have lots of them and I am looking forward to using a few.

I make good time. I get to where the trail comes out near I-86 and crosses the Seneca Indian Reservation for a few miles before coming out on private land on the other side. I've been hearing gun shots for the past few miles, and it is clear to me now that they are coming from the reservation as hunting season is right around the corner. I decide not to travel across the reservation and instead take the hunting bypass route to Salamanca. I will get a motel for the night. It's more than eight miles from where I now stand, which will make for another thirty-mile day.

I make it to Salamanca just as darkness descends. I check in at the historic Dudley Mote where the woman at the desk sees my pack and cuts me a hiker trash rate. Up in the room, I order dinner from a flyer. Within a half hour, I am enjoying some delicious Calzones. It's been a long day. I have no problem falling asleep.

Sunday, September 15
Trail Day 164
Miles hiked: 24
Telemark Motel - Ellicottville, NY

I greatly enjoyed my stay here at the historic Dudley Motel. After a continental breakfast, I pack my gear and hit the road to hike back to the trail in Bucktooth State Forest. Soon the trail crosses through some private land where the trail is in bad shape. It mostly follows an old rutted logging road with standing water in most places. This is a disappointment as I have heard great things about the FLT, but it isn't off to a great start.

Eventually, the trail emerges onto a country road past a golf course and continues off-road in Rock City State Forest. This is an improvement over the section I was just on. Along this section of trail I meet two hikers. Hence, I meet Keith and Cindy, out for the weekend. They have been working on hiking the entire FLT end-to-end in sections. I am pleased to find out that they know about the NCT and they seem impressed with my story of attempting to hike the entire thing. After snapping a photo with me, we part ways and I discover how this forest got its name. There is an old CCC camp located here complete with an actual rock city and the trail goes right through it. From here, the trail passes through Holimont Ski Area where it winds among and across the many ski trails. The markings here are few and far between and I manage to lose the trail a few times.

Eventually, I get back on track and hike on down to NY-242, where I turn and head to Ellicottville. I have a food drop here, but today being Sunday, I'll have to wait until tomorrow morning to get it. In town I find that most of the "motels" are actually restored Victorian style houses, well out of my price range. To find an affordable motel I need to hike over a mile further to the south end of town to the Telemark Motel. Once inside I make a call. I'm on the phone with Irene, the editor of both the FLT and NCT quarterly newsletters. I had been in contact with her a few days earlier and she wanted to come down to meet me and take me out to dinner. I tell her my whereabouts and she says she will be here in about an hour.

I get a nice shower in and then watch some TV as I wait for Irene to arrive. Before long, she is outside to pick me up and we head to the brewery in town for a nice burger and great beer. We have a nice conversation about my trip so far—my estimated schedule through the rest of the FLT, and what I plan to do when I finish. Irene is going to try and set up a few more interviews for me once I arrive in the Watkins Glen-Ithaca area to help promote the trail. Afterward, Irene drops me back at the motel and she heads back home. *Thanks for the delicious dinner Irene, it was nice meeting you.*

Monday, September 16
Trail Day 165
Miles hiked: 20
Boyce Hill Shelter - FLT

I slept in this morning for some much needed rest. I head across the street to Burger King for some breakfast first thing. Then it's pack shouldered and I'm hiking back into Ellicottville to retrieve my package at the post office. After getting everything squared away, it's time to hit the trail again.

The hike begins on private land with some gorgeous trail. This section has lots of switchbacks to ascend and descend the sides of large hills and bluffs. After a brief roadwalk the quality of the trail decreases again with more rutted and wet logging roads. The next section is again in good shape across land donated to the FLTC, complete with a campsite. Then, the trail follows NY-242 for more than a mile before it turns into Boyce Hill State Forest. As I am looking for a place to pitch my tent, I come across a shelter that isn't marked on the map. It must have been built very recently, as there is also scrap lumber lying around. Oh yes, this will do just fine.

Tuesday, September 17
Trail Day 166
Miles hiked: 28
Sixtown Creek Campsite – FLT

It got cold last night and sleeping on the floor of the shelter was no comfort. I didn't sleep well, so getting out and going is difficult. Before leaving camp I find a small piece of lumber that will work great to replace my bear anchor I lost back in Cook Forest. I'm heading back into the heart of bear country now, so I will need it if I expect to keep my food to myself.

After an hour of hiking, the sun comes out and it warms up quite nicely. Some well-maintained trail takes me through Bear Creek State Forest and some private land until I reach Kingsbury Hill Road. At this point, the trail is again unfortunately a victim of low maintenance. It hasn't been cleared or mowed in some time and I am faced with more swarms of bees. I make it through this time without being stung, but have a difficult time navigating this section.

Once inside Bush Hill State Forest, a temporary reroute has been marked by flagging and shows up on my map. But, I am only able to find the first flag. The trail goes somewhere across a wide open field and it's anybody's guess as to exactly where it leads. After heading straight in the direction I think the trail most likely goes, and keeping my eyes peeled for flagging, I become lost and have to bushwhack back to the road. In the process, I become tangled in brush and severely cut up by multi-flora rose. After crossing a barbed wire fence and a rather deep, muddy drainage ditch, I make it back to the road. I take a moment to drop my pack, wet my handkerchief, and wipe the blood off my legs.

Taking a break now, I look at my map and find the best way to hook up with the trail again at the entrance to Farmersville State Forest. Pack shouldered again I roadwalk the next several miles to find the trail and head in. I am pleasantly surprised to find the trail through Farmersville nicely maintained. After this, I have a long roadwalk to Swift Hill State Forest where I plan to pitch for the night.

It is evening now and I have almost completed this section, but there is a designated campsite on private land only a few miles further that I could make before dark if I hurry. I decide to go for it and follow the trail out of the forest onto an abandoned rail grade and on the outskirts of the little berg of Higgins. I pass along the edge of several farms and find the blue-blazed spur trail that leads to the campsite. This little trail takes me past a small private waterfall and through a guy's front yard before crossing the road and arriving at a small campsite. I arrive right at dark, set up camp, hang my food, and drift off to sleep.

Wednesday, September 18
Trail Day 167
Miles hiked: 19
Hesse Private Shelter – FLT

There is a picnic table at the campsite so I cook breakfast first thing this morning. Looking at my maps, there appears to only be one spot to camp within the next thirty miles of trail, so today will be a shorter day to make use of the shelter located there.

This morning I follow the blue blazes out to the road, where I am immediately greeted by two angry dogs at the house where the trail crosses the front yard. With no way around, I decide to take the high-water route to avoid an unpleasant scuffle with these dogs that are not happy about me being there. After the bypass route, I join the trail again off County Road 19, and head on in... or should I say up.

The trail through this area is all on private land, mostly along field edges and fence lines. For the most part, this section is decently maintained so navigating it is not a problem. At Camp Sam Wood, I stop at the shelter to take a break before continuing. The trail leading away from here is a little dangerous as it follows very closely to a fence line... an electric fence line! I have to walk slowly as there is less than four feet between the hedge and the fence, and I don't want my pack or my trekking poles to brush against the hot wires.

I navigate around without being shocked and hike the rest of the way to reach the Genesse Valley Greenway. The Greenway is an abandoned towpath that has been converted into a trail for hiking and biking, and leads into Portageville where it joins the Letchworth trail to bring a hiker around a loop through Letchworth State Park. Along the Greenway, I make good time, but soon am confused as the maintained path suddenly ends. To this point the path had been freshly mowed, but here suddenly it stops and is overgrown with lots of poison ivy. Careful not to get too much of it on me, I tiptoe through the tree line separating the Greenway from the service road and hike the rest of the way into town on the road.

In Portageville, I stop in for a late lunch at the Letchworth Pines Tavern where I am one of only a few people here. I order a full meal of burger and fries. The bartender, Seth, asks me where I'm headed. Like so many before him, I give the full account my journey. He responds by paying for my first beer, a nice cold PBR. **Thanks Seth, I appreciate it.*

After enjoying my meal, a few more locals come in; most ask me the basic questions. Then it's time to move on, hiking across the highway bridge and picking up the trail again on private land with some fine overlooks of the countryside. I end the day at the private Hesse Lean-to and make myself at home for the night.

Thursday, September 19
Trail Day 168
Miles hiked: 24
Pond Campsite - Gas Spring State Forest - FLT

I had a nice rest in the Hesse Shelter and I waste no time in getting going this morning. The hike leads me through private land, and out to a short roadwalk where I bail off and head to the convenience store in Dalton. I need to refill my water supply before continuing on, as this is the last reliable source that I know of. From here, it's a long roadwalk to the little berg of Swain where the trail again takes to the woods on an old rail grade.

Many blazed loop trails exist in this area and I'm not quite sure of the purpose. The only visible purposes are a few archery targets, which indicate this may be part of an archery range. Whatever the case may be, I make good time on the rail grade.

The next chunk of trail is very interesting as it is all on private land and goes directly up a creek. Not beside the creek...but directly up the creek! I've been hiking a lot of places, but I've never been on a trail like this before. The creek bed is set in steps, varying in width and height, and the trail follows this for about a quarter mile. It is slow going because even though the water is low, the creek bed is still slippery, most of the rocks being incredibly flat and smooth.

Out of the creek now, shortly I come to a trail intersection. A spur trail leads from here to Bossard's Cabin, available for hikers to use (except during hunting season). I want to check it out, but I still have a long way to go, so I hike right on past. Right after this there are many electric fences that need to be crossed through some cattle pastures. Luckily, gates have been installed to allow hikers to travel this section more easily. But, I still need to be careful not to get zapped while unhooking the gates. I make it through the gates and over a few stiles without incident.

Shortly after traversing an old tractor road past an old barn, the trail heads uphill toward an open meadow with great views of the mountains behind. Soon the trail reaches Gas Spring/Klipnocky State Forest and I make it to the campsite located adjacent a small pond. There I call it a day and pitch my tent among the pine needles.

Friday, September 20
Trail Day 169
Miles hiked: 29
Burt Hill Shelter - FLT

Over the course of my hike through the great state of New York, I have noticed the pattern of the Finger Lakes Trail. Many of the area's public lands are little specks of state forest land and the trail weaves its way from one speck to the next, crossing private land in between to connect one forest to the next. I have also noticed that the sections through the state forests are all very well marked and maintained, and the private segments haven't had nearly as much care. The diversity of this trail certainly is one of the more interesting things about it and makes for a very enjoyable hike.

Today's hike brings me through a nice long segment through Klipnocky and Bully Hill State Forests, followed by a roadwalk into Hornell where I stop for a break and some surprisingly good pizza at the gas station. The day has turned very hot and I have an uphill climb leading out of Hornell, so I need to be well hydrated. While at the gas station, I take time to check my email and send in a call to Bruce to let him know of my location. Folks who have been following along with my hike are expecting me to finish sometime in the next few weeks, so I let Bruce know where I am and where I expect to be the next few days.

I also take time to check the weather; a thunderstorm is due to hit sometime tomorrow, shortly after noon. I should get as far as I can today to try and beat the weather (if possible). So instead of spending the night in Hornell I push on for a few more hours. The trail leads me across some private land and into Burt Hill State Forest where I stop for the night at the shelter here.

Saturday, September 21
Trail Day 170
Miles hiked: 17.5
Super 8 Motel - Bath, NY

I'm up fairly early and get hiking right away to try and beat the impending storm. The trail today is entirely on private land and half on roadwalk. After an hour or so, I stop at the edge of a farmer's field to have a quick snack and glance at my maps. As I am studying the map, from the corner of my eye, I see something move. I am completely surprised to see a lynx standing in the middle of the trail, staring at me, less than twenty feet away!

I've never seen one in the wild so this encounter is a real treat. If you've never seen one, a lynx basically resembles a giant house cat with a short tail. It spends a few seconds staring at me, as with the pack I'm sure I look strange. After realizing that I'm a person, it quickly retreats into the corn nearby and vanishes. The quick encounter didn't allow enough time for a picture, for which I am greatly disappointed.

The rest of the day proves to be largely uneventful. A short section along a probable esker allows for some terrain changes, and then a short section through an active archery range adds to the experience. At NY-415, I turn from the trail toward Bath and manage to reach town a little before 1:30 p.m., and check into the Super 8 Motel. No sooner have I reached my room on the third floor than the thunderstorm begins.

Yesterday when I checked my email, I had a message from Peggy of FLTC. She said she would like to help me out when I reach the Hornell area, so I give her a call. I let her know that I have made it to Bath right as the storm hit, and that I am staying in town tonight. She says she wants to take me out to dinner and we make arrangements for her to pick me up in an hour. When she arrives, we head toward Hammondsport to an authentic Mexican restaurant.

While waiting for our orders, Peggy asks me some interview questions about my hike. She hopes to get me a few more interviews in Watkins Glen once I arrive there in a few days. The food is delicious, and Mexican food is difficult to find on the trail besides fast food joints. Once back at the motel I say goodbye to Peggy, and she wishes me luck as I continue on the final leg of my journey. *Thanks Peggy, for your encouragement and treating me to that fine meal.*

Sunday, September 22
Trail Day 171
Miles hiked: 22
Just south of Rhinehart Road – Sugar Hill State Forest, FLT

I slept in this morning to recover as much as possible before hitting the trail again. By the time I have had breakfast and packed my gear, it is almost 11 a.m. before I am out hiking. On my way out of town, a woman pulls over in her car and rolls down her window. "I saw you walking and thought you could use this." She hands me a twenty dollar bill. Hence, I meet Karen.

She asks me my story and I give her the quick rundown. She seems very inspired by my journey. She has a dream to hike the AT once both of her kids are in college. After a brief conversation, she is gone. *Thank you Karen for your generous donation. I wish you the best of luck on your future AT thru-hike.*

Today's hike is mostly on private land, but the trail is well maintained for the most part. I reach the highlight of the day fairly early where the trail follows some field roads around sunflower fields to a sheltered bench with great views to the south. After stopping to admire the view, I sign the trail register nearby and continue on.

Some interesting features of the trail today is a short segment along an abandoned railroad (with rails still in place) and a short section through some vineyards. The day ends with a long road-walk where I make good time, and I make it to Birdseye Hollow State forest and pitch for the night. Despite the late start I manage to get in a solid twenty-two miles.

Monday, September 23
Trail Day 172
Miles hiked: 26
Twin Shelters – Birdseye Hollow State Forest, FLT

Today's hike takes me through some finely-maintained trail through many state forests, with some roadwalk connectors in between. Within the first few miles I pass by Birdseye Hollow County Park and an old foundation. Once out of Birdseye Hollow State Forest, I have a long roadwalk to bring me into South Bradford State Forest. Here, I reach an intersection with the Great Eastern Trail. This is the northern terminus of the GET, which parallels the AT on the west side of the Appalachian Mountains.

After snapping a picture of the sign, I turn and follow this trail a short distance to the Moss Hill Lean-to where I stop for a break. In the log book inside, I discover a note addressed to me. It is from Jo, a fellow Minnesotan who earlier this year completed a thru-hike of the GET. We had spoken once before I began my hike back in March, and she was very excited to hear about my trek over the NCT. Like me, she is also a regular on the SHT and heard about my hike at the annual meeting.

More unusual is the fact that she has family in my home town, which doesn't even show up on most maps. (What a small world we live in.) Inside is a coupon, "valid for one free beer." *Thanks Jo, I will keep this and cash it in sometime whenever our paths may cross.*

The hike continues through Goundry Hill, then Sugar Hill State Forests. At the northern-most point of this section the trail passes by a very old cemetery atop a hill; providing a great view north toward Lamoka and Waneta Lakes. I have a cell signal here and I have a text from Peggy. She has a TV news crew set to meet me in Watkins Glen around 11 a.m. tomorrow, and she will be there as well. With that in mind, I need to make it as far as I can today to minimize chances of being late tomorrow.

I finish the day hiking through Sugar Hill State Forest, passing one shelter where I originally intended to spend the night. Instead, I push on another mile and a half to a pair of shelters complete with picnic tables and a fire ring. I am a little surprised to be the only person here. This site is clearly intended for groups. Excited to finally reach Watkins Glen State Park tomorrow, I manage to cook my dinner and hang my food just as darkness descends. I settle into one of the shelters for a night of rest.

Tuesday, September 24
Trail Day 173
Miles hiked: 20.5
Dunham Shelter – Finger Lakes National Forest, FLT

I managed to have a restless sleep last night as the cold descended and it was hard to stay warm. As a result, I got a later start than I wanted, and I'm not sure if I'll be able to make it to Watkins Glen by 11. I feel guilty now, as I have an entire group of people depending on me to be there. With nothing to do but hike, I get started as soon as I am able, hiking as fast as possible to reach Watkins Glen State Park.

I have been looking forward to reaching this place since before starting my hike. During my research for this trek, I came upon many fantastic photos and videos of this place and have waited to experience it for myself. When I arrive I am not disappointed. It looks even better in real life, just spectacular!

This three-mile segment of trail I am on traverses Glen Creek, which is actually more of a river. Lots of history can be found here, even pre-dating the CCC days the entire trail through the gorge has been literally carved into the side of the gorge. Sheer walls tower above, stone steps, tunnels and bridges are abundant to allow access to view the many spectacular waterfalls.

As I descend into the gorge and reach the lowest level, I am immediately reminded of Rivendell, the hidden valley where the Elves dwell in Tolkien's great work. This place is absolutely breathtaking. I wish I could spend more time here, but unfortunately I have a time crunch and need to be moving on. I have no doubt this three-mile section of trail will be the highlight of the entire Finger Lakes Trail, and one of the best highlights of the entire NCT.

Right at the end of the gorge is the town of Watkins Glen, a fine trail town if there ever was one. I had sent a text earlier to Peggy to let her know I would be an hour late. Sure enough, I arrive at the Chamber of Commerce just before noon. When I arrive, I am surprised to find three separate camera crews there, all ready to hear my story. A few newspaper editors are there as well, and after taking a few moments to find a good spot, the interviews begin. It's a strange feeling, being in the woods for days on end and suddenly be in the middle of civilization with cameras and microphones shoved in your face. I don't mind it the least bit, as my goal to raise awareness and interest in the trail is dependent upon interviews like these.

After the interviews are over, I head to the post office to retrieve my next supply package. As I am heading into the building Peggy flags me down. With her is her coworker, Kim, and they say they would like to take me to lunch. There's no way I can say no to that. We find a nice establishment with some good food and excellent beer, and I give Peggy an update of my hike since I saw her a few days ago. Kim has many questions for me. She just graduated college a few years ago and still has the adventurous spirit in her. What a fun time here in Watkins Glen.

Back at Peggy's car it comes time for another sad goodbye. She and Kim need to hit the road and head back to work. *Thanks Peggy for all you have done for me the past few days. And thank you Kim, for tagging along to meet me.*

I decide to linger in town for awhile before moving on. I find a nice ice cream joint right near where the trail exits the park. I find it to be some of the best ice cream I have ever tasted. I make conversation with Pete, the owner, and he wishes me luck on my journey. I finally leave town and follow the trail along the shore of Seneca Lake, one of the Finger Lakes. A short section of trail just outside of town takes me past a nice creek gorge complete with a waterfall.

Most of the remainder of the day is a roadwalk to the Finger Lakes National Forest. I stop outside the bar in Burdett for a quick break. As I am leaving, I run into Melven, a local. He just saw me on the news and wants to know more about my hike. Wow, that was fast! The interview was mere hours ago, incredible.

I finish the roadwalk and begin my hike through the Finger Lakes National Forest. I am only about a mile from the shelter there when I lose daylight and have to find the shelter in the dark. With my head lamp on, I make it there without any trouble and settle in for the night.

Wednesday, September 25
Trail Day 174
Miles hiked: 25
Riemann Woods Campsite - FLT

I was up and moving early this morning; it was still dark. I begin the hike early, trying to get as far as possible today. The hike leads through Texas Hollow State Forest before crossing NY-228 at the

Veterans Memorial Park. I stop here for a break to refill my water before continuing on.

The next stage of the hike brings me through Connecticut Hill Wildlife Management Area, passing through a nice gorge and over the summit of Connecticut Hill (the highest point for about forty miles in any direction). After that, is a most enjoyable section through Stevenson Forest Preserve with giant Hemlocks all around. I stop underneath one of these giants to have a last snack of the day before hiking the few more miles to the Riemann Woods Campsite. There, I call it a day.

Thursday, September 26
Trail Day 175
Miles hiked: 31
Shindagin Shelter - FLT

Today's hike brings me through Robert H. Treman State Park. It's not nearly as impressive as Watkins Glen, but it has many of the same features; lots of carved stairways into the side of the gorge and many impressive waterfalls. Unfortunately, the main route through the gorge, the Gorge Trail is closed for repairs. This is very disappointing, but I'm still able to see most of the main attractions from the Rim trail. There are only a few people out and about in the park today so it is a very peaceful hike.

From the park the trail crosses lots of private land before reaching Danby State Forest. The trail through the state forests continues to be well marked and maintained. Exiting the forest the trail heads on private land and over Eastman Hill and along a high cliff edge for a good distance. With all the trees blocking the view it's hard to see just how far down this cliff goes, it has to be a few hundred feet straight down.

Crossing NY-119 the trail follows an abandoned rail grade for a short distance before turning east and heading through Shindagin Hollow State Forest. I reach the shelter there after dark and spend a little time filtering water from the nearby creek before calling it a day.

Friday, September 27
Trail Day 176
Miles hiked: 34
Home of Jon and Jennifer – near Cortland, NY

I've got a drop box waiting for me in Blodgett Mill—a good forty-three miles from here. I'm going to have to get in some serious miles to make it to the post office there before noon on Saturday, so I'm up and hiking at first light. After leaving Shindagin Hollow State Forest, the hike is mostly a roadwalk with a small section of trail around Potato Hill State Forest, then around a trailer park to Robinson Hollow State Forest. I take a break at the Kimmie Lean-to before continuing on through Hammond Hill State Forest, along some field edges and past a microwave tower.

Once in Kennedy State Forest, I pass many opportunities for loop hikes: the orange blazed Spanish loop, the blue blazed Swedish loop, the yellow blazed Lithuanian loop, green blazed Irish loop, and orange blazed Virgil Mt. loop. After crossing the Virgil Mt. Loop for the second time, the trail turns north and loops back around over Greek Peak and Virgil Mt. before descending down to the road.

I stop on the corner at The Gatherings Restaurant and Cabins for a break. I'm just about to leave when a guy pulls up in his truck and on his way inside stops to chat with me. Hence, I meet Justin, who lives just down the road and was going to get some takeout at the restaurant. He recognizes me right away. As it turns out, one of his classes at the local college has been following my progress. I tell him my plans about getting to the shelter just a few miles up the trail and leaving early so I can make it to Blodgett Mills in the morning to get my package. He then invites me back to his place for dinner, says he will drop me off back on the trail early morning, as he needs to head to Pittsburgh for the weekend anyway. I accept his offer and we load my gear into his truck. We head not even a mile down the road to his place.

When we arrive, I am greeted by two more people: Jenn and Jon, owners of the house. Justin is renting a room upstairs and says I can crash on his couch for the night. Justin explains to them who I am and how he ran into me at the restaurant. They are excited to host me for the night and to hear my story. Before long, I am invited out back to their patio complete with a nice fire pit, and I am served a nice glass of red wine. As dinner is cooking, Jenn and Jon give me the tour of their backyard. The creek runs right through their property and they explain to me the recent history of the area and how recent floods have changed the terrain of their land.

Just as darkness is descending, I am served a great meal of steak and potato wedges while I converse with my new friends. Jon gets a fire going, and after dinner we all sit around and have s'mores with their two kids. I haven't had a s'more since my night at the schoolhouse back in White Cloud, MI. What a treat.

Jenn hands me her business card before her and the family retire to bed. I am close behind, and Justin shows me the way upstairs to his apartment where I crash for the night on his couch.

Saturday, September 28
Trail Day 177
Miles hiked: 25
Home of Bill and Mary - Chittanengo, NY

Yesterday, as I was sitting outside the Gatherings Restaurant, I made a phone call to Mary. She is involved with both the Adirondack Mountain Club (ADK) and the Central New York Chapter, NCT. She wanted to host me for a day as I approached the Onondaga section of the FLT, which is about a day's hike away now. We made plans for her to pick me up at the end of today, somewhere in Taylorsville State Forest at one of the two trailheads there. (Right when I got off the phone with her, I ran into Justin, and the events of last night transpired.)

I didn't sleep well last night. On top of getting to sleep pretty late and getting up really early this morning, all in all I only got about four hours of sleep. Justin fixes us a quick breakfast and then he drops me back on the trail at 6 a.m. We shake hands and he wishes me luck as he drives away and heads to Pittsburgh.

The hike begins in Tuller Hill State Forest. I need my headlamp for the first half hour or so as it is still dark. When I reach the Woodchuck Hollow Lean-to where I planned to spend last night, I take the headlamp off and put it in my pack. Now light out, I make good time to the north end of the forest, then through a section on private land and reach West River Road. The next six miles are on roads and I make it to Blodgett Mills before 10 a.m. to retrieve my package.

I take a break outside the post office and make a few phone calls. Bruce left me a voicemail so I call him back first thing. He tells me about an opportunity to do some serious networking at the upcoming National Scenic and Historic Trails Conference in Tucson, AZ. There is a scholarship program available for college students or recent graduates, to attend the conference as a trail apprentice and learn how to get into the trail business. It also allows them to provide their own insight about the needs of the younger generation. He wants to know if I would be interested in applying so he can get the paperwork started while I am still on the trail. It sounds like a great opportunity, so I tell him to go ahead and get started.

After an hour I am ready to continue on, so I shoulder my pack and head out of Blodgett Mills on a roadwalk to reach Hoxie Gorge. At the creek, I navigate around several blowdowns and lose the trail in the process. After spending twenty minutes walking around in circles trying to find the trail, I finally get back on track, frustrated as I discover it was a badly marked turn that threw me off track.

The next section of trail is through some private land to Baker Schoolhouse State Forest. At the trailhead a sign is posted. Apparently, the trail dead-ends at the forest boundary ahead because the landowner on the other end withdrew their permission for the trail recently. Looking at my map I realize it will add several miles to detour around this section. After walking along busy NY-41 for several miles, I find the trail where it heads up a steep embankment on some stairs into private land.

Soon I am in Taylor Valley State Forest and am climbing up Mt. Tego. Toward the top I have a cell signal, so I give Mary a call. With the short sleep last night and the extra miles hiked today, I don't have enough energy to make it over the next ridge to the second trailhead where we planned to connect. I ask her to pick me up at the first one instead, which is just a few miles away. I hammer out the last miles and reach the trailhead off Cortland-Two Road. I'm there no more than a minute or two when a car comes down the road toward me and stops. Hence, I meet Mary in person.

We load my gear into her car and enjoy a nice chat en route to her home in Chittanengo. When we arrive, I bring my gear inside and meet her husband, Bill. Mary shows me to the room where I will be staying, and I unload my gear and get a hot shower in before dinner. At the dinner table I am served a delicious bowl of beef stew with a cold beer, and even apple crisp for dessert.

During our conversation at the dinner table, Mary mentions that the Onondaga Chapter of ADK is having a reception for me tomorrow at Highland Forest County Park. This means I will be able to sleep in tonight and get some much-needed rest. Before I turn in for the night, Mary says it's fine if I use her computer to check email and anything else I need to do. I take the opportunity to fill out all the paperwork that Bruce has forwarded to me about the National Trails Conference, and within an hour have it all filled out and sent in. Fingers crossed this works out in the end.

Sunday, September 29
Trail Day 178
Miles hiked: 12
Rose Hollow Campsite - FLT

It was so nice to sleep in this morning. Immediately, when I get up I am treated to a great sausage and egg breakfast. After that I spend awhile sorting through my gear and looking over my maps to make a tentative plan for the next few days.

Around 10 a.m. we load the car and head for Highland Park for the banquet. The Lodge where the banquet will be held is an impressive facility. There is a large balcony on the north side that provides a sweeping view of the countryside. Quite a few people have shown up to meet me and hear my story; most of them members and volunteers of ADK, FLT, or NCT. We enjoy a nice spread of food while sharing stories about the trail. Afterward, we all stand on the balcony for a group photo. It was a pleasure meeting everyone who attended: Anne and Bill, Mike, Tony, Kathy, Peg, Brian, Laurie, and Lucy. I apologize for leaving anyone out, a few names are escaping me. There were perhaps five others... again, sorry.

It surely was an enjoyable afternoon. After a few hours it is time for me to hit the trail. However, and I say farewell to everyone as Mary and Bill load me into their car and we head back to Taylor Valley State Forest. I say goodbye for now, but I will be seeing them again in a few days. It is after 2 p.m. when I get on trail again. After following the trail through the forest and over Mt. Roderick, it follows the road for the next mile before heading back into the woods.

Along the road segment, I meet a few horseback riders out for an afternoon ride. They clearly don't know that the NCT is not meant for horses—even though there are "no horses" signs at almost every road crossing. But I don't have time to stop and argue with them so I let them by and continue on my way.

Back in the woods, the trail crosses a neat stone water crossing made out of large flat boulders to cross a creek before crossing the road and entering Cheningo Day Use Area. Many switchbacks lead out of the day use area and toward Allen Hill where the trail leaves the forest. A brief section across private land leads into Cuyler Hill State Forest where I will be camping for the night.

I pass the first campsite along Wiltsey Glen with an impressive fire pit, but continue on to the second site to use every amount of daylight I have. Soon, I come to an orange-blazed spur trail leading to Rose Hollow campsite where I will pitch for the night. No sooner do I set up camp than darkness descends and I turn in for the night.

Monday, September 30
Trail Day 179
Miles hiked: 26
Backyard of Eric and Camory - near DeRuyter Lake

I am excited to wake up this morning. I have less than three miles
to go to reach the beginning of the Onondaga Trail that the NCT
follows away from the main FLT. This is exciting because it means
I am just one step closer to reaching the end of my hike at the edge
of Adirondack Park. However, it also means I will be leaving the
FLT behind, which has been one of the best highlights of this trek
overall.

I hike the three miles within an hour and am standing at a road
crossing where I see the blazes change from white to blue. It's nice
to have the company of the familiar blue blazes again. The Onondaga Trail begins on private land, where it mostly follows along
the wooded field edges, a few small cemeteries included. Just outside the village of Cuyler, the trail follows the road for the next
two miles before again entering private land on a tractor road behind a farm and heading uphill into the woods. I stop toward the
top to take a break and enjoy the nice view to the southeast.

From here, the trail travels through Morgan Hill State Forest for
the remainder of the day; taking me past several campsites, a shelter and right on the rim above Tinker Falls. I originally intended
to hike the spur trail down to the base of the falls, but I simply
have no time now. Within Labrador Hollow Unique Area I stop
at the summit of Jones Hill to admire the view. The land drops
off steeply at a cliff just in front of me, and this is designated as a
hang-glider launch point. No gliders up here today, just a young
couple sitting enjoying the view.

I have a cell signal up so I make a call. A guy named Eric emailed
me a few weeks back saying he would be interested in helping me

out when I was in this area. We have a brief conversation and I tell him my situation. If he would be willing to pick me up at the end of the day at a road crossing I wouldn't need to take a shorter day to camp within the forest boundary. He is very enthusiastic to help me out so we make plans for him to pick me up at the end of the day.

The rest of the day is a very enjoyable hike along well-marked trail, mostly through the state forest and the rest on private land. Some wetter areas on the private land has some boardwalk with wire mesh stapled on top to provide traction. (Good thinking by the volunteers who maintain this section.) I am only about a mile away when darkness descends and I have to pick my way carefully to avoid getting caught in a fence or going off track along the field edges.

I make it down to the road without incident and hike a few hundred feet to an intersection. I see a truck waiting on the side of the road and two guys talking in a farm driveway. Hence, I meet Eric, here to pick me up and shuttle me to his home near DeRuyter Lake. Also here is Scott, owner of the farm and maintainer of the section I just passed through, which happens to cross his land. It turns out it was his idea to put the mesh down on the boardwalk to give extra traction. *Thanks for allowing the trail to cross your land Scott, and for keeping it well maintained.*

After conversing for a few minutes along the side of the road, I load my gear into Eric's truck and we head for his home. He explains that some of his children are currently sick with a flu so he says it's up to me if I want to stay in the house or camp out in his yard. With the hike through the Adirondacks coming up in a matter of days, now would be the worst time to get sick. I decide to play it safe and pitch my tent in his backyard for the night. When we arrive, I find a nice level place between his back door and his fire pit. As I am setting up camp, he gets a fire going first thing, accompanied by two of his young children. With the fire going he tells me to relax while he gets some dinner ready. Within a few minutes, I am served a delicious warm bowl of soup from his wife Camory. We spend awhile around the campfire sharing stories about the trail. The kids seem fascinated with my gear and the stories of my hike.

Eventually, it is bed time for the kids and I decide to turn in as well. Eric says he will be ready to go at first light as he has to be at work at 7 a.m. Works fine for me. I end the night by putting out the fire and settling in for a comfortable night of sleep.

Tuesday, October 1
Trail Day 180
Miles hiked: 31, +1
Home of Bill and Mary - Chittanengo, NY

I slept well last night so getting up early is no problem. I'm all packed up and ready by six. We load my gear into Eric's truck and he drops me off in front of Scott's farm where he is out and about. Eric hands me an apple to take for a snack, and with a hand shake he is gone and off to work. *Thanks for letting me stay in your yard last night, it was a pleasure meeting you and your family.* One final "good luck" from Scott and I am hiking down the road toward Highland Forest County Park.

When I arrive, I am disappointed to find that a dense fog has settled in, so I am robbed of the great view from the balcony of the Lodge. I stop in to refill my water and then continue on. A little ways east of the Lodge I manage to take a wrong turn and don't realize it for the better part of a mile. Luckily for me, all the intersections are numbered so I am able to look at the park map and find exactly where I am. I backtrack to the point I lost the trail and pick it up again, I simply wasn't paying attention and missed the point where it turned from the main path. Exiting the park the trail is a roadwalk passing along the north shore of DeRuyter Lake. The fog has lifted somewhat and the sun has pierced the clouds. I am reminded of Minnesota, Land of 10,000 Lakes. Such a pretty scene.

After passing through DeRuyter State Forest I take a detour into the village of New Woodstock, as the next trail section is now closed for hunting. From here it is a roadwalk to the boundary of Tioghnioga WMA where the trail follows the west boundary. I am disappointed to find this section overgrown in many places, but I make it through without too much difficulty. Coming out onto a service road I have reached the end of the Onondaga Trail and will now turn north onto the Link Trail that will lead me to Canastota and the Old Erie Canal Trail. I have officially left the Finger Lakes Trail behind.

The Link Trail starts off as a roadwalk then crosses some private land to an old rail grade that has been maintained to a nice six-foot-wide path. More roadwalking leads to a section through some private land and a very interesting sculpture park. Like Lakenenland back in Michigan, the owner of this park has displayed his artwork just for the enjoyment of the public, and has allowed the trail to pass through it. This segment brings me into Cazenovia where I stop for a break. I give make a phone call to Bill, as he and Mary were planning on meeting me again tonight. We make plans for him to pick me up at the end of the off road section north of Cazenovia in about two hours. With no time to waste I shoulder my pack and continue on.

The trail leading out of Cazenovia is yet another Gorge Trail, the third for this state. It is aptly named as it parallels the river and has a few small waterfalls and rapids along the way. This is a most enjoyable hike, mostly on abandoned rail grade that has been well maintained. I pass many people along this stretch, some walking, some on bikes, and some out for an evening jog. I'm able to make good time and make it to within about a hundred yards of Freber Road when I recognize Bill hiking down the trail toward me. Well if this isn't good timing I don't know what is!

We load my gear into his car and head to Chittenengo for dinner. At the restaurant, we talk about my experience on the trail the past few days, and my immediate itinerary for days ahead. Bill takes the opportunity for some trail publicity by informing our hostess about my hike. She asks me a few basic questions and seems impressed by my journey. I am again disappointed that she has never heard of the NCT, even though it is right here in her back yard. Hopefully one day we can change that and get more people interested in the NCT.

We head back to Bill and Mary's house where I will again be spending the night. Mary offers one of her smaller packs to use tomorrow so I can travel lighter. I accept her offer gladly as my goal is to make it to Rome, which is a good thirty-four miles away. I head to bed pretty early so I'm rested for the long day tomorrow.

Wednesday, October 2
Trail Day 181
Miles hiked: 34
Quality Inn - Rome, NY

I'm out and hiking fairly early this morning with a lighter pack to make it easier to cover the long miles. I hike the Link Trail the last eleven miles or so along farm edges and into the town of Canastota where I have a drop box waiting. This box is important as it contains all the maps I will need to get through the Adirondacks. Adirondack Park is mostly a wilderness area roughly four times the size of Yellowstone, only it's controlled by the state, which makes it unique. To navigate this vast area I got the wonderfully detailed waterproof National Geographic Maps, five of them to cover the entire park. Back in the planning stages of my hike I had the luxury to make my own route through the park, as the final plan for the NCT has not been finalized. I hope to reach the edge of the park day after tomorrow and at least get a few miles in before dark.

At the post office now I receive my package and send a few things home, including a few souvenirs I received at Highland Forest County Park, and all the maps since Watkins Glen. The clerk can tell I have a story to tell, so I give him the quick rundown of my hike and that I am now about two weeks away from finishing. He is very impressed and wishes me the best of luck...he even covers the cost to mail my package home! *Thank you sir, every bit of trail magic is precious.*

The rest of the day is spent along the Old Erie Canal Trail, mostly a crushed limestone surface canal towpath clear from here all the way to Rome. This section proves to be mostly uneventful except for the unseasonably warm temperature, hovering around 85 degrees. In the middle the towpath is interrupted for a hike along dangerous NY-46, and afterwards I manage to witness a barge go through the canal at Lock 21. The hard surface of today plus the long miles I've put on since crossing into New York have put a number on my feet. By the end of the day they are screaming at me.

At the Old Erie Canal Village on the outskirts of Rome, Mary and Bill are there to intercept me. I exchange packs with Mary, getting my big heavy one back. Thus, it is also time for another goodbye. *Thank you Mary and Bill for all you have done for me these past few days.*

I hike the remaining few miles into Rome and check in at the Quality Inn right as darkness descends. The rest of the night is spent laying in bed and caring for my feet. I am planning on sleeping in tomorrow; I haven't taken a break since Lisbon, Ohio and have covered long miles since then. I am overdue for a break. However, I have only a few more days until I am in Old Forge,which is my next resupply point. Once there, I planned to take one last zero day or two before hammering out the remaining miles of this amazing trail.

Thursday, October 3
Trail Day 182
Miles hiked: 25
Headwaters Motor Inn - Boonville, NY

I am definitely overdue for a rest day, I slept in until almost 11 a.m. With much reluctance, I get some food in me and head out with pack shouldered to another unseasonably hot day. Today is almost entirely a roadwalk and my feet are screaming at me right away. Right across the street from the motel is Fort Stanwix National Monument, a reconstructed Revolutionary War fort that the trail passes through. I have to bypass the fort however, because of the recent federal government shutdown, in effect until further notice.

Just outside Rome, I spot a small parking area and a flat grade in the woods on the left. It's not on my map, but I decide to follow it and it dumps me back out to the road at the fish hatchery. I have nearly eighteen miles of roadwalk along NY-46 to reach some off road trail just south of Pixley Falls State Park. Along the route I can see for the first time the Adirondack Mountains in the distance. From Pixley Falls to Booneville the NCT follows the Black River Canal Towpath, mostly a grass trail intended for skiing in the winter. I enjoy this section as it is much easier on my poor feet with the soft grass cushioning. All around most of the trees' leaves have turned red and some have already dropped their leaves. Fall is definitely in full swing now.

It is already dark when I finally enter Boonville and make my way through downtown, and stop in a bar for a drink to get rehydrated. A few of the locals see my pack and ask the usual questions. They wish me luck and continue on with their conversation. I linger for awhile and then ask the bartender where the motel is in town. He says it's down the road about a half mile on the outside of town. With nothing left to do, I make my way to the Headwaters Motor Inn and check in. For dinner I order a few calzones from the brochure in the room, and after gorging myself and looking over my maps to plan for my entry into Adirondack Park, I crash and instantly fall asleep.

Friday, October 4
Trail Day 183
Miles hiked: 29, +2
Gull Lake Shelter - Adirondack Park

I woke up early this morning to get an early start to make up for lost time. After a quick breakfast I'm out the door and hiking before 6 a.m. The trail heads out of Boonville on the BREIA Canal Path, but it is still dark outside and I am unable to find where the trail leaves the covered bridge in Ester Park. I decide to not waste time and just hike this portion on roads. It will be roughly the same distance by road, possibly a little longer.

Right as the sun comes up the rain begins, not a downpour, but just enough to make everything soaking wet. Within a few hours I am in the town of Forestport and I find the trail where it follows one of the village streets to an intersection with a diner on the corner. I look around and see no more blazes after this one on the corner. This may be the last blue blaze I will see on this trek as the rest of the trail between here and Crown Point is unofficial.

The rain letting up for the moment, I stop outside the diner for a break to let my feet rest. A guy from the power company, whose truck is parked nearby, walks over and wants to hear my story. I tell him my story so far, and how I am now only days away from finishing. He congratulates me and gives me a piece of fruit from his lunch box to tide me over this morning. He also points me in the right direction to get to North Lake Road where the trailhead to enter the park is located. It turns out, it's the same road I am on now, it's just uses a different name here. Thanks for your help sir.

A few miles up the road is a small grocery store where I stop to purchase a small box of raspberries. This may be my last chance for real food for at least a week. Kind folks working the counter here.

The rain coming down again, I continue on and soon cross the "Blue Line" into Adirondack Park. Soon I am standing at the trailhead for the Stone Dam Lake Trail, planned to be the NCT someday. I sign the trail register with my intended itinerary before heading on it. Many people are rescued from this vast wilderness every year, I'd prefer not to be a victim myself.

The trail starts out in nice shape, making for an enjoyable hike. However, after a few miles I run into trouble. There is supposed to be an intersection up ahead where I should turn left to head towards the shelter on the shore of Gull Lake. However, I am greatly confused when the trail I am on dead-ends at the Chub Pond Shelter. According to the map, I missed the turn almost a half mile back. Carefully I retrace my steps, but hike over a mile the other way until I again turn around and hike back to the shelter. I do this two more times before finally becoming frustrated, almost to the point of tears.

I stop where I am and just sit on the ground. I can't believe this is happening. I'm only three miles in to what is supposed to be the best part of the whole hike and I am utterly lost. If the trail is here it is not marked at all, and is lost amongst the brush. Realizing I may have no choice but to hike back out the way I came and hike to Old Forge on roads, I take one last look. I head back and spot a small trail marker on a tree in the middle of a beaver pond. Suddenly it hits me. The trail intersection I was looking for has been completely swallowed up by a beaver pond as a result of a recent dam. The trail I was on was a reroute around it to get to the shelter.

Keeping my eye on the marker, I begin to carefully wade my way across almost waist-high water in some places and make it to the other side without completely falling in. Once on the other side, it takes only a short search to pick up the trail again. Thank goodness, I am back on track! However, I wasted an hour walking back and forth to try and find this trail that I now have very little daylight left to hike almost four miles to the shelter.

With no time to lose, I pick up the pace to find that trail conditions here have decreased quite dramatically. Unfortunately, the section I am on now is open to snowmobiles in the winter and so it is very wide and wet. With all the rain we just had the wet spots are pure mud. I sink up to my knees in some places, making the hiking very slow and sloppy. I hope my entire hike through the Adirondacks isn't like this.

Despite the setbacks and the temporarily crushed spirits, I make it to the shelter a little after dark. I hang my food and spread out my gear in the shelter just as the rain comes again. Glad to be in for the night with a roof over my head.

Saturday, October 5
Trail Day 184
Miles hiked: 18
Adirondack Lodge – Old Forge, NY

As I wake up in the shelter this morning I can't see more than five feet out. An extremely dense fog has rolled in. I spend some time to cook breakfast and then head out as soon as I am ready. From the heavy rain last night the trail is once again a mud bog, more sinking up to my knees as I struggle to make it through the low areas. After a few hours however, I finally make it to the McKeever trailhead parking lot. From here it will be all a road walk along NY-28 to reach Old Forge where I will be taking a much needed rest.

There is a constant stream of traffic heading into the Adirondacks today. Everyone is coming up to see the last of the fall leaves. A few miles short of Old Forge I begin to feel a sharp pain behind my knee. I try to slow my pace but it's not helping much and the pain is getting worse. What a heck of a time to score an injury. I should have taken a rest day back in Rome or even Watkins Glen to give my legs a break, and now I regret not doing so. This may not have happened otherwise.

With much painful struggling, I do manage to make it to the edge of Old Forge but I need to stop on the side of the road for awhile to give my leg a rest. As I am just getting up to make the final push into town, a car pulls up and stops. "Need a ride?" Hence, I meet Veronica, up here for the weekend to do some day hiking. I am only a short distance from the place where I plan on staying and I need to get some supplies before settling in. I find out from Veronica that the grocery store is clear on the other side of town, a few miles. So without any further thought, I accept her offer for a ride to the grocery store.

Along the way, she asks me where I'm headed and I give her the rundown of my journey, and how I am now about ten days away from finishing. She is very excited and congratulates me on a job well done. As she pulls in the grocery store, I unload my gear from the back of her car. As I am leaving, she hands me a piece of paper with her number and email address on it. "I'll be in the area all weekend, let me know if you need anything." *Thanks Veronica, it was a pleasure meeting you.*

At the grocery store I stock up on fresh supplies to last two full days. Being Saturday, the post office is now closed so I will have to wait until Monday to get my package. After walking out of the store with enough to happily gorge myself over the next forty-eight hours, I take a break outside and enjoy a fresh orange juice and a box of cookies, before finishing out the day by walking back over a mile to the Adirondack Lodge where I will be staying.

On the way there a woman flags me down and comes over to chat. Hence I meet Michele, a local. She saw me along the road and could tell I had a great story to tell. We spend a good while talking about both of our experiences—mine on this long journey I am on, and hers about a quest to hike all the 46ers in the Adirondacks. Adirondack Park has forty-six mountain peaks that are at or above 4,000 feet elevation, and it is a goal of many to eventually conquer them all; Michele being one of them.

She can tell I am exhausted so she doesn't want to hold me up, but she wants to hear more about my journey. She hands me a piece of paper with her number on it and says she wants to treat me to dinner tomorrow night. *That is awfully nice of you Michele, I will definitely take you up on your offer.*

After parting ways with Michele (for the time being), I finally make it to the Adirondack Lodge. I took time while I was in Rome to reserve a room here for two nights, and it is all ready to go when I arrive. No sooner have I checked in than a thunderstorm rolls in and lingers the rest of the night. After draping all my gear over the backs of chairs and on the table to let it dry out, I take a nice warm shower and settle in for a weekend of rest.

Sunday, October 6
Trail Day XXX
Miles hiked: 00
Adirondack Lodge – Old Forge, NY

The Adirondack Lodge is a nice place. The structure is designed with that classic north woods feel. Good continental breakfast, spacious rooms with balconies on the upper level, they even have a heated indoor pool. Yes, I sure picked a good place to take a day off.

My legs hurt in various places; a lot of strain has been put on them from pushing on this past month with no rest. I have had mostly shin splints and a strained muscle behind my knee, but not nearly as bad as it was yesterday. It rains the entire day today so I am unable to enjoy the balcony outside my room. I spend some time looking over the maps for Adirondack Park trying to find the quickest way through. Originally, I had planned a route that would get me through the park while staying on trails for about ninety percent of the time. This adds some mileage but it's more true to the experience of a thru-hike.

However, after being about two weeks behind my original planned itinerary (and my strength being depleted little by little every day), I am no longer comfortable taking the longer route. As soon as I leave Old Forge I will be starting the most difficult part of my entire hike, right at the end. Winter could come any day now and I definitely do not want to get stuck in a bad situation. I find a new route leading out of Old Forge on roads to the

Northville Placid Trail (NPT) where I can pick up my original route that will take me into the High Peaks. By doing this, I can still see the major highlights that I intended, and I can cut out an entire day of traveling.

With my mind made up, I make a call back home to inform my family of the changed route so they know where I will be if anything bad happens. Afterward, I give Michele a call. She regrets to inform me that she will not be able to make it tonight like she hoped, but she still wants to treat me to dinner. She has a gift card for a nice pizza joint down the road that she wants me to have. After getting off the phone I head downstairs to the lobby and she is there with the card in hand. After a brief conversation she wishes me luck and is gone. *Thanks for your generous donation Michele, and for your kindness. It was a pleasure meeting you.*

Monday, October 7
Trail Day XXX
Miles hiked: 00
Adirondack Lodge – Old Forge, NY

Last night at midnight, the severe weather sirens went off. I realized when I woke up that I definitely need another day of rest, so right away after breakfast I check in for another night. The woman at the desk informs me that we are in a tornado watch for the rest of the day; very unusual for this time of year and for this area in general. At the moment it is warm and sunny, so I head to the post office to retrieve my package that will get me through the rest of New York. Inside is my winter gear, enough food for a week, and a bear canister. Hikers traveling through the High Peaks are required to use bear canisters for their food. They are heavy and bulky, so for the next week I will be a little heavier than usual.

As soon as I get back to the lodge, the wind picks up and the rain comes again. It's definitely not a good day for hiking. Toward evening though, the rain quits and I take the opportunity to use Michele's gift card to get a fine dinner at Tony Harper's Pizza Shack. Back at the Lodge I stock my bear canister full of food and pack up my gear in preparation for the final leg of my journey.

Tuesday, October 8
Trail Day 185
Miles hiked: 26
Golden Beach Campground – Adirondack Park

I decide to sleep in this morning but still get going at a decent time. After one last breakfast, I head out and hit the road, literally. The entire day is a road walk as I head east out of Old Forge on NY-28 through the little village of Inlet and along many lakes. It is nice today; sunny, fairly warm and no rain. It is a very enjoyable, if uneventful hiking day.

As dusk approaches, I pull off into the trees amongst a few removed sites of Golden Beach Campground right on the shore of Raquette Lake where I pitch for the night.

Wednesday, October 9
Trail Day 186
Miles hiked: 23.5
Catlin Bay Shelter #1 - NPT, Adirondack Park

I woke up this morning to a banging sound out by the road. As I emerge from my tent, I strain my eyes through the trees to see many large yellow trucks parked barely a stone's throw away from where I am. The Department of Transportation must be doing a last-minute project along the roadway to prepare for winter. In fear of getting in their way or being blocked from getting out, I break camp as quickly as possible and hit the road again.

Like yesterday, the hike is almost entirely a roadwalk. My goal is to reach the first shelter out of Long Lake on the Northville Placid Trail by nightfall. Despite the long road walk, I am provided many nice views along the way. I stop for a break outside the Adirondack Museum in the little berg of Blue Mountain Lake. Lots of tourists are out and about enjoying the nice weather.

Once I reach the village of Long Lake, I stop for one last break before hiking the last few miles to the trailhead for the NPT. At a house across the street I see a guy with his dog and another hiker standing in his yard talking. The dog owner flags me over as I pass by. As I walk up he explains what he is trying to do. He recently got the new dog and is trying to familiarize him to hikers so he won't chase them every time one walks by. What a good idea, I wish the folks down in Ohio would have gotten the memo to do this.

After spending a few minutes with the dog, the other hiker and I turn away and head up the street to the trailhead. Hence, I meet Max, currently on a thru-hike of the NPT and one of the few long-distance hikers I have seen this entire trek. We reach the trailhead and sign in to the trail register where we part ways. We both had planned to stay at the first shelter on Catlin Bay, but I have just enough daylight to make it to the second one instead. And Max noted that my pace was much quicker than his, so he probably won't catch up to me. *Happy Trails Max, I wish you luck on completing your journey in a few days' time.

The first few miles of the NPT are in very good shape, decently marked and maintained, very good quality for a wilderness trail. I am excited to see what the next few days have in store. I reach the second shelter (which is actually marked Catlin Bay #1) just as darkness descends and I am officially in the High Peaks Wilderness.

Thursday, October 10
Trail Day 187
Miles hiked: 24
Duck Hole #2 Shelter - NPT, Adirondack Park

Breakfast this morning is some good ol' power bars. I made a decision not to carry any meals that require cooking into the High Peaks. It saves space allowing for more dry foods like power bars and saves weight by not having to carry any fuel or the meals themselves. As a bonus, it saves time, breakfast is quick, and then I am on the trail at first light.

I am impressed with the NPT as I head east, deeper into the High Peaks. It has many nice views of lakes and rivers, is well marked and maintained and is for backpacking, only so I don't have to worry about deteriorated trail because of bikes or horses. This trail was also the first one established in the Adirondacks, and possibly the first in the entire state of New York. From being well-known it is fairly well-travelled and the tread is easy to follow.

At one point, I come to a place where the beavers have been at work again. The trail ahead is completely submerged by at least two feet of water. Rather than getting my feet completely soaked I decide to detour around, which takes some time and carefully planned footing to avoid slipping and falling into the newly formed pond. On the other side, I come across two hikers hiking the opposite direction. Hence, I meet Luke and his father Steve out on the NPT for a few days. They ask if I'm thru-hiking and I say, "Yes, but not the NPT." I tell them my story and they are utterly surprised and impressed at my accomplishment. They seem interested in finding out more about the NCT, so I give them my website address before continuing on. After a firm handshake from both of them I continue on down the NPT.

The highlight of the day occurs while crossing two rivers. Some very impressive suspension bridges have been constructed to allow hikers to pass over the river gorges safely. The one over the Cold River is really impressive as the water rushes over a short waterfall, and some intense rapids move right underneath your feet as you pass over. Right on the other side is an Adirondack shelter, where I stop for a break to admire the view. I have no doubt this is probably one of the best shelters in the area and I can tell it is also heavily used.

Later in the day, I run into an obstacle in the form of many blow downs. This is a classic situation in which most of the trees are too high to climb over, but too low to crawl under. Luckily, someone has been through here recently and has marked a very narrow reroute through the debris with pink flagging. For the better part of a mile, I pick my way through this maze, ducking under trees and climbing over others until coming out on the other side. The rest of the day proves to be uneventful as I make it to a pair of shelters known as Duck Hole. There, I call it a night within view of an ancient wooden dam.

Friday, October 11
Trail Day 188
Miles hiked: 14.5, +1.5
Feldspar Shelter – High Peaks Wilderness, Adirondack Park

I slept well last night. Good thing too, as I will surely need my energy today. The trail continues the steady climb I have been taking since approaching Old Forge and gets steeper as the day goes on. Within a half mile of leaving the shelter, I come to a trail junction where I turn right and leave the NPT behind and head east into the center of the High Peaks and toward the highest of them all, Mt. Marcy. If I make good time today I can summit and make it to the shelter on the other side before nightfall.

The hike today is gorgeous, lots of cascading waterfalls and some interesting wooden suspension bridges to cross. There are many trail junctions to contend with as well, but so far I have managed to turn the right way and stay on track. I noticed back in my room at Old Forge, that these wonderful maps from National Geographic have marked the trails on the map to match the color of the markers on the trail, very helpful for staying on track.

The trail in this area becomes increasingly rocky and choked with roots, and mud. I have no doubt this trail once allowed horses in the not-so-distant past. In a lot of places a narrow-rutted track weaves its way between large boulders and amongst tangled tree roots. As I reach Lake Colden I have another trail junction, complete with a ladder leading straight down the side of a short ledge and onto a wooden dam. From here I am provided my first up-close view of Mt. Marcy, very impressive indeed.

I encounter lots of hikers along the trail today, probably out to enjoy the last few decent warm days this year. Late afternoon I am on a steady yet steep uphill climb toward Mt. Skylight, where I will turn left and head up and over Marcy. I meet a group of many day hikers coming down, asking if I am heading toward Marcy. They tell me to make sure to turn left at Lake Tear of the Clouds instead of right, they made that mistake and had to backtrack. As I reach the edge of the Lake I see a trail leading off to the left, but no sign. So far most of the intersections have been marked with a sign but this one doesn't have one.

Taking the hiker's tips, I take the left turn and start hiking up again. Before too long I can tell this trail is not the correct one. It is too steep in many places for even a day hiker to clamber up, and there are no markings of any kind. As I reach an opening in the tree canopy, I look northeast in horror as I am still looking Up at Marcy! I turned too early and ended up on the adjacent mountain. "Well shit!" I was doing so well at staying on track and then right at the critical moment I took a wrong turn. I turn back with a heavier heart as I retrace my steps to the point where I left the main trail.

With the time wasted scaling the wrong mountain, I don't have enough time left in the day to make it clear down the other side of Marcy. Unfortunately, I am above 3,500 feet now, and there is no camping allowed at this elevation unless at a designated campsite. With no options left to me, I turn right and head back down the trail to the latest shelter over a mile away. At this stage in the hike there is no worse feeling than climbing down a mountain knowing you have to climb back up in the morning.

I find going down to be harder than going up, and after scrambling over boulders and through pools, I make it to the Feldspar Shelter where some other hikers are just preparing dinner. Hence, I meet Mark, Chris and Steve, three friends out for the weekend to bag a few 46ers. I ask kindly if they wouldn't mind if I bunked with them for the night, and they respond by making plenty of room for me to move right on in. This is the first night on this entire hike that I have had to share a shelter with other hikers. Strange, being this close to the end.

While we enjoy our dinners we share hiking stories. They ask where I hiked here from and I spend a brief time telling them my story and that I expect to finish on Monday. They seem impressed and congratulate me on a journey nearly completed. We spend some more time swapping stories until darkness sets in and we settle into the shelter at our own pace. I am the first one out, as I have a big day tomorrow.

Saturday, October 12
Trail Day 189
Miles hiked: 25.5
Chapel Pond Tent Area – Dix Mountain Wilderness,
Adirondack Park

I am the first one awake this morning, and as I retrieve my bear canister and start chowing down on breakfast everyone else starts to roll out of bed. By the time I have my gear all packed and ready for the day, the other guys are just getting their breakfast going. Steve insists they take a picture with me before I head out so they have proof they met the youngest guy to hike the NCT. After a firm handshake from each of them I turn and begin my ascent to the top of Mt. Marcy, only a few miles away.

When I reach the first trail junction where I am to turn left to go up Marcy, I realize how I got thrown off track yesterday. The hikers I came across were not clear with their instructions. They told me to turn left at Lake Tear of the Clouds where they should have said turn left AFTER Lake Tear of the Clouds. The intersection was clear on the other side of the lake from the trail I took by mistake yesterday. I am here now however, and I turn and begin my climb up New York's highest mountain.

The climb to the top is very steep, I need to stop for a short break many times. Before too long, I am above timber line and I have a sweeping view to the east. With no trees to block the wind, it gets more difficult to climb uphill as the wind is constantly pushing me sideways. The trail here is bare rock, nothing to nail a marker too. Instead, there are a few paint blazes right on the rock face and at places where the trail turns some very large rock cairns have been built to help guide hikers to the top.

The mileage from the shelter is just shy of three miles, but this climb seems to go on forever; by far the most difficult climb I have hiked in my career. About halfway up, I meet another hiker coming down. He says he has scaled Marcy many times but never from the north side, so he's trying it the other way this time. He appears to be the only one out here besides me.

Finally, at a little after 9:30 a.m., I am standing on the top of Mt. Marcy. The wind is very intense up here and it gets cold very quickly. There are a few more hikers up here taking a rest behind some boulders to get out of the wind. Within a few minutes lots of people arrive from the other side. I ask one of the women from a passing group to take my picture. After several nice shots I stop and admire the magnificent view. Being the highest point in the entire state at 5,344 feet, I have a 360-degree view all around. Most of what I can see are the other 46ers, but in the distance behind many of the peaks I can see a wide light ribbon. Alas, I set my eyes on Lake Champlain and the finish line for this hike, nearly thirty miles away. Day after tomorrow I expect to be standing on the very shore of that lake at Crown Point, the Eastern Terminus of the NCT.

My trip through the High Peaks in these gorgeous Adirondack Mountains will no doubt be the highlight of this entire trek, a very fitting end to this long journey. Unfortunately, future NCT hikers will not have the same experience I have had. Currently, there is no official route for the NCT through the Adirondacks. They have been doing a routing study over the past ten years and are now close to a final solution. However, the route will not go anywhere near the High Peaks. For whatever reason, the current stewards are worried that routing the NCT over Mt. Marcy would damage the area due to over-use. This makes little sense to me, as the NCT will never be as popular as the AT where thousands of people attempt it every year.

To put it in perspective, the NCT has been around for more than thirty years... and I am only the fourth thru-hiker! It's a shame that future NCT hikers will be robbed of this grand opportunity due to a misconception about the use of the trail. I can only hope that in the future those in charge will change their minds, and the NCT can be routed over the path I have taken through this vast wilderness.

The climb down is much harder. I have to go slow to avoid falling flat on my face. I encounter lots of people on their way to the top, of course it must be Saturday. By the time I get to the bottom my knees are on fire. I've gone this entire hike without many aches and pains, and now here at the very end are my knees not the least bit pleased.

I have more intersections to contend with on the far side of Marcy. My original plan was to bag five more of these 46ers on my way out to Port Henry, but with the time it took to get over Marcy (with my heavier-than-normal pack on) and the fact that there are no campsites between here and there, I decide to take a detour. This will ensure that I will have a legal place to camp at the end of the day. My detour will add some mileage, but it will have much less elevation change making for an easier hike.

The trail is still in rough shape in some places, more mud holes and large boulders to contend with. By the time I reach the Johns Brook Lodge (a large cabin right on the trail) the trail has turned into a nice gradual downhill descent to a trailhead parking lot just outside of Keene Valley. The trailhead is swarming with people, most of them anxious to get out and spend this fantastic weekend in the High Peaks. I stop here to take a break before continuing on to Keene Valley. I am not surprised to find the little village also swarming with people.

It's late afternoon now and everyone is out and about looking for a place to have dinner. I decide that isn't such a bad idea and find a nice little diner across the street. As I go in I am surprised that

I am the only backpacker here and there appear to be no open tables. Just as the booth nearest to me opens up, a group of three is in line to take it. They notice me as they are just sitting down and they ask if I want to join them. There's no way I can turn this down. I set my pack outside on the porch and then join them at the booth. Hence, I meet Darlene, Ben, and Caroline; on their way home from a day hiking the High Peaks.

We spend lots of time talking about our hiking adventures, they seem very impressed with my accomplishment. It turns out they are from just a little south of Rome, so they knew exactly where I was two weeks ago when I had to bypass Fort Stanwix because of the government shutdown. Soon our food is served and we chow down. To my amazement they offer to cover my tab. *Thank you dear new friends, I really appreciate it.*

I have only a few miles left to go to reach a designated tenting area right along Hwy-73. After saying goodbye to my new friends, I arrive just before sundown and set up camp, only a few other campers settled nearby.

Sunday, October 13
Trail Day 190
Miles hiked: 27
Crown Point State Historic Site

Looking at my maps in my tent last night I realized I have only twenty-seven miles go to reach the end of the trail at Crown Point. From here it's almost completely a roadwalk, mostly downhill. There's no stopping me now, I am finishing today!

I am up at first light after a quick breakfast and heading south along NY-73 on my way out of Adirondack Park. This turns out to be one of the most scenic roadwalks I have had along the entire trail. After crossing underneath I-87, I get onto country roads and reach a trailhead for the Crowfoot Pond trail. I take this trail across to Crowfoot Road on the other side, and there to hike straight into Port Henry.

The trail is much wider here than normal, and fairly flat, but with nearly all the leaves being down now I need to watch my step to avoid falling on my face as every rut and rock is hidden. Despite this, I manage to make decent time and emerge from the end of the trail onto a gravel road right along the lake. After passing probably a dozen homes, the road widens out and the sun comes out, making it fairly toasty. Soon an ATV comes driving up the road and the operator stops right next to me.

I won't go into a lot of detail about what transpired, but apparently I had been trespassing on private property when I emerged from the Crowfoot Pond Trail. The guy on the ATV is a landowner who lives on this road, who said he would report me for trespassing. I tell him I had no idea I was trespassing as the map shows the trail coming clear out to the road, and said nothing about the road itself being private. If I had known I would not have taken that route. I always respect private property ownership.

He asked me where I am parked, and he has a rather awkward expression when I reply "North Dakota." I show him the map as proof of my intentions, my route being clearly marked. I only chose this route because it was the most direct to Port Henry. If I had known it was private, I would have gone around, sparing me from this very uncomfortable and confrontational experience. After talking with him for more than ten minutes, I humbly apologize for trespassing, and let him know I intend to inform the Adirondack Mountain Club of my experience and tell them they should remove that trail completely. One day people less aware than me are going to come along and get into a bad situation with these angry landowners.

Please ADK representatives, I advise removing the Crowfoot Pond Trail completely so there is absolutely no confusion for future hikers.

After parting ways with the landowner, I pick up the pace down the rest of the 'private' road. The guy warned me about his brother who "isn't as nice" as he is, and I would like to avoid any future confrontations. I manage to make it within sight of the intersection that will bring me onto paved county roads right around a corner. And just then, a large black pickup pulls onto the road. Trying not to draw any extra attention to myself, I just stare at the ground hoping they will pass me by. As it speeds past I hear the brakes come on just a few paces behind me. Not daring to look back, I continue on until I step onto the pavement and county property.

I continue the fast pace all the way into Port Henry, nearly six miles. Once there, I finally get a chance to sit down and have a break outside a gas station. The town of Port Henry is right on the shore of Lake Champlain, and as I arrive in town it is clearly visible in the background. I have only seven miles to go now to reach the end at Crown Point. I need to catch my breath though, so I take time to enjoy some comforts (ice cream) and rehydrate in the shade. I am amazed at how warm it still is up here in the mountains in mid-October. It is not at all uncommon for it to have snowed many times by this time of year. I am not complaining, I enjoy the nice weather and I am no lover of winter. I'm glad it stayed away long enough for me to reach Lake Champlain on a nice sunny day.

After my extended break, I hammer out the remaining seven miles to Crown Point. I am greeted by one final NCT marker at the gate and then follow the trail up to the old British fortification. I scamper along the old ramparts getting several good shots of the fort and the lake in the distance. It is a gorgeous setting here at the old fort, situated on a peninsula jutting out into Lake Champlain.

To the west are the Adirondack Mountains of New York where I have spent the past week in vast wilderness. To the east loom the Green Mountains of Vermont, where runs the famous Long Trail and a portion of the AT. On the far side of the fort I arrive at a kiosk overlooking the lake and the Lake Champlain Bridge leading into Vermont.

On the Kiosk is a map of the entire NCT with the caption:
Eastern Terminus

I've done it! I've hiked the North Country National Scenic Trail from end-to-end!

It seemed like an impossible task when I was way back in the snow-covered plains of North Dakota over six months ago. Back then, I had doubts I would ever make it to the end, but I knew I would just give it my best effort. But here I am, after 201 days of hiking I have made the 4,600-mile pilgrimage through seven northern states to this spot near the New York/Vermont state line.

It's approximately 4:30 p.m., there is one tourist near the kiosk to take my photo in front of the bridge and kiosk. I have mixed emotions as I stand here. I am happy that I have accomplished this amazing task; one that has been my dream for the past three years. However, I am also a bit sad. There is no one here familiar, no one to shake my hand, no one to share this moment with. Without any further delays, it's time to give my family a call back home.

I make the call, telling them I have made it to the end. There is much excitement on their end, but a little sadness on mine. Next to call is Bruce at NCTA HQ. He's very excited as well, both for my accomplishment and with the good news that I have received one of the scholarships to attend the National Scenic and Historic Trail Conference in a few weeks out in Tucson, AZ.

Wow! The good news just keeps coming in. With one last call to make, I reach Chris from Champlain Area Trails (CATS). He sent me a voicemail about a week ago and told me to call him back. He was hoping to hike with me as I approached Crown Point. Unfortunately, it's too late for that, but we make plans for him to come meet me tomorrow morning as I cross the bridge into Vermont.

Across the street from the fort is a state park campground where I head over and pitch for the night. I am provided a nice view across the lake to the North with the bridge directly in front, all lit up with the coming of evening. Those last few phone calls completely depleted my battery, so I let it charge for about an hour in the bathhouse while I enjoy my dinner. Afterward, I read some more of Tolkien before retiring to bed...a mixed bag of emotions as a pillow.

The Lake Champlain Bridge- *Photo from John and Dove Day.*

VERMONT

October 14 - October 17, 2013

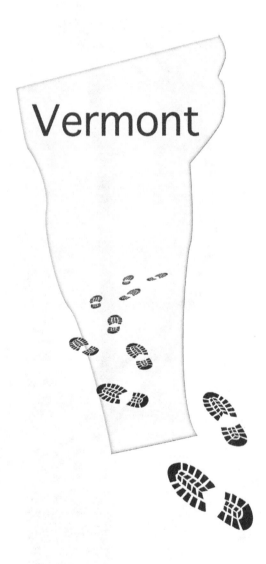

Monday, October 14
Trail Day 191
Miles hiked: 22.5
Inn on the Green - Middlebury, VT

I am tired this morning, as I had a restless sleep last night. As I emerge from my tent, I am grateful I finished the trail yesterday as opposed to today. The sky is completely overcast with a light drizzle off and on, and the air is much colder than yesterday. To make matters more gloomy, last night as I made camp, I realized that today is Columbus Day...post offices will be closed! Therefore I will have to wait until tomorrow before I am able to retrieve the package I have waiting back in Port Henry. I hope that someone in Middlebury will be willing to shuttle me there in the morning.

After a quick breakfast, I head over to the guard station by the Lake Champlain Bridge and wait, as Chris of Champlain Area Trails will be joining me shortly. As I am waiting, a reporter shows up with his camera. Hence, I meet Alvin, here to get a quick story about me. He takes a few photos of me in front of the NCT Terminus kiosk and asks a few questions as more people start arriving. Here to meet me and hike with me across the bridge are Melinda, Elizabeth, John, and Chris. Melinda and Elizabeth both brought some trail magic with them—a package of delicious brownies and a bottle of freshly made apple cider. With all greetings exchanged and trail magic in my pack, we all set off across the bridge into Vermont.

You're probably wondering why I am hiking into yet another state; particularly, one that the NCT doesn't go through? I found out during my research for this hike, that the original plan for the trail when it was laid out in 1980 was to have it continue into Vermont and connect with the Appalachian Trail via the Long Trail (LT). At the time however, the Green Mountain Club (who is charge of maintaining the LT) was concerned about over-usage, and so they pulled their support for the trail and forced it to end at Crown Point. Now, it has been a generation later and they have changed their minds and are actually quite enthusiastic about the idea of establishing the original route. I decided way back in the early planning stages to hike the proposed extension to the AT, rather than quitting at Crown Point. I need to get home somehow anyway and there happens to be an Amtrak station in Rutland only a few miles off the AT. (May as well make it official, rather than just hitching a ride or roadwalking the rest of the way.) So for the next several days, I will be hiking in the great state of Vermont.

On our trek over the Lake Champlain Bridge, the group is anxious to hear about my journey. As we cross, I share as many of my experiences as possible in the small amount of time we have before reaching the Green Mountain State. On the other side of the bridge is another historic site known as Chimney Point, and in the parking lot is a vehicle with a man waiting outside. Hence, I meet John of the Middlebury Area Land Trust (MALT). He is here to talk with me about the route through this area and give me some maps that will help get me to the Long Trail.

At this time, the group I came over with needs to head back, as they have jobs to get to on this Monday morning. I say goodbye to the nice people I just met as they turn and head back to New York. I spend a few minutes talking with John as he describes the route to get me in and around the town of Middlebury before heading to the Long Trail. MALT has their own set of maps for a loop trail they have been developing over the last decade that completely circles the town known as the Trail Around Middlebury (TAM). My route will take me over the northern and eastern half of this trail, but first I need to find my way there and for that John has printed me a special map that includes the temporary roadwalk to the first trailhead.

After thanking John for his help in navigating this area, I shake his hand and I am off to chart new territory.

The roadwalk begins down busy VT-125 right along the shore of Lake Champlain. After a few miles, I come to an intersection and turn east onto Town Line Road toward Snake Mountain. Along this road a car pulls up and down goes the window. It's a local, Jim, who is wondering if I need anything. I tell him I know exactly where I'm going, and he wishes me luck as he drives away.

Before too long I reach the base of Snake Mountain, a solitary peak standing between the Adirondack Mountains of New York and the Green Mountains of Vermont. Once again, being the Tolkien fan that I am, I can't help but make a comparison to the Lonely Mountain. There is a short section of existing trail here that I was looking forward to hiking. John had warned me that a portion of it has not been maintained in many years, but that I could probably find my way through if I was looking for a challenge. I decide to go around as I don't have enough time today to risk losing the trail.

Circling the base of the mountain, I find my way to the other side where I pick up a new section of the TAM completed just last year in anticipation of the NCT being extended through Vermont. I am pleasantly surprised to find the trail well marked, despite being mostly along and even through farm fields, there are even a few blue blazes. After only two miles I come to a trail intersection, a spur trail leads off to the right to Bittersweet Falls. I drop my pack and walk the short spur, but arrive to find the waterfall completely dry. I take a few photos and head back, noting that there is a perfect spot for a future campsite right near the falls.

The trail continues along farm fields to another trail junction, this one being the original TAM. I take the north fork. After crossing a stile through some pasture guarded by many cattle, and along a few more fields, I arrive at the Otter Creek Gorge Preserve and enter the woods. As I enter, I am again pleasantly surprised with the quality of this trail. Here in the woods it is very well marked, and official TAM markers are tacked to the trees every few hundred feet. Suddenly, I emerge onto a narrow suspension bridge hanging above Beldens Falls. What a spectacular little trail this TAM is turning out to be.

The last section of trail takes me along the river's edge among some large boulders through Wright Park. On the south end of the park I have a roadwalk that will lead me into town where I will need to find a place to spend the night. As I arrive downtown, I am surprised to find John waiting for me in front of a little café. He seems surprised that I have made it here so soon, despite it being almost evening. We spend a few minutes talking and he mentions that he wanted to offer to drive me to Port Henry tomorrow to pick up my package. *Thanks so much John, I greatly appreciate it.*

After we set a time for him to pick me up in the morning, he points me in the direction of a few motels and he leaves for the evening. I decide to spend the night at a place called Inn on the Green, located very close to main street. The Inn is actually a restored Victorian style house, and it doesn't appear to be too busy at the moment. I head on in and ask about pricing; having no doubt it is well out of my range. I decide it is worth the stay though, I have spent much less money on this trek than I thought I would, and I have only three days left to go. I head on in, got a room on the second floor.

Even the inside of the old house is just like it was two centuries ago, although now has modern amenities (TV, running water, WiFi). The kind woman behind the desk hands me a menu and she explains that at this Inn the guests have the option of being served breakfast in bed. I've never had this experience before. I take a few minutes to fill out what I want, and then it's shower time first thing. After charging my phone, I check it and find that I have a voicemail from Ron Strickland, founder of the Pacific Northwest National Scenic Trail and the Sea-to-Sea route (C2C). He is currently in Boston, heard about my hike, and wants to meet up with me somewhere on the Long Trail. Wow! Another opportunity to meet a trail legend.

I call him back and we make plans to meet at Maine Junction, the point where the AT and LT diverge (if you are north-bound on the AT). Just as I am about to start my dinner, there is a knock at the door. The housekeeper has just made a fresh batch of chocolate chip cookies and she offers me one. Oh boy, if these aren't the most delicious cookies I've ever tasted I don't know what they are.

I spend the rest of the night unpacking my gear, figuring out what I can cram into the bear canister to send home in the morning and then drift off to sleep.

Tuesday, October 15
Trail Day 192
Miles hiked: 21
Sucker Brook Shelter – LT

I decided to sleep in last night, and awake to a knock on the door; must be time for breakfast. As I open the door, a young woman brings a large tray full of various pastries, some cereal, yogurt, and juice right to the foot of my bed. This is just strange, never in my life have I had this kind of service. And, oh my, is the food ever good!

After finishing breakfast, it's time to head out to meet John so we can head to Port Henry to retrieve my last food drop. During the ride, John gives me the history of the TAM, starting with his involvement as trail coordinator. He includes plans for the future of the trail; including getting the section through Snake Mountain opened up and connecting the TAM to trails currently in existence in the Green Mountain National Forest. The NCT will one day be routed over these trails to reach the Long Trail, which it will then follow south to its junction with the AT. Hopefully, this will all become a reality in the next few years.

We arrive at the post office in Port Henry just as it opens, my box is there. I grab it and we go again. The drive takes longer than it should because the road between town and Crown Point is down to one lane due to some road work. Finally, we make it back to Middlebury where we stop in at the MALT office. Here, I meet Carl, the executive director, as well as Jon and Joanie. They are pleased that I am using their trail as part of my cross-country journey, and are looking forward to working with the National Park Service, and NCTA in the future to complete the extension of the NCT once it gets approved. Joanie takes a few notes from our conversation for a short article in their newsletter.

After my brief visit, it is time for John to drop me off back at the Inn so I can continue on with my hike. I thank him for everything he has done for me the past two days and after a firm handshake he is gone. It takes me about a half hour to get everything packed, and then I am out the door.

First stop on my way out of town is the post office, so I can mail home my bear canister and get rid of a lot of extra weight from things I will not need these last few days. After a brief roadwalk, I've got an uphill climb on the TAM through Chipman Hill Park, followed by a gradual descent into Means and Battell Woods. On the south side of Battell Woods, the TAM crosses busy VT-125 into Jeffrey Murdock Nature Preserve. But, I need to head east, so my journey on the TAM will end here. I turn left onto the busy highway and head east into the Green Mountains.

After a few miles I reach the small community of East Middlebury where a guy in a pickup flags me down. "You hiking the Long Trail?" I respond that I am on my way to it. He then asks if I need a ride, and seems rather confused when I decline his offer. "You know it's about fifteen miles from here right? Uphill the whole way." I thank him again for his offer, but kindly refuse. He wishes me luck as he drives away. I bet I know exactly what he is thinking as he drives away..."Just take the ride dummy!"

No sooner do I leave the little village, than the uphill climb begins and I am in the Green Mountain National Forest. Man, I wish I could have taken that ride. The constant uphill climb has already worn me out. The road here has no shoulder, and there is a steep drop-off into a river far below on one side. Luckily, there are not too many cars out on the road today.

About halfway to my destination, I pull off into a little wayside rest and inspect my pack. Since entering the Adirondacks, one of my shoulder straps somehow became frayed and started to slowly come apart. It's to the point now where it could snap at any moment. Rather than risk it failing while out on a rocky trail, I take the time here to patch it up as best I can. I only need to make it for two more days, so a little duct tape will do the trick. After ten minutes of pack surgery I am hiking uphill again.

Late evening, I finally arrive at a trailhead for the Long Trail and see the infamous white blaze. There are a few cars parked here and some people taking photos of the entry sign. The Long Trail was the first long-distance trail in the US, designated in 1910. Stretching from Massachusetts to Canada, the AT is superimposed over it for nearly half of its length. According to the sign, I have 4.6 miles to go to reach the first shelter, where I intend to spend the night. I have maybe an hour of daylight left so I need to move fast. Without any delay, I take a large gulp of water, snap a photo of the entry sign and head on in, or UP I should say. I now know how the LT got its reputation, it is well marked and maintained but very challenging. The rocky trail makes it treacherous to hike, especially when wet, but the scenery is spectacular.

I manage to make it to the shelter just as darkness descends, and I am greeted by two other hikers who have already set up for the night. Hence, I meet Dave and Brooke, out on their last day of a multi-day trek. I hang my food and head back to the shelter where we swap some hiking stories. I tell them of my journey and how I am now basically on my way home; just taking a detour to hike as much trail as possible before boarding that train home. They tell me they are greatly inspired by what I have just accomplished and are so glad they had the chance to meet me. *Thank you dear new friends, it was great to meet you as well.*

Wednesday, October 16
Trail Day 193
Miles hiked: 17
Rolston Rest Shelter - LT

I'm up at what appears to be first light. It's hard to tell as the sky is completely overcast. Dave and Brooke are up as well and we all get moving at exactly the same time. Unfortunately, we are heading in opposite directions, so I will not see them again. I snap a picture before shaking both of their hands and wishing them well as they reach their destination. *Happy trails new friends. It was a pleasure.*

The sun tries to peek out, but it remains overcast the entire day as I hike through and then out of the Joseph Battell Wilderness. The trail is very rocky most of the way and choked with roots. Like the AT, this trail gets so much use that in many places the tread is a deep ravine, worn down over the years by thousands upon thousands of hikers traveling its length. There is a lot of elevation change today, but towards the end of the day the trail does level out quite a bit and I've got a gradual downhill to the Rolston Rest Shelter where I set up camp for the night.

I've still got some time left before it gets dark, so I enjoy a nice dinner and after hanging my food spend some time reading some more from Tolkien to pass the time. About a half hour before nightfall, I hear voices coming down the trail from the south. I look in their direction and see two women hiking toward me. As they enter the cleared area around the shelter, they greet me with a standard "Hi", and look for a place to set up their tents. I'm a little confused by this, as these shelters are designed to fit eight people and it saves the trouble of having to set up your tent at all.

When they seem unable to find a level place behind the shelter, I ask why they are setting up their tents when I am the only other person here. I explain that these shelters are designed for eight people, and we are all supposed to share. Hence, I officially meet Maggie and Sarah, out for a two day trek on the LT. Apparently, they thought since I was here first, that the shelter was all mine. But I correct them on this, and they happily decide to move their things into the shelter rather than pitch their tents. Good thing too, just as darkness descends a light rain comes and continues most of the night. From my experience on the FLT, these shelters are a lot drier than your tent when you wake up in the morning.

We spend a little while talking, and they begin by asking me where I am coming from and where I am heading. They seem flabbergasted when I explain that I have walked here all the way from North Dakota, and that I will officially be done tomorrow when I reach Maine Junction. I find out that Maggie is from New York, and Sarah is from Maine. Every so often they decide to meet somewhere between them and go for a long hike. This time it happened to be this section of the LT.

Before too long, it is time to settle into bed. And as my head hits the pillow I am suddenly hit with the realization that tonight is my last night on the trail. All the mixed emotions I had when I reached Crown Point come rushing back, and I am filled with sadness. Hiking this great trail for the past six and a half months has become my life, and a life that I have grown to love. The trail is my home. This is it, tomorrow it's all over. This is my last night on the trail.

Thursday, October 17
Trail Day 194
Miles hiked: 06
Red Roof Inn - Rutland, VT

I awoke fairly early this morning, but I only have six miles to hike today so I take my time getting moving. I retrieve my food bag first thing, and eat most of what's left of my food while conversing with Sarah and Maggie as they cook their own breakfast over a stove. Around 9 a.m., I'm finally out on the trail and hike the five miles to Maine Junction, where I reach the white blazes of the infamous Appalachian Trail. This is the end of my hike as this will likely be the future Eastern Terminus of the NCT once Congress approves the extension.

I'm here before noon, so I have about an hour to wait; Ron Strickland is heading out to meet me at this spot around 1 p.m. I snap a few pictures and take a video here at the sign, and then set my pack down and use it as a chair. I have a cell signal so I use this time to make my Amtrak reservations for the ride home, day after tomorrow. In the meantime, I enjoy sitting in front of the sign here on the AT and reading many pages of Tolkien. Soon Maggie approaches and says, "Hi", on her way out. She stops to chat for a few minutes while she waits for Sarah to catch up. She takes my picture in front of the sign just as Sarah comes down the trail.

As the two of them depart back toward their car, Maggie hands me a piece of paper with her number on it. "I'll be in town until 5 or so," she says, and with a smile she turns and hikes away.

A few minutes later, I hear two men coming up the trail from the south, and I recognize one of them. Hence, I meet Ron Strickland face-to-face, and he has brought his friend Walter, along that lives in the area. We take many pictures in front of the sign and exchange greetings. We've got a mile to hike on the AT to reach the trailhead parking lot off of Hwy 4, so we head out and talk along the way.

Ron has been busy for a long time. He founded the Pacific Northwest Trail that goes from Glacier National Park to the Pacific Ocean in Washington State. Since then, he has been working on a much more ambitious project. He envisions a coast-to-coast trail that will allow hikers to literally travel the width of the entire continent, from one ocean to the other. He calls it, the C2C Route. The plan is to one day connect the PNT to the NCT, one of only two gaps in the proposed trail's area. The other gap, is the gap I have just hiked between Crown Point and Maine Junction, which is seemingly very close to being approved. Only two hikers have completed the entire proposed route, Andrew Skurka and Nimblewill Nomad.

I've known about the concept of this trail from doing research for this hike, and it is a fascinating idea. The current plan is actually to extend the NCT further west into Montana to connect with the PNT there in Glacier National Park. I am opposed to this idea for several reasons. Once you leave Lake Sakakawea in North Dakota, there are no more lakes, no more forested lands. These are characteristics that define the North Country for what it is. As soon as you go west from Lake Sakakawea, you are no longer in the North Country, you are in Big Sky Country. Extending the trail westward, I think, would diminish some of the character of the NCT. And, at 4,600 miles long, it is already impossible to hike the entire thing having fair hiking weather the entire time. It would make more sense to me to create a new trail between the two existing trails, one that is more definitive of the character of the region. Ron and I agree on this idea and have come to call it the Big Sky Trail (BST).

We talk about a few more issues regarding the National Trail System in general, and he seems pleased when I inform him that I have won a scholarship to attend the National Trails Conference in Tucson in a couple weeks. We arrive at the trailhead off of Route 4, and he informs me he has a gift for me in his trunk. He hands me two books that he has written himself, one being the new guidebook for the NCT, the other being a book called, *Pathfinder*. *Pathfinder* outlines the work that goes into creating a new trail, based on his experience with the PNT. He takes a few moments to write some encouraging remarks and sign them before handing them to me. I see some papers sticking out of the cover of the NCT guidebook and I discover that it is all the information he has gathered about the future BST.

At this point, he needs to get back to Boston, so once again I must say goodbye to a new friend. **Thanks for the gift Ron, and driving all this way to meet me. It was an honor meeting you and I hope our paths cross again.*

Originally, I had intended to hike an extra day on the AT, going over Mt. Killington and hiking into Rutland from the south. However, with the events of today, I decided it would be more fitting to end the hike here instead. Walter agreed to shuttle me into Rutland where I have a reservation at the Red Roof Inn. After checking in, I immediately strip down and take a hot shower. My muscles are extra tight from the intense terrain I've been hiking the last week, and the hot water does much to relieve some of the tension.

Afterward, I check my phone. It's almost 4 p.m. I give Maggie a call. She is still in town and she suggests we have dinner together. We make plans to meet in fifteen minutes at a restaurant across the street from my motel. I arrive a little early, but only find myself waiting about five minutes before Maggie shows up.

We are seated right away as the place is completely empty. We both start off with a beer and spend the next several hours talking about our many adventures. Maggie has been to all but four states. She had even gone to Alaska. I relate to her the crazy adventure I had there while on an internship for the BLM and Forest Service where I was working on a historic preservation project a few years back. I went into detail of how the nearest town was almost two hours away, how the only way to get to the site was by river, and how we managed to get caught in a 100-year flood while working on our project.

I shared how the road we came in on got washed out, so we took a nine-hour detour through Canada to get back to Alaska. And, how some of us didn't have passports, how we spent three nights in a hostel in a small town in The Yukon Territory during a music festival and each drank the Sour Toe cocktail, and how after only three hours of sleep, I had to drive an old Volvo station wagon with a leaky tire and a manual transmission six hours through a foreign country. I also told her how I had the chance to take the first stage of the inside passage cruise to Juneau and then fly home.

As it turns out, we have visited a lot of the same places and even met some of the same people on our travels. Maggie tells me how in 2010 (while I was in Alaska) she was wandering through parts of the Pacific Northwest; particularly Idaho and Wyoming working on various projects. She met some of the same people there that I would meet a year later while working on another internship in the same area. A guy in Cody, WY was one of the people we had in common, along with some forest rangers from the Shoshone National Forest. Talk about small world!

As I finally realize it's dark outside and the restaurant is now full of people, I know we have to be well past time for her to make the long drive back to New York. She doesn't seem to mind, and we stay a little longer. Finally after 7:30 p.m., we get up and leave, as a whole line of people were waiting to get into the restaurant... oops! In the parking lot I walk Maggie to her car and it is time for another sad goodbye.

Even here, at the very end of this hike, the partings are no less difficult. *It was a great pleasure meeting you Maggie. Thank you for making this last day on the journey of a lifetime even more memorable.*

"Not All Who Wander Are Lost."
(J.R.R. Tolkien)

Future Eastern Terminus North Country Trail - Ron Strickland and Strider.

EPILOGUE

On October 19, 2013, I headed to the Amtrak station in Rutland to board the first of three trains that would bring me home to Minnesota. It was my first time traveling by rail and I enjoyed the experience. I had to change trains in Schenectady, NY, and then again in Chicago. Just as I said I would way back in Michigan's Upper Peninsula, I gave Jeff a call, the lawyer I had met with the large group camping at Craig Lake. Unfortunately, it was the weekend so he was not in Chicago at the time, but he had already heard that I had completed my hike and congratulated me.

Instead, I ate a quick meal at the train station and then spent the few hours I had walking around the city. I took a trip down to the Lake Michigan Shore and spent some time by the fountain. I stared across the water, knowing that beyond the opposite shore some 120 miles away was the NCT.

Two days after leaving Vermont, the train pulled into the Twin Cities station after 10 p.m. It was snowing as I stepped off the train. There to greet me were my parents (the first time seeing me since I was home for the wedding back in August). It was good to see them, but I was also a bit sad to be home. The trail had been my home for over 200 days, and now it was gone. A week later ,the whole thing felt like a dream, a distant memory, but one I would never forget.

I had a little break from the awkwardness two weeks after completing my thru-hike as I flew down to Tucson, AZ for a week to participate in the Partnership for the National Trail System Conference. I had applied for a scholarship while I was still on the trail in New York and ended up winning one of them. I was flown down with fourteen of my peers as a trail apprentice, and spent the next week meeting and mingling with experts from all walks of the trail community. Representatives from the National Scenic

Trails, the National Historic Trails, and Federal Land Managers all met to discuss issues facing the trail system and to brainstorm ideas for the future.

We trail apprentices were there to observe, learn, and on the last day, present our own findings. I'm still in touch with many of the people I met that day, and I became fast friends with most of the other trail apprentices. It was another stepping stone that would lead me to where I am today.

One thing that often gets overlooked before you begin a thru-hike, is what might happen to you after you finish. I had heard stories about hikers having trouble readjusting to life back in the real world, and I expected I would feel different when I returned home. But, I had no idea the post-trail adjustment would hit me so hard. It doesn't happen to everyone, but I'd say that most of us suffer a bit after returning home from a thru-hike. It's a very real phenomenon, and it's difficult.

When I returned home, the post-trail depression hit me hard. I had trouble sleeping and didn't enjoy things I had usually liked. I had to sleep on the floor for the first week because it was closer to the life I had known of sleeping on the ground, or the hard floor of a shelter. Sleeping in a bed for more than a few days at a time was strange. Some issues came up with my family and friends, it was often hard to connect with them on the same level again.

There were now the expectations of civilized life. One thing that's really hard getting used to is showering when you're not actually dirty. It feels incredibly wasteful, so why should I have to do it at least every other day? The answer is because in the "civilized" world it's unacceptable to smell bad—and my family made that point very clear after the first few days. I also had to constantly ask myself, why I had so many clothes? Two sets is all you really need right? One for sleeping and one for hiking.

Coming back, I had the urge to get rid of most of my stuff, it all just felt like unnecessary clutter.

I got the feeling pretty early on in my hike that the trail was actually a living entity, full of knowledge and experiences that surpassed anything I had ever known. Returning home I felt out of place, even had a sense of lost identity. I felt alone in a world where no one in my normal circle had a shared experience or knew what I was feeling. Living in the dirt, drinking from water that was shared with wild animals was intoxicating and life changing. I didn't know what the "real world" was anymore. Was it life on the trail surrounded by the natural world? Or is it this "synthetic world" where most of us spend our day-to-day lives?

What ended up making it a little easier in the end, was knowing that it would pass and that the feelings of depression were just a physical reaction of my body trying to cope with the dramatic lifestyle change. In the early days of the fallout, I took a weekend trip back to the North Shore where I had spent so much time with friends and as a solo hiker, places I knew well and had formed so many memories. My first stop was to Jay Cooke State Park. The iconic Swinging Bridge had been repaired, recycled with as much of the original material as could be managed. It brought some comfort knowing they used parts of itself to rebuild, but at the same time it wasn't exactly the same as before, and never would be again.

It was quite a literal translation of a metaphor that now applied to my life and hung over me like a cloud; a dark cloud building in the west just before it summons enough energy to generate a thunderstorm. The bridge was me, I would never be the same again, and at the time I didn't know for better or worse. It lasted more than three months, but I finally came out of it. I probably would have been at the mercy of that dark cloud longer if I hadn't received a few opportunities to return to the trail as an intern the following spring. I moved to Fargo, ND to set up basecamp as I spent the next year on a big project.

On my spare time I got back on the trail as much as possible, either hiking new sections or volunteering with the existing chapters to build new ones. It was nice to go back for multiple days and hike some of the areas that had been completely covered by snow during my thru-hike. I got to finally see the waterfall in the Sheyenne State Forest in North Dakota, I hiked the entirety of the Sheyenne Grasslands without snowshoes, and I hiked the eleven miles between Itasca and Lake George that I had bypassed because of snow. I even found the spot in the park where I had gotten lost.

In addition, I traveled around giving presentations of my adventure on college campuses, community buildings, and at various outdoor events; keeping true to my mission of raising more awareness for the NCT. During my college years, if you had told me that after graduating I would become a public speaker, I would have said that you were crazy. I used to suffer from varying degrees of stage-freight depending on the situation, but my experience on the trail had changed all that. Returning to the "real world", I found that my confidence in any situation had skyrocketed.

In the year following the thru-hike, a lot of things happened. I once again received a scholarship as a trail apprentice for PNTS, and headed out to Lake Tahoe to participate in another conference. This one proved to be a bit more beneficial, as it was only the National Scenic Trails in attendance, and did not include the Historic Trails. Many of the topics and issues for up for discussion applied closely to concepts related to my project. It gave me the chance to reconnect with a few of the other apprentices, met some new ones, and reinforced many of the professional connections I made at the Tucson conference. I also hiked a few miles of the PCT; now having set foot on all the Triple Crown trails.

About a month later, I took a short trip to Michigan for the filming of a music video dedicated to the volunteers who selflessly give their time to maintain this trail. I reconnected with several trail angels who helped me out during the hike. And, I finally got the chance to meet Ed Talone and hear some of his inspiring stories from his 1994 thru-hike. Ed and I still talk often to this day, and at our meeting the first four thru-hikers have all met each other at some point, a full circle.

In 2015 I ended up moving to Michigan for a more involved role in the operations of the trail. It was another weird adjustment to make, but in a good way. Nearly everywhere I went hiking, I would run into someone who knew who I was, and I had reunions with many of the people I met along my journey. Even stranger were the return visits I made to a few specific places along the trail two years after having hiked thru on foot. To this day, I don't think I've had a stranger feeling than pulling into a campsite or trailhead with your car to a place you visited on foot with everything on your back. It's very disorienting.

It's been three years since my journey ended, and it still affects my day-to-day life. I think about the trail every day, about the things I saw, the experiences I had, and the people I met. Despite the incredible scenery found along the trail, the folks I met along the way—the magnificent trail angels and volunteers—ended up being the most memorable part of the hike. What the future holds I do not know. But I do intend to finish the entire C2C Route.

I've found that once you complete your first long-distance hike, you're pretty much ruined for life. The trail constantly calls to you. You're always thinking about the hike you already did, and at the same time planning and looking forward to the next one. For me, it'll probably be the PNT next, including the potential Big Sky Trail through North Dakota and Montana, a trip of about 2,000 miles.

In the meantime, I'll do what I can to ensure these trails stick around for future generations. It would be a tragic loss if these magnificent trails ever ceased to exist, and rob the opportunity from so many prospective hikers to be able to experience life on the trail and undertake the adventure of a lifetime.

Strider's Total Mileage:

North Dakota – 437.5
Minnesota – 846
Wisconsin – 209
Michigan (UP) – 531.5
Michigan (LP) – 578.5
Michigan (Total) -1110
Ohio – 967.5
Pennsylvania – 241
New York – 692
Vermont – 66.5

NCT (Total) – 4,568 Miles

ABOUT THE AUTHOR

Luke Jordan grew up on a farm in central Minnesota where he spent much of his childhood running around outdoors. His favorite and most inspirational place to visit was the North Shore of Lake Superior. He was awe-struck by the beauty of the region, and soon started venturing out on his own.

During his college years, he began backpacking and volunteering for trail organizations, particularly on the famed Superior Hiking Trail. Seeking a degree in Natural Resources, he developed quite a diverse background with invasive species, trail development, and historic preservation. In December of 2012 he graduated from St. Cloud State University and decided to pursue a dream that had been almost three years in the making.

With his college years behind him, he was ready to strap on his pack and attempt a grand adventure over the North Country National Scenic Trail. He succeeded, and became the fourth person to successfully thru-hike the trail. The journey helped connect him even more with the natural world and restore a bit of his faith in humanity.

Known on the trail as Strider, he continues to share his story and inspire others to get out and hit the trail on their own adventures.

Luke "Strider" Jordan/*Art by Haley Frost Creative*   395

TESTIMONIALS

"The North Country Trail is the hidden gem of the North American hiking system. It is one of most challenging and diverse trails in the world. Strider's love of the outdoors and thirst for adventure lead to an attempt of the North Country Trail as his very first long distance trail thru-hike, an out-of-the-box choice for sure. His writing gives us a glimpse into the unique challenges and rewards of the NCT. I am grateful that Strider has taken the time to share his stories and experiences from this amazing footpath!"

-Jennifer Pharr Davis – Author, speaker, hiker

"During these modern times it is easy to think that thru-hiking pioneers are of a bygone era. From Earl Shaffer's 1948 inaugural thru-hike of the Appalachian Trail to Eric Ryback's 1970 trail blazing thru-hike of the Pacific Crest Trail we have since moved on to speed records both supported and unsupported as well as land speed records for yoyo's and flip-flops. But America's National Scenic Trail System is much bigger than just those two trails. It is comprised of eleven trails which may not sound impressive but those eleven trails pass through, up and around, but usually up, some 18,000 miles of America's treasured lands. One quarter of those miles comprise just one trail, the North Country Trail.

"In 2013, a 22 year old man set out to become just the fourth person to thru-hike the 4,600 mile North Country Trail. I was delighted to read Luke Jordan's new book documenting his epic adventure along that behemoth of a trail. It is a story of a young man embracing one of the ultimate thru-hiking challenges and a trail community in turn embracing him the entire way. The book is a testament to true grit, the lure of the trail and the kindness of strangers through the voice of one of today's thru-hiking pioneers."

-Bart Smith – Long distance hiker, photographer and author

Made in the USA
Monee, IL
01 June 2024

59239123R00233